GREAT DAY COMING

GREAT DAY COMING

A MEMOIR OF THE 1930S

HOPE HALE DAVIS

STEERFORTH PRESS

SOUTH ROYALTON, VERMONT

For information about permission to reproduce
selections from this book, write to:
Steerforth Press L.C., P.O. Box 70, South Royalton, Vermont 05068.

Library of Congress Cataloging-in-Publication Data
Davis, Hope Hale.
Great day coming: a memoir of the 1930s / by Hope Hale Davis.
p.   cm.
ISBN 1–883642–17–5
1. Davis, Hope Hale. 2. Communists — United States — Biography.
3. Communism — United States — History — 20th century.
4. Communism and psychoanalysis. 1. Title.
HX84.D284A3   1994
3335.43'092 — dc20   94–31548

Manufactured in the United States of America

First Edition

For Claudia Flanders, OBE, JP
Once known as
Project Revolutionary Baby

The conversations reproduced in this memoir are drawn from memory reinforced by notes written soon after the event. In all cases they record scenes in which I took an active part. Although the language may not always be literally exact, the speeches represent the personalities and thinking of the speakers and the essence of the talk.

Hope Hale Davis

There's a great day coming,
There's a great day coming,
There's a great day coming by and by,
And the workers shall rise and gain their freedom on that day,
Are you ready for that day to come?

CHAPTER 1

In February 1933 a taxi took me through a blizzard from Greenwich Village to Presbyterian Hospital. The countdown of Project Revolutionary Baby had begun.

At our left, all the way up Riverside Drive, dwellings made of oil barrels, scrap lumber, corrugated tin, and cardboard crowded the strip of park by the Hudson. Every city had a Hooverville, named for the failed president blamed for the Depression.

"You don't really mean to bring a child into this!" my friends had cried.

We had our answer to that, Claud Cockburn and I. "Would we have let a depression scare *us* out of being born? Then what right have we to think our child will be a coward?"

Before I started the project, pregnancy had been the great danger, as it was for all my young women friends in New York. We lived lives of risk; writers represented the spirit of the twenties. We spent our days pursuing success and our nights gaining what we thought of as experience. But even before I met Claud I had felt the lack of something essential — something I would never have admitted I needed, or why I needed it.

By the fall of 1930 I had made an early mark in advertising and was now the first female promotion manager of the humorous weekly *Life,* at a salary of four thousand dollars a year. Even though it was twenty percent less than the five thousand dollars paid my male predecessor, who had alienated everybody, I felt lucky and rich. Courting advertisers of Pierce-Arrows and Bugattis seemed an amusing, unreal game. But something was wrong with a day that began with buying a five-cent apple from an unemployed architect who stood shivering at the entrance to my building.

A woman who lived above me spent exhausting days getting babies adopted. Yet how many of the hundreds of children needing homes could she place? A woman lawyer involved in juvenile delinquency described jammed courts and hasty, indifferent judges. I knew the slums poured out more and more angry kids. All these problems interlocked. What could be done?

I was ready for what Claud would tell me. Not that he spoke seriously, at first. After we discovered we were the same age and had published fiction — he in *Dial* and I in *The New Yorker* — what charmed me was his gaiety, his mischief, his wit. Tall and gangling, wearing glasses that hid his best feature, he kept people laughing with tales that made the world seem delightfully absurd. But when we were alone he took off the concealing glasses and said that something could be done about the problems I thought so hopeless. We could sweep away all these disgraces at once and build a new society that would rule them out forever.

He liked his work as the junior New York correspondent of the *London Times* and liked his colleagues (one of them had brought us together). But the job served only as training, he said, for his real future. As soon as he had what he needed he would go back to England and help make the revolution that he said had to come. When he warned his chiefs that he might be leaving they offered him almost any post in the world if he would stay, had suggested that he might some day become the foreign editor and even the editor. But he had given all this up with a smile, for the chancy life of a revolutionary.

This made him irresistible — knowing that within the frivolity and fun was what he called *"un homme serieux."* This gave our hours in bed a quality beyond comparison with my earlier quests for experience. But our time together was soon to end.

My realizing this led to Project Revolutionary Baby. All I asked of Claud was a marriage certificate — necessary then for the child's sake. I wanted what a woman has traditionally asked of a lover going off to war — his qualities, his heritage.

I was sure I could carry on the project alone. In 1931 I had been given the chance to create a new magazine to be sold in department stores. Its quick success, I thought, was due to designing both the fiction and articles to help our readers solve their problems, and in the Depression problems were desperately tangled.

"Since my husband lost his business," a woman might write to our Beatrice Fairfax, "he won't come to bed till after he thinks I'm asleep." Then one of my fiction writers who understood how male pride affects virility would create a story in which the wife helps her husband build a confidence based on more than a weekly paycheck.

With an unemployed friend engaged to act as liaison, I would put together the next month's magazine in the hospital. A practical nurse already hired would give me and my new young maid a few weeks start. The pediatrician and I had figured out a breast-feeding schedule to fit my working day.

Claud had sailed for England in July, the baby well begun. But during June, those mornings in the sunny Hotel Lafayette café when he helped me get down a few spoonfuls of cream of wheat before I set off to work, his interest in the project changed. He wanted more to do with that child (named, a bit prematurely, Paul Alexander) than he had foreseen. As the time of our parting came near he wondered if it need be for very long? Why shouldn't I, in fact, come over soon and work with him for the revolution? I could help educate the English masses, using the skills I had learned with my magazine. As to child care, nannies were plentiful in England now, and when the revolution came, he said with assurance that impressed me, he would have perquisites.

Naturally I had hoped he felt as strongly as I did that what we had together could not be given up. But I would never have asked to share his life. For a romantic of the twenties the man had to do the asking — begging, really — overcome with passion. Also, paradoxically, my feminist pride had kept me silent. But now I could plan to work with him, play a part in the great change that he was sure would come.

On February 18, 1932, the night of our wedding, Claud's cousin, Alec Waugh, had given us a party. Claud repeated a toast he had heard in Washington from the French poet and ambasssador, Paul Claudel. In English it said simply, "May you be to him like good bread." In French, and in Claud's voice, it sounded lyrical. Good bread, he lovingly pointed out, was something of which a man could never tire. The real meaning may not have occurred to either of us: that a wife should be something a man went on consuming for his own nourishment all their lives. Perhaps it just seemed too natural to notice. As it turned out, the wish would be given almost no chance to come true.

As the day of Claud's sailing came closer I began to doubt my courage. I sent an S.O.S. to my sister: I needed my nephew, Roy. And that twelve-year-old's excited exploration of the steamship *Dunquerque* saw us through the parting. Afterward I searched out every Abbott and Costello film playing in greater New York. Hunched down in a dark theater, surrounded by the noise of laughter, with Roy gasping and choking until he cried, I was able to add my sobs to his and get the worst of my weeping over before he left for Washington.

I hadn't doubted my courage before, though I had wondered — rhetorically, at least — about its source. "Why am I so sure of the rightness of having a child," I'd written in my journal a year before, "so sure that I take on this reponsibility with no security but my own earning power? And in a world shaking on its foundations?" I didn't try seriously to find an answer, and would have rejected any that suggested its real source, which took me a long time to discover.

While I was in Presbyterian Hospital both Hitler and Roosevelt came to power. I read the news between my earnest sessions with Trotsky's *History of the Russian Revolution.* Meanwhile I tried hard to enjoy my private room, meals I could choose from a menu, back rubs given by graduate nurses — all this and nursery care for six dollars a day. My daughter Claudia with her flailing fists and crest of pink-gold hair, was a triumph. She sucked my breast as if with love, but I often cried as I nursed her.

"It's just postpartum blues," my doctor said. She was Jean Corwin, heroine of Barnard's early battle to get women admitted to

4

Columbia's medical school. I didn't know her history, but I sensed that she liked my being on my own. I didn't, not at all. I had my friends, and my sister had come from Washington, but only Claud's special kind of appreciation was worthy of Claudia.

"It is amazing," I wrote him, "to feel respect for a creature with a heelprint the size of a nickel." I was sure he would find her fascinating. But starting his behind-the-news bulletin, *The Week*, required his constant presence.

Claud and I had saved two hundred dollars in gold pieces for my doctor. Though charmed, she could only let them trickle briefly through her fingers before Roosevelt called in all gold. Banks were failing everywhere, and for several days they all had to be closed.

On my first morning at home I met my landlady in the hall. The last time I had seen her she had been wailing, "Whatever am I going to *do?*" Probably few of her tenants were able to pay their rent. Owners had mostly stopped evicting, for that would leave the apartments empty and no hope of payment. Park Avenue duplexes were being secretly offered free to any respectably dressed people who would have lights showing in the windows. These offers were seldom accepted; it cost too much to keep up appearances.

That March morning my landlady's jubilant cry astonished me: "Everything's going to be all *right!* I heard Roo-sevelt on the rad-dio, and he says so!"

Roosevelt's inaugural voice had reassured the whole country. He had become everyone's father — a father not only caring but powerful, the kind in short supply just then.

Yet twenty million people were still out of work. My brother in Iowa, a chemist who had taken salary cuts but kept his position, wrote that one of his unluckier colleagues with a Ph.D., a hungry family, and nothing else, had offered to clean the local racetrack enclosure without pay, stipulating that he should be the only one allowed in after the last race. That season he and his family lived on lost coins, the rare bill carelessly dropped, and the even rarer uncashed winning ticket.

At home I was planning the June issue of *Love Mirror*. One day my secretary arrived, I thought, to bring the May issue. Instead she brought news that one of our backers, who had been stealing the

5

profits, had now absconded, and the printers had stopped their presses. We sat down to our last task together, telling our faithful contributors the news that would be as bad for them as for us.

I called my sister. "Come and stay in the shack," Mimi said at once. She meant the cabin where they had lived while building their house on a Virginia hillside. It was surrounded by woods, with boisterous little "runs" rushing through miniature gorges to the Potomac. I was fond of my brother-in-law Rollo and their two boys, but the thought of Mimi made me hesitate. She had proved her love generously, from dressing a doll for me when she was fourteen and I was four, to this warm welcome. Yet sometimes, unpredictably, she could become my enemy.

In this mood of doubt and indecision I had a bad dream. Claud and I are lying in my big bed with Claudia between us, just as I pictured us in my scenarios. Resting on his elbow Claud is looking down at her, smiling. But what is he doing? Quite consciously, still smiling, he is letting ashes from his cigarette fall into the baby's eyes.

I hated and resisted the dream. Claud was always so considerate of everyone around him.

I was still worrying over Mimi's invitation when the publisher Delacorte asked me to create a new magazine for his group. I loved being offered jobs, and in 1933 it seemed like a Nobel prize.

Cupid's Diary, I told myself, was no worse than *Love Mirror,* a name forced on my magazine as companion to *Movie Mirror.* But this would be a "pulp," following the Delacorte pattern. Their kind of happy endings, instead of the ones that readers might actually work to achieve, offered fantasies like stowing away on millionaires' yachts. Also, could I ethically take it on when I might leave soon? My summons from England could come at any time. I cabled Claud.

His first answer was a radiogram dated April 14, 1933. It read: REFUSE JOB. AWAIT LONG CABLE TOMORROW. The second was dated the fifteenth: SCHEME I HAVE FOR YOUR COMING OVER HERE IMMEDIATELY HAS TEMPORARILY GONE AWRY. BEST TAKE COTTAGE NEAR WASHINGTON. LOVE TO YOU AND CLAUDIA.

The two radiograms are in my hands as I write this, their folds still crisp. Those capital letters, typed by some operator decades ago, make me feel that the choice is still open, that I could still decide against Washington, escaping what I thought then would be only the minor dangers of family life.

I don't think the choice was mine, but I had the illusion that I was doing my own thinking. Of all the illusions I grew up with, that one has lasted longest — if it is an illusion — maybe even till now. But in April 1933 I weighed the pros and cons objectively, I thought, then acted on my soundest judgment. I would go to Virginia. It would not be for long.

CHAPTER 2

Union Station! In my memory all marble columns and majestic spaces, it had meant excitement to me since age fourteen. That fall — it was 1917 and the Washington streets were full of officers bustling to their desks, booted and spurred — Mother and I had fled from Iowa after my stepfather's sudden death. She was sad, but how could I resist this moment? With the Capitol dome in the background there stood my smiling brother-in-law whom I had never met. And beside him Mimi, a new gentleness about her, my tiny nephew in her arms.

Now in the spring of 1933, helped down by the parlor-car porter, I was the new mother with a baby in her arms. Their welcome made me feel like the prodigal son.

As Mimi took my blanketed bundle and met Claudia's wide blue eyes, she seemed once again newly gentle, and wonderfully strong. I counted on her strength.

Mimi had a look of vigor, with bold cheekbones where the color kept moving as if with a life of its own. Her eyes were large, dark gray, set within deep luminous hollows that gave a sense of import to her most casual glance.

In Virginia the redbuds and magnolias had come out. As we climbed among the tamaracks to the half-hidden cabin my feet welcomed the springiness of pine needles. The scent of crushed sassafras seemed the breath of home. But I checked that thought; my home was in the future, not yet imaginable.

The part of the shack you saw first, with its chimney poking up from the steeply pitched roof, looked like the wicked witch's hut in a fairy tale. You entered dimness; in the faint light from one high window the woodstove crouched like a lurking black animal.

A passageway led back beside a makeshift closet to a quite different room, large and light, its screened walls open to the woods, with canvas curtains that would roll down in times of wind and rain. Rollo and the boys had placed my studio couch at the far corner, and Claudia's crib across from it in an alcove behind the closet. They had set up my desk diagonally opposite and connected my lamp for working at night.

Settling in, I thought of Mother arriving at a Missouri log house, years before I was born. Father's health had broken down while he was a high school principal in Iowa, studying at night for the ministry. His doctors gave their current solution: a change of climate, mountain air. Land speculators were advertising the Ozarks as "a cure for whatever's wrong with the body, mind or pocketbook." Father had gone south first, and after a time Mother followed with the children — three then, who had come in quick succession.

It was evening by the time the wagon could get them there from the train, and the children were hungry. Father had set up the stove, Mother recalled in her memoir, and she made johnnycake for their supper. "But Father could hardly wait to show me our spring, where we would cool our food.

"The first thing I saw as we neared the spot," she wrote, "was a little stream sparkling from out of its half-concealing thicket of wild roses and elderberry. All along the bank the bushes grew up and met in a graceful green arch, the brilliant pink of the roses mingling with the delicate white of the elder blooms."

Did she remember the scene so lyrically, I wondered, because she had shared it with Father? Still, I could hardly envy her, knowing what was ahead of her. I didn't envy anyone. How could I? And if I had to wait, what better place than here on this hilltop with the dogwood blossoms drifting like white moths among the pines?

And the wait might not be long. In May Claud wrote of "a new magazine being started, a sort of English version of *Time,* with a good deal of money behind it, and they want me to edit it . . . I am sure that out of all this we shall presently be in the position that we talked about. I mean, where it would be possible for you to put to use over here your vast experience and especially what you learned on *Love Mirror*."

But June came, bringing only an emissary. Harrison Brown, a rueful, rakish journalist who was "flabbergahsted" at the beauty of "Claud's bonny kid." This kind of appreciation from a man who was not Claud seemed almost to hurt physically; I had to try not to resent him for seeing Claudia now, while Claud was missing her.

I remembered Mother's description of Father's joy in their first child, with his "silvery-golden hair." (Claudia's hair was a pinker gold.) "When I would get the baby all ready for bed except putting on his nightclothes," Mother wrote, "Father would take him in his hands and hold him up high to gaze on his cherubic beauty."

On one of the hottest days Gardner "Pat" Jackson brought his wife Dode out from Washington. They came in the same Essex coupe in which Pat and Claud, the year before, had covered the march on Washington of thousands of World War veterans, demanding their promised bonus now, when they were out of work. The same Essex, one late night of 1927, had carried petitions bearing three-hundred thousand signatures to the Boston State House, in a last desperate effort to save the anarchists Sacco and Vanzetti from execution.

"What a pet!" Dode cried at first sight of Claudia, and asked how I could bear not to have Claud see her now. Before I could answer Pat broke in, urging me to go to England.

I mustered all my arguments, about how the baby was not meant to be a burden to Claud, that our marriage had been just a technicality. Pat's square bulging forehead, already red in the heat, seemed to steam. He insisted that no marriage was ever just a technicality. Experience of life gave a man perspective. Let Claud get one glimpse of his child, and his ideas would change. I said quickly that Claud already loved her. "I'm amazed," he had written soon after she was born, "to feel such strong emotions about a creature I've never seen."

"So take the next boat!" Pat Jackson shouted.

My nephew Roy came round the corner of the shack when they had left. "Are you going to go?"

I asked him what he thought. At twelve, with his bristle of fair hair above blue eyes that seemed both puzzled and amused by what they saw, he was a person to be taken seriously. A few decades later he would be a member of the Academy of Science. But that day he spoke as one of his age. What he really wished, he said, was that Claud would come here. And I knew he was remembering the evening last year when I had followed Claud to Washington and brought him out to dinner.

The meal hadn't started as I hoped. Rollo, always preoccupied by domestic projects, talked at length about eradicating groundhogs. But Claud listened intently, his brown eyes brightening, and began to impersonate Mrs. Groundhog.

" 'Cor, Alfie, wot you sayin'? Footsteps up above? That's the product of a fevered imagination if I ever — *Poison,* is it now! If I wasn't sure your head was screwed on straight, Alfie, I'd think you was touched. Blockin' up our exits — Bloody paranooie, my lad. That's the size of it."

Remembering gave no comfort, nor did telling Roy that Claud couldn't leave his news bulletin just now, when it was becoming essential reading even for world leaders.

As July went on Claud's letters and cables dwindled and then stopped. Reading *The Week* I could imagine how frantically he was racing around to get his inside news. Patience, I told myself, was the least he could ask of a revolutionary partner.

The heat lay like a damp blanket over the Potomac valley, and I waded through the days as if through some kind of resistant steam. The pages of my books, mildewed, stuck together. As I rolled the softened paper into my typewriter I found it hard to think up the Young Love plots that editors wanted. But after a few misses a check for fifty dollars came from *Family Circle* for a tale that ended with finding a lost letter behind a radiator.

Hagar Wilde (who would soon write *Bringing Up Baby*) invited me on a cruise to Bermuda. I declined, fearful of missing my summons to England. But her husband had become editor of *Radio Fanfare* and could assign me interviews with stars coming through Washington on "personal appearance tours." The day I spent with the handsome Cuban crooner Tito Guizar caught me in an ordeal I hadn't expected. With his young dark-eyed wife and elaborately bassinetted baby in the hotel room, he kept me listening for an hour to the joys of a new father.

My interview with Colonel Stoopnagle and Budd came as a relief. An oddly-matched pair who had brought new thousands of sophisticates to the radio audience, they never stopped inventing their comedy. Thinking of my nephews, I invited them out to dinner. And at the table they perfected the famous dialogue in which Bud asks the Colonel for the secrets of his profession, which consists of stuffing the cotton in pill bottles. As the solemn questions went on, the Colonel seriously disclosing the techniques by which he foils the most determined attempts to get the cotton out, both Herbert and Roy did what I had heard of without believing — fell off their chairs and rolled on the floor.

One day a mint copy of *Miss Lonelyhearts* came from Pep Weinstein. His earlier book published under the name of Nathanel West, *The Dream Life of Balso Snell,* told from the point of view of a flea in the armpit of Jesus, had left me puzzled. But *Lonelyhearts* touched me closely, too closely. He had transmuted what he had laughed at in the letters readers had written to my magazine into pathos I found almost unendurable now. Though the book was inscribed to me, I sent it to Claud as soon as I read it. Whether he received it or not I never learned.

In August a letter from my favorite contributor, Ellen Kerkhoff, had a postscript that disturbed me.

She began by warning me against hoping to "write on the typewriter with one hand and change diapers with the other," especially in the wilderness. You could only do that in New York, she said. "Darling, don't you think you should come back? I can find a day nursery for the baby, a good one, either at a very nominal price or no price at all. And I'll find you an apartment, one fairly large room and bath, cooking, heat and so on, for thirty a month. There are such things as screens, you know, to put up in front of the baby." She added, "You should think about this, Hope."

But what I thought about were her final lines: "Bill Furth who is on *Time* magazine told me that Claud was the London representative of the magazine now."

So the *Time* deal that was supposed to take me to England had materialized. And I had heard nothing more about it from Claud.

Reading Ellen's letter now, I suddenly feel impatient with the young woman who read it then. Why didn't she act on it? The hard life Ellen described didn't scare her. Something else may have — the idea of giving up, failing.

My morale needed the boost that came with the visit of Harry Buckland — tall, with dark blond hair worn longer than American men's, and the offhand manner of Rugby and Cambridge, now with an added M.D. He was heading for New Zealand to inspect his sheep station before starting his London practice.

To me Harry represented a bygone phase of my life. 1930 had ended the decade of the sexual revolution, which I had gladly thrust behind me. But geographically he and I shared spectacular memories. I brought out my album and we looked at pictures of us waterskiing on the Lake of Zug, where friends of his had restored a tenth-century castle. In another we stood with the famous Swiss guide Signorelle near a high Alpine shelter, with sharp white peaks all around us, where *The White Hell of Piz Palu* had been filmed. Harry and I had seen the movie together in the innocent days when its maker had not yet been linked with Hitler. That afternoon as we looked at the album I doubt if I even spoke the name Leni Riefenstahl, much less imagined meeting her, and meeting her in a way that led to calamity.

Harry inspected Claudia with a doctor's eye and found her perfect. But my health troubled him. I was thin, and had had a series of infections. On a day when the temperature and humidity both stood near 100, Claudia had turned away from my breast, once and for all.

Harry prescribed a sea voyage, proposing to change his booking to a suite for us all, including a nanny for Claudia. "We'll stop at Tahiti and any port you choose."

Like Ellen's letter, Harry's invitation might seem like fate's offer of another way out. And maybe it did give me a slight twinge of nostalgia for the old footloose days. But I wrote Claud that the quest for romance in the South Seas was "banal, no adventure at all compared to the ones I've cast my lot with." And I enclosed a snapshot showing Claudia intently studying *The Week*.

These photographic expenses were adding to my growing debt; the checks for writing never seemed to catch up. Rollo was a statistician, and their household had always operated on a budget. I remember that the one for 1917, when Rollo earned $1750 a year, allowed them fifty cents a month for wine. Now, with Mimi's job at the National Research Council, they could afford their generous impulses. But impulses were different from a steady drain. Once, when Rollo offered to advance the pay of a neighbor girl to look out for Claudia a few hours a day while I worked, I saw Mimi's lips tighten, though we all knew it was a good investment. I didn't realize how mixed her feelings about me were, though I should have caught a clue the night Rollo brought a couple from his office out to dinner.

Making conversation, I asked where they came from — everyone in Washington came from somewhere. When she answered, "Fredonia, Kansas," I said, "I was almost born there."

"Almost?" she asked, and I told about Father having just taken up his best post, as superintendent of schools in Fredonia, when he caught typhoid and died two weeks after arriving in town.

"I saw that arrival," our guest said.

As a child, sitting with her family on the porch, she had listened for the train whistle, then waited. And there came the family: four children, each carrying a piece of luggage and a pillow, with chubby Grafton, age six, bringing up the rear. Father and Mother led the procession, and "She's in the family way," whispered across the porch.

I felt a strange sense of dislocation, seeing the procession pass, me present merely as a pregnancy, the only way my father would ever know me. Preoccupied with these thoughts, I didn't think how Mimi might be feeling. She had walked in that procession, at age ten, and could remember what happened afterward. Having been her father's darling, she lost him; an aunt came and helped them move back to Iowa, to the household where there was no room for her and eleven-year-old MacFarland. They were sent to an aunt and uncle who were almost strangers. She must have felt abandoned even by her mother, waiting those two long months for my birth.

If I hadn't been so absorbed by my own sensations I might have realized how deeply rooted were Mimi's mixed feelings about me. And I might have wondered if I should keep on expecting her support for a hope that grew more and more unrealistic day by day.

I must have known how unrealistic it was. When the postman signaled me with his klaxon's *ooh-wah-wah* at the foot of the hill, I ran leaping down from flagstone to flagstone. But the clutch of my chest muscles came less from hope than the fear of disappointment sure to follow.

I wonder whether anyone was fooled by my efforts at cheer. I knew Mimi counted on me — fresh from the New York scene — to help liven things up when her academics and statisticians came out to play tennis. But sooner or later the talk came back to the Depression and Roosevelt's latest plans for dealing with it. This always left me impatient. Hearing the calm, inconclusive weighing of the pros and cons, I longed for Claud's vivid certainties. "These schemes of Roosevelt's sound so wonderful," I wrote him, "I wish I could ask someone who knows history what the catch is."

Why didn't I get busy and *study,* figure things out for myself? If only I had done my own thinking! I can't be sure it would have sent me toward a more prudent path, but surely I'd have looked with a clearer eye before I leaped, and been warier about the terrain where I landed.

Still, I was a child of the twenties, when only a man's word carried the real authority. The writers in style — even female — showed a woman acting not only most romantically but most honorably as faithful handmaiden to an irresistible male.

Consciously I despised Hemingway's idiot heroines. I had wept when Helen Hayes died for Gary Cooper in *Farewell to Arms;* in fact staying to the end made me late in feeding Claudia. But even with tears streaming down my face I noted that this nurse went to her death without ever having uttered an intelligent word.

I didn't realize that below my consciousness Mother was backing Hemingway. How often she had said, speaking of Father, "There was nothing I might ask him that he couldn't tell me." It was with men as teachers that I fell in love. For all Claud's charm, without my trust in his thinking, his political vision, he could not have kept his hold on my imagination.

Mother would have urged me to ask for my guidance from God rather than Claud. Still, she often observed that the answer might come in unexpected form.

The summer had almost ended when Mimi announced that Dr. Corell was coming to lunch on Sunday. I knew that professor, had composed a limerick about him, rhyming "courtly" with "portly." This time he was bringing a guest. I asked in dread, "Not another economist?" Indeed he was, this guest, though a fledgling, still a graduate student at Columbia, hoping for a job in the New Deal. Continuing to protest in that frivolous, unsuspecting way, I think I even considered possible methods of escape.

CHAPTER 3

I am trying now to imagine what that stranger saw when he stood outside the screen door in the glare of the August sun.

It would have looked cavelike, this part of my cabin, the rafters and beams dimly glimpsed like the ribs of some rough mythical beast that had swallowed us. But he was not fanciful; he would have seen a young woman in a faded blue sundress bathing a baby. The sash was tied around my head to hold my hair back in the heat.

Sometimes since then I've looked back on this picture — all the light from the small window caught in a dazzle from the splash of water around the baby's glistening body — as a sort of entrapment.

Such an idea would never have come to me then. I was phrasing a letter to Claud — still another, newsy, and oh so self-reliant. I responded rather absently to Claudia, who was pronouncing syllables in her purposeful way. "What language is she speaking?" an amused voice asked at the door. Slavic, he thought.

Claudia twisted to see him, almost slipping out of my grasp. He stepped quickly to the foot of the bath-table and caught her flailing feet. Introducing himself as Hermann Brunck he gave me Rollo's message: better hurry if I wanted a drink. Then he started talking to Claudia in what sounded like Russian. She laughed suddenly as if catching the joke.

Maybe entrapment could have worked both ways. A seeming absence of danger might pose a danger. If he had been striking in any way, or come on strong sexually, I'd have caught warning signals.

But how could I feel any threat from this man, with his easy, un-affected manner and scholarly shell-rimmed glasses, his sandy hair receding from his forehead?

He was sturdy, but not tall, compared to Claud's willowy six feet four. And though Claud took a genuine interest in other people, he could hardly enter a room before he became the center of a group listening and laughing. They would hear some comic tale such as his being swindled at age eighteen in a Budapest castle by a shady count teaching him Hungarian. Claud's sort of self-mocking humor required a special kind of assurance — maybe cultivated only in England.

This man's confidence was different, but real. He expected people to take him seriously, and I responded, though maybe sublim-inally, to the way he held himself in his gray linen suit, and even the burnished glow of the heavy brogues he wore. My conscious interest was in his knowledge of Russian.

A little, he said: just what he had picked up during three weeks in the Soviet Union last summer. He stood waiting with the towel for me to wrap the baby in.

While I powdered the crevices in the baby's solid pink body he talked about Moscow, the parks of Culture and Rest. They really swarmed, he said, with people playing games (soccer and chess), lis-tening to concerts or just sitting reading. Everyone had learned to read, and they were all reading!

His manner of speaking — the inflection pure American but with a European edge of precision — gave a convincing effect of accuracy. Since he had come to Washington for an interview at the National Recovery Administration, he might clear up some of my confusion. "Does your taking a job at NRA," I asked, "mean you believe in Roosevelt's grand schemes?"

He said he doubted if even Roosevelt did, or knew what he would do from one day to the next. "He's like a blind sculptor."

That statement caught my attention, as it deserved to. Later I could see more than one meaning in it. But that day I heard it as he intended — simply dismissive. I told him it was the first straight talk I'd heard since I left New York.

Four months, he remarked, was a long time to go without straight talk. That startled me; this man knew exactly how long I had been here. As I carried the baby to the open part of my cabin I imagined Mimi talking to Dr. Corell as if I'd been abandoned. But if he had passed that idea on, his friend gave no sign of it, asking what kind of unstraight talk I'd been hearing.

Roosevelt's fireside chats made me uneasy, I told him. They sounded so appealing that I wanted to believe in them myself. But everybody listened as uncritically as my mother listened to the minister reading the Bible.

This happened in New York too, he said. And I quoted my friend Sheila, widow of the great radical writer Paxton Hibben; she had laughed in real relief, saying we needn't bother any more about making revolution — Roosevelt was doing this for us.

"Far from it."

Putting Claudia into her crib, I heard about the loss of a perfect chance to take over the banks and create a rational monetary system. The bankers had been in Washington, on their knees — yes, a couple of them literally kneeling — ready for any cure the president prescribed. And Roosevelt had just let them patch up the old system that had failed. In the middle of a description of Senator Bronson Cutting of New Mexico putting his head down on his desk and weeping, a sudden silence fell.

I looked over my shoulder. He had turned on my desk lamp, which for Claudia's sake I had shaded with a blue-velvet evening cape. Under the light he studied the picture of Claud, asking if it was my husband. I told him it was a photograph of a painting, which of course showed him as the artist, Berta, had seen him. (Had wanted to see him, I added to myself — serious, thoughtful, steadfast.) And recognizable, of course, with his full lips, high forehead resting on his almost abnormally flexible bent-back fingers; but the deep shadows below the even line of brow gave his eyes an unlikely soulfulness. Berta had left out his wit and gaiety, his mischief.

When Claud had gone to Berlin, straight from his clique of esthetes at Oxford, Berta had taught him what it was to love a woman. And during that first year of his work at the *Times,* she and her friends had made him seriously political. She may well have been afraid of his other side — his lightheartedness — afraid it would take him cheerfully on from her to the next love, as indeed it had. When he met me he had decamped precipitately from the apartment of the radical feminist Suzanne LaFollette; among the papers stored with me was her scathing goodbye note.

"People never turn out to be like your image of them," Hermann was musing. Seeing my startled look, he explained that he must have imagined Claud from the style of *The Week,* which he read at the John Reed Club — its irreverent tone, its audacity.

That voice was truer than the painting, I said. But I felt vaguely disturbed. Those mimeographed pages could evoke Claud powerfully, even painfully, for me. But this man had never met him. He seemed almost too perceptive.

He and his friends would like to know, he said, how Claud got his information, sometimes from sources close to Hitler. I couldn't enlighten him. Months earlier Claud had hinted at "lacunae" in his letters. He was fairly sure that they were being opened.

I was tying stiff cuffs over Claudia's elbows, and she began her usual struggle against them. Her face flushed red and hot; she grunted and gasped. Hermann came over, asking what this was all about. I had made the cuffs, I told him, from a Children's Bureau pattern, to prevent thumb sucking. They were recommended by a committee of the most prominent pediatricians in the country. Hermann still looked troubled, and as we left he paused outside the door, listening to Claudia. He had a doctor friend in New York, he said, who thought a baby's use of the opposable thumb was one of evolution's survival features. I asked if his friend was an established pediatrician. How wonderful it would be to forget all those warnings about dental structure and let her go free. But no, Ben was just starting out, and it would have seemed irrelevant if I'd been told his last name: Spock.

At lunch the tennis guests began talking excitedly about the new Civilian Conservation Corps. It promised to take thousands of city youth off the streets and into the woods, restoring the national parks. They would learn forestry and even building skills, repairing bridges and canals and reservoirs. I couldn't see anything wrong with it until Hermann spoke. He saw a possible danger in having the CCC under the control of the army. With demagogues like Huey Long and Father Coughlin, the radio priest, inciting them, this could become a fascist force like those in Europe.

He had spoken reasonably, but met protests so vehement (Rollo's cocktails always potent) that I admired his calm response, agreeing that Colonel George Marshall didn't seem a fascist type. And in any case nobody could really be sure what strength our history might have given us, since no country had ever before had a hundred and fifty years of democracy.

But later, walking in the woods, I asked him if we really had time, the way things were going, to look at all sides of questions? Hermann's judicious answer — that it depended on the direction things were going, which we couldn't tell at the moment — made me impatient, and I started walking faster. Catching up, he asked if my sense of hurry could be partly due to some deadline of my own.

I don't think I admitted it aloud, but I may have sighed over that deadline, long since passed. I turned away from the thought, suddenly walking out along a fallen log that bridged the stream.

Hermann stood on the bank watching me. Then he asked in a curiously neutral voice if my husband and I might have made two plans, one of which prevented me from carrying out the other.

I smiled at his formal language, but probably gave my usual line, about how Claud had to be free for what he had to do. And I added what I had been telling myself all summer: "Claudia was strictly my idea."

Does a crucial moment always hold some element of farce? As I spoke those words Hermann's foot slipped on the boggy bank. There was a sucking sound, and he swore.

Something broke in me, some tension. I laughed and laughed, unable to stop, watching him pull his foot from the muck. I felt a delicious release.

With a stick he started cleaning his shoe. Then he raised his head; and giving me a level look he began without transition to talk about the Hoovervilles I had mentioned at lunch. "What makes them important is the waste. Thousands of men living in those shacks who could be building decent houses."

This was what I had missed all summer. I sat down on the log and listened as if to music while he cited figures, the numbers of unfinished buildings all over the country, climaxed by the statement that would always seem conclusive: The construction industry had come to a stop because under capitalism building could only be done when somebody made a profit from it.

In a curious contentment I sat watching the water of Windy Run flow clear as brandy below my sneakers. He said that Hooverville on Riverside Drive could be seen every day by the graduate students at Columbia. "An ivory tower with a view."

I asked if that wasn't a good reason to come out of the ivory tower. And maybe this was the first time I noticed the European way his shoulders moved. And the first time, too, that I challenged it: Why did he answer with just a shrug? He had sounded like a Marxist.

When he said his Marxism so far was only theoretical, I mimicked his shrug. "Oh well," I said, "a theoretical Marxist is better than none."

"Marx wouldn't agree with you," he answered seriously. "Remember, 'Theory without action is barren, and action without theory is blind.'"

Deep below consciousness I may have heard the echo of what Mother so often quoted: "By their fruits shall ye know them. . . . Faith without works is dead."

When I recall that we paused beside the chestnut tree I may be telescoping memories, perhaps because of the poignancy this one would take on. But I can see his hand resting on a silvery smooth trunk, both of us looking up to where each branch began a soaring sweep, only to come to a bare, jagged end.

Years ago, I told him, a sudden blight had swept this part of the country. Until then the chestnut blossoms must have been beautiful in the spring. In Europe they still were, Hermann said, his voice so nostalgic that I asked him — though this seemed unlikely, with Hitler there — if he missed Germany. He said he had been pretty

24

thoroughly Americanized in Plainfield, New Jersey, where he had gone to grammar school. His family had already taken out their first citizenship papers when they happened to choose the month of July 1914 for their holiday in Germany. His father, a reserve officer, had gone into active duty as a cavalry captain. But no one could have been less warlike. Speaking with a tenderness that struck me as unusual from a son, Hermann told how his father had been in and out of hospitals most of the four years. "But not from combat. He literally had no stomach for war."

Seeing the gentle curve of his lips saying this, I remembered the propaganda of my childhood, showing spike-helmeted *boches* (this meant beasts) driving bayonets through Belgian mothers.

Near the end, when the army was taking old men and boys, Hermann himself had become a very young *Oberleutnant*. But the famine and inflation after the war were worse. He had actually gone through, I realized, what I had glimpsed only from the billions of marks worth of postage on the letters that came to the office where I worked.

His first mention of his mother may have come then, when he spoke of how women struggled to satisfy their children's constant hunger. Amazingly his mother had organized, quite early in the war, a branch of the *Frauenfrieden* — women for peace. And she, a devout Catholic, having observed that the priests on both sides were urging their young men to slaughter fellow Catholics in the trenches a hundred yards away, had left the church.

How different she sounded, I thought, from my own mother, who could never have given up her faith. Once committed, she made everything in her life fit in with it. "Anyway, she believed President Wilson," I told Hermann. "'A war to end war.'"

His mother had no such hope, Hermann said. She had lost her illusions early. He didn't go on, and it was only later that I learned the story, and still later that I began to see this as a piece in the puzzle of her son's life.

The path skirted the edge of the cliff; we looked out over the treetops across Key Bridge to the battlements of Georgetown University on the heights of the far shore. Beyond the river's southward curve was the white oblong of the new Lincoln Memorial; straight east the Washington Monument was a stick of chalk against the hazy sky, and farther still the dim dome of the Capitol. Somewhere between, too low to see, was his Commerce Building.

"Not *my* Commerce Building. Not yet, if ever." When he had gone for his interview he said it had seemed to him like some modern version of Inferno, hellishly hot (no air-conditioning, though finished as late as 1931) and wildly chaotic. Everyone was racing somewhere to find somebody who was racing somewhere else because the phones in those ten thousand cells kept breaking down. His possible chief was cut off in the middle of what sounded like an essential conversation with an official of the seamen's union who had been hard to reach.

Did I make up some aphorism then about all important things starting in heat and chaos? Whatever I said must have suggested how the scene excited me. For he turned and asked how I could have kept away from it so long. Not waiting for an answer (we both knew it) he went on in a matter-of-fact tone that gave his statement even more force: "You could walk into any of those agencies and be snapped up on the spot."

The good feeling came over me in a rush — I had forgotten how good — that the world wanted what I could do. For a moment I gave myself up to it. But only a moment. To consider taking a job here would mean I had lost faith in the great future Claud and I had planned.

Coming back we heard waking-up chirps from the cabin. Roy, who had been on watch, came to meet us with a praying mantis in a jar. The great green insect swayed from side to side, its tiny face wearing the sanctimonious look that reminded me suddenly of an elder who took up the collection in church when I was small. The insect's forelimbs were folded in a pose of piety that did not quite hide the knives underneath.

Roy said that her descendants — if she was a female, as he hoped — would kill thousands of pests in his father's garden. That should make up (he giggled) for her biting off her husband's head when she was through with him.

As I carried Claudia out to dress her I heard a murmur of what sounded like scientific conversation. Hermann was giving Roy the same serious attention he had given the adults at lunch.

I was putting Claudia into a gift dress of blue organdy. As I brushed her hair she heard Hermann's step and looked over her shoulder, then turned coquettishly away from him. After a moment she turned back, holding out her arms. They were very round, with a fruitlike bloom. Sometimes a baby could seem more voluptuous than a woman.

She let him pick her up and carry her to the other room. When I went in she was sitting within the circle of his arm, playing with his keys. I asked if he was as experienced as he looked. He said there was a baby in Chicago he knew fairly well.

Almost before the thought had time to enter my mind I asked the question: "Yours?"

"Conceivably."

I laughed at his choice of words. But the atmosphere in the room had changed. He was no longer just a chance guest who happened not to play tennis and whose politics interested me, but someone human and individual, with a past perhaps (like mine) a little problematic.

Roy had come back to say that Mimi's boss had demanded to see Claudia. A behaviorist whose studies proved that babies needed stimulation, he carried out his theories by old-fashioned poking and prodding, while strongly enunciating baby talk in Claudia's face. I couldn't entirely protect her; he was an eminent psychologist, the chief this year of Mimi's division at the National Research Council. To forestall his jealousy I took the baby from Hermann as we walked down the path. But I kept the feeling of rapport. He must be as preoccupied with that mother in Chicago as I was with Claud.

This was not strictly true; like most human situations, his was complicated. But when I murmured that we were more or less in the same boat he didn't deny it.

He said he'd let me know how his interviews turned out. Either way, he added, he would send me some books from New York.

CHAPTER 4

The next week his first book arrived — *The Coming Struggle for Power* by John Strachey. Two weeks later a baby pen was delivered. "It's an investment in work-feasibility," Hermann wrote. "When it pays off, you can reimburse me for half its cost. The other half is strictly between me and Claudia."

It took five minutes to decipher those few lines, even though I had had some practice since he left. He had written to me every day or so, and perhaps in one of my answers I had described Claudia's comic look of outrage when pine needles pricked her knees as she crawled around where I sat typing. I felt uneasy about accepting the pen, but he was right; it made concentration much easier, and soon did pay off.

At first his letters had caused me problems. Claud was the one I wanted letters from and Hermann's handwriting was almost illegible.

But I soon began to value them, even when they were only brief accounts of talk among the Marxists in the John Reed Club. He reported their ridicule of his prospective chief, General Hugh Johnson, and the campaign to get industry's compliance with the National Recovery Administration. The president was helping; in his Fireside Chats he urged consumers to buy only where they could see the NRA sign with its blue eagle and the words We Do Our Part.

"The crazy thing is that it's working," Hermann said, "even on me." He had accepted the Washington job, in spite of misgivings.

Letting a whole industry get together to set prices and limit production had the effect of canceling all the hard-won antitrust laws, but in return for this the industries had to let unions be legalized. Also, for the first time in history child labor was prohibited. This and the minimum wage of fifteen dollars for a forty-hour week seemed advance enough to balance almost anything. Women in the cotton mills had been earning four or five dollars a week for such long hours that they worked through winter weeks without seeing daylight. Children spent their childhood rushing from one loom to another tying threads with their tiny nimble fingers, until they collapsed with tuberculosis and their little brothers and sisters took their places.

Gradually I began to look forward to his letters. He was making me see the schemes and patterns, the power plays behind the events in the news. They helped me wake up from my heat-drugged days of waiting, to exercise my mind (to a limited degree, at least). I began transcribing some of his reports and sending them to Claud; soon in an issue of *The Week* I recognized an item of New Deal gossip Hermann had picked up from his friend John Donovan.

John had already started at NRA, working in the unit set up to enforce Section 7a guaranteeing the right of workers to organize. Hermann's ambivalence about this "wild-eyed red" was a bit like the mix of attraction and resistance I had felt in grammar school for the bad boy of the class. But Hermann had come much farther from eighth grade than I had. It was a long time before I really understood this, and by then it was too late.

In September he wrote of watching a huge Blue Eagle parade down Fifth Avenue, which had lasted from morning till midnight, people marching all that time, bands playing "Happy Days Are Here Again," the atmosphere festive and exhilarated. "They think everyone will have a job tomorrow, at thirty a week," Hermann wrote. "They're in for a big come-down." And yet their excitement had been infectious. "It was just a matter of numbers, I suppose. All those millions marching together. Nothing has ever been seen like it. I kept thinking what a kick you'd have got out of it."

I suppose I did catch the significance of his beginning to see things with my eyes and be affected by my imagined response.

30

But what surprised me more, when he arrived for Sunday lunch again, was the impact of his actual presence. I was physically conscious of him from halfway across the room. Even at that distance I noticed that the fan of lines his smile imprinted at the corners of his eyes gave him an endearingly friendly look. I was relieved that he volunteered when Rollo announced that the tennis court needed rolling after the morning's rain. I wasn't ready for another walk in the woods. During Hermann's weeks of absence something had changed between us.

I settled Claudia for her nap, got into shorts, and was passing the house when Mimi called me in. She pointed down to where the men were working, stripped to the waist, the sun bright on their bodies. Hermann was bending forward, pushing the roller; highlights moved on his wetly gleaming arms and shoulders. Glancing at me, Mimi made a remark that sounded as if she had planned it. "Very few males can take off their clothes without looking ridiculous," she said. "Your Teutonic lover may be one of them."

I suppose I demurred at the word "lover." But why not, she wanted to know? Why not a little refreshment after all these long virtuous months? Wasn't my fidelity misplaced, anyway? I could not agree. My fidelity had not been a matter of virtue but a choice and a passion.

I doubt if I said much of this to her — I was a little too wary for that. From my earliest childhood she had been able to win my confidence so easily, and she still could, even though she had betrayed it so often.

When I was nineteen a scenic artist who had come to Washington to take charge of his sets at the opening of Eddie Cantor's musical *Kid Boots,* had walked into the boarding house where I lived, and seeing me at the top of a ladder trimming the Christmas tree, had within an hour proposed to me. I was working as a stenographer for $22.50 a week; even with night classes at George Washington and art classes at the Corcoran I felt locked into a life without future. This stranger was attractive, talented, and his work exciting; he would introduce me to the world of the theatre. He wooed me with Shakespeare passages he had memorized from the paint bridge high above the stage where famous classic actors were declaiming. But I sensed some danger in him, and after weeks of doubt asked Mimi what she would do in my place. Without a moment's hesitation she said "I'd marry him tomorrow!"

I learned later why she wanted me off and away. She'd been having an affair with a man who had begun to write me long letters full of advice on my reading and my painting.

Families can absorb even betrayals; they have to. I had fled to Mimi from that dangerous marriage. All this time hers had been the home I could bring my friends to, for weekends of lavish food and drink. And here I was this summer with my baby.

Mimi had a way of making intimacy with her deliciously inviting. Now, when she invited me with a tilt of her head, I followed her.

Entering her bedroom always gave me a feeling of disorientation. The house had been built economically, its only aesthetic indulgence the large living room with casement windows and alcove for Rollo's Steinway. The sleeping space was meant to be purely functional. But surrounded by all this bare wood and tile, Mimi had created for herself a boudoir, the boudoir of somebody's mistress — as in fact it usually was. For within view were her trophies: an exquisite tiny liqueur cup of worked silver brought from Russia during the revolution by a journalist who had once occupied my cabin; an oil sketch done by Charlie, my first love, with whom at age eighteen I had gone sketching along that same shore; a turquoise necklace in a French enameled tray, tossed there with topaz earrings and a bracelet of garnets and pearls, worn home casually from some academic conference.

From a shelf at the head of her bed she drew out a small book and read aloud a passage about a woman being like a fruit whose rich flesh should be parted and savored slowly. Then with hardly a pause she began speaking dreamily of the techniques of making love, describing the ways a woman could help a man prolong their pleasure, how she could tease and tantalize, vary her stillnesses and rhythms, distract and delay and postpone, recharge and add seduction, heighten the waiting, deepen and glorify the climax.

Mimi's tone was soft, with a full timbre that was new to me. Her normal way of speaking was midwestern, practical. Now, though, this hot day as she lay there on her daybed, her full breasts molded in linen of the same coral color pulsing in her cheeks, her voice melted into my own mood.

Hermann, showered and dressed in his gray suit, spoke casually, almost impersonally, proposing that I go with him the next night to meet his friends. When I hesitated, Mimi (who from the first had stipulated "No baby care!") said at once that she could put Claudia to bed. And so it was arranged.

CHAPTER 5

When Hermann said we were going to the Newspaper Club, I envisioned the large elegant dining room paneled in dark wood I had imagined from Claud's letters written on Washington Press Club paper. This place turned out to be a bleak speakeasy with bare bulbs hanging from the pressed-tin ceiling. Almost in the first minute I saw a cockroach as big as a mouse moving along the wall. "It's the 'in' place for New Dealers," Hermann said, and that night it was crowded.

John Donovan had saved a place for us at his table. He was fierce-browed, with sharp features and a lock of dark hair falling over his forehead. He studied me intently while we were being introduced, as if measuring me for political possibilities. Before I could worry about the result I was being greeted from across the room by Gardner Jackson. He insisted on taking me over to see Dode, presenting me to everyone we passed as "Claud Cockburn's little lady."

On the way back my hand was caught by a red-haired office colleague of Jackson's, Mary Taylor. Drawing me down to sit beside her, she asked how I had liked being identified as someone's little lady. Not wanting to go into that, I said Pat probably meant it kindly.

Mary laughed. "And Pat thinks of himself as a raging feminist." Her voice was low, with a gurgle of amusement. I felt an immediate liking for her. She knew *The Week*, which her friend Rodney Dutcher, a columnist for the Scripps-Howard syndicate (a huge man, shouting in another corner) called required reading for Washington journalists.

Mary talked between gusts of smoke from a cigarette in a long holder held between prominent teeth on which were flecks of tobacco and a smudge of lipstick. For some reason this added to her charm for me. I found myself admitting having designed the format of *The Week*. This led to questions from her that drew from me what amounted to a resumé. Before I went back to Hermann's table I had promised to start work at the Consumers' Counsel office Monday morning.

I think it is possible to be drunk on decibels. Of course I had other reasons to feel intoxicated, but I had been thirsting all summer for this kind of noise. And these voices were full of the excitement of history, of making history happen. Leaving the club I heard one woman cry over the clamor: "Carl Sandburg next week! Imagine, culture in the White House!"

It was cool outside, and Hermann hung his jacket around my shoulders as we waited for our taxi. When it came he declined my offer to drop him off in Georgetown where he was staying with Dr. Corell. I didn't insist. It had been so long since I had ridden home in a taxi with a man after a party.

As we moved west on K Street, Hermann reached for a cigarette from his jacket pocket. The pocket was over my breast, and I felt the touch of his fingers through the cloth. I glanced over to see whether he had been as aware of it as I was. In the flare of the lighter his face wore a look of concentration, and he didn't speak at once. Then he went on with what he had been telling me, about how he and his friend Ernst were putting each other through graduate school. This was Hermann's year to work and send a stipend to Ernst at Columbia.

Crossing Key Bridge I pointed upstream, to where the steep banks closed in, the water dark with moving shadows. Roy sailed his canoe up there among the rocks and rapids, I told Hermann. Mimi and Rollo believed in letting the boys take their own risks. "But are they equipped to assess them?" Hermann asked.

Maybe not, I had to agree. Then I thought of my own risks. "Maybe nobody ever really is," I said.

It was then, as we spoke of risks, that he told me the story that I would remember and ponder, searching for clues.

One spring when he was fifteen he took a river trip with a professor at the *gymnasium* who had helped him make up his Latin when he entered the school from America. They were paddling kayaks, and the river was high. In the middle of a rapids the professor's boat caught on a submerged crag and went under.

And Hermann had saved him. I guessed this at once, though he had not been about to tell. This professor, he went on, had wanted him to study philosophy instead of engineering. Hermann had been tempted, but had not let his parents know how strongly. For his father counted on his following in his footsteps, and he had, though he thought now that this had been a mistake. When he had finally left engineering for economics his father had accepted his decision; even in those early days he might have understood. He told me all this as if he felt it important for me to know.

The other important talk on that ride began when he reached again for a cigarette, noting that I didn't smoke. I suppose I prattled on, as I tended to do, mentioning some scientific discovery about the effect of a mother's smoking on a baby's heartbeat. When he spoke of my having made a responsible kind of decision, I looked at him quickly. "You sound surprised," I said. "And I can understand why."

He doubted if I did quite understand. "Put it that I try to limit my expectations of people."

Those words hung in the air for a minute while I tried to be sure I had taken in their meaning. They seemed to have portent for us. In fact everything we said to each other on that ride seemed to be telling us more about each other than we might have learned from years of acquaintance. What I learned — or could have, if I had listened with the ear of someone more inclined to delve, to wonder, to suspect, to doubt — might have made me hesitate. But my ear heard what I wanted — maybe needed — to hear. And having heard it I could give only one answer, as we climbed the hill to the cabin and he asked if he could let the taxi go.

37

CHAPTER 6

When I went to work in the office of the Consumers Counsel, our chief was Frederick C. Howe, an old reformer who had helped clean up Cleveland before World War I. Later he had fought for woman suffrage with his wife, Marie, the biographer of George Sand. Her recent death, Mary Taylor said, had desolated him.

His welcome was benevolent, and I must have answered respectfully. But the word "reformer" had given me my cue to hear the click of his false teeth and note that his hair was too dark to be true.

What I didn't know, or have the perception to guess, was that this old liberal was braver than most of the radicals around. He would defend the consumer against the meat packers and the dairy industry when others (like Secretary Wallace, who talked righteously about "the forces of evil") would surrender. And my chief would be fired for his courage.

If I had looked up his *Collier's* article of 1917, I might have seen him differently. "I want woman suffrage," Howe wrote, "because it will also free men." His article recalls that Wendell Phillips had said negro slavery was bad enough for the blacks but worse for the whites. The master was chained by shackles that bound the slave. "I want woman suffrage," Howe concludes, "for what it will do for woman, for what it will do for men, for what it will do for the muddle we have made of politics."

By 1933 women had been voting for over a decade, without doing much about the muddle. But Dr. Howe was youthfully hopeful. He had taken this job, he told us, because he was "selfish." His kind of selfishness had been explained in that article: "I cannot myself be happy in a world where there is so much poverty, so much hunger, so much suffering that can so easily be cured."

This spirit had brought hundreds of people to Washington. And (however daringly different I might think myself) it made a team of us — five oddly assorted women who filled the small room in the old marble-columned Department of Agriculture building.

I sat across a double desk from Mary Taylor. At Mary's left was Iris Walker, a practical working Democrat, widow of a congressman and our liaison with Capitol Hill. I had dismissed her at first glance as a clubwoman type; she was, and to our advantage. In a few months I would be producing radio programs in which the president of the General Federation of Women's Clubs would ask questions of Dr. Howe, eliciting consumer information that would have startled her if she had not been too preoccupied with her performance to notice. Others noticed, all over the country.

Anne Carter, the severe-faced woman opposite Iris, was a member of the Woman's Party, whose feminist position I couldn't understand; for the sake of equality they were ready to give up the few humane concessions women had won in the workplace. At a small desk in the corner sat Margaret Thompson, untrained and idealistic, an English Fabian.

Mary herself was a Norman Thomas socialist. I was told this scornfully by Nathaniel Weyl, a twenty-two-year-old economist in the adjoining office. Nat himself, Pat Jackson whispered to me in awe, was "a card-carrying Communist."

Later, as a Communist, I would have to try to think of Mary, a Socialist, as our enemy. But she was a passionate fighter for consumer rights and a shrewd, effective strategist. She loved the outwitting and circumventing required to get okays on what we wanted to publish in the *Consumers' Guide*. The old-line information chief rightly suspected our agency, since any helpful knowledge we might give the consumer would outrage the powerful interests the Department of Agriculture had always served, or at least appeased.

Mary knew how to bring forces to bear; her voice on the telephone was a soft, conspiratorial murmur that filled me with a delicious suspense. The names she spoke flashed like a neon sign with power: Tommy "The Cork" Corcoran, ever at Roosevelt's elbow, along with Ben Cohen, nudging the president in directions they (sometimes because of Mary) wanted him to go; Bernard Baruch, who had sixty members of the House and Senate in his pocket; Harold Ickes, the "old curmudgeon" over at Interior, a Republican but incorruptible; Robert Moses, with whom Mary had worked in New York, creating Jones Beach, and whom now, despite his intransigence, she thought the New Deal needed; Molly Dewson, who could set Democratic wheels moving in complex patterns to drive through some pet project or appointment of Mary's; Doris Fleeson, a journalist whose influence in the newspaper world brought support to whatever side she and Mary decided was the right one on any question.

Mrs. Roosevelt became more and more important to us. Each week Mary and I went to her press conference, held in a sunny upstairs sitting room in the White House. Some of the newspaper women asked her the personal kind of questions supposedly of female interest, and she answered innocently. Telling about her privileged girlhood, she recalled her English boarding school where they spoke French at meals. When they wanted bread they had to say "du pang." But if I giggled later over her pronunciation — how amusing to be in the position of laughing at the first lady — Mary quickly set me right. Like other New Dealers, Mrs. Roosevelt was learning on the job. Mary and I carefully planned our questions to inform her about problems we thought urgent. A quick study, she needed only to have her interest stirred and we could count on action.

Of all possible ways of getting power I think Mary really preferred intrigue. At first I didn't connect it with her heritage. When she called herself "black Irish," I stared at her auburn hair and gold-brown eyes. She explained that her forebears had been Protestants in Catholic Ireland. Sent to Mount Holyoke for a lady's education, she had chosen the least ladylike profession possible, becoming a newspaper reporter. For several years she had covered Spain for the *Chicago Daily News*. She had had many lovers (if she wanted to sleep with someone, I heard, she simply told him so) without any desire to marry. But now she was ready to break all her rules to wrest her Scripps-Howard columnist, Rodney Dutcher, from his wife and young son.

I caught the clue when I learned (to my amazement) that her father had been a Presbyterian minister. She had been raised a Calvinist, taught to do what she ought to do, I told Hermann. And then, growing up in the twenties, she found she ought to rebel. "So she's more conscientiously wicked than any really wicked person."

Hermann delighted in such paradoxes. And if he saw that this one also applied to me he didn't say so. Maybe he didn't see it any more clearly than I did. He seemed to have a high opinion of my intelligence, and I tried to do nothing to undermine this precarious situation. I suppose both of us really had the illusion that I did my own quite reasonable thinking.

Each night he asked me about my day, and at first I reported, as I had to Claud, only the odd and comic, such as the battle between our newly hired Hearst "sob sister" and the old-line chief clerk. After decades of pouncing on latecomers and subtracting half an hour from their annual leave, he couldn't deal with anyone's wanting to work all night. To tease him Milly had started dutifully reporting to him each five minutes she took to go to the toilet.

These anecdotes didn't suffice for Hermann. He demanded *my* news. For example if I told about an official lunch for George Russell, the poet A.E., he wanted to hear any questions I had asked. I began to understand that whatever had happened to me interested him. When at last I could believe this I relaxed as I never had with any man. Always before, though unaware of it — in fact scornful of the idea — I had felt the effort of trying to please.

Hermann's own reports often mentioned John Donovan, who was causing an uproar at NRA. Although he worked in the unit that was supposed to protect labor unions, when he began talking of a union in NRA itself they called him a Communist. "Which he is, of course," Hermann said cheerfully.

John was pressing him to join the Party. But Hermann knew that would mean being under orders, at whatever risk to his career. He had always been successful, and he enjoyed the feeling. (I liked his frankness about this.) He kept putting John off.

We usually did this reporting, those first weeks, in the rumble seat of the family Marmon. Theoretically Hermann lived with Dr. Corell, but since he seldom spent a night there Mimi saw no sense in his going to a restaurant for dinner and then coming out to Virginia by taxi. In any case, the whole situation, with Claudia being cared for by Mimi's maid's niece, would last only until my appointment went through. Like many others in that frantic first year of the New Deal, I had gone to work without waiting to be officially hired.

On the day in December when the document came, assuring me $3200 a year, I moved into an apartment near Rock Park that Hermann had found. "With a view of Paris rooftops," he said proudly, "or a reasonable facsimile. And equidistant from zoo and nursery school."

Knowing no better, I had presented Claudia, aged eight months, at the Kalorama Day School. In the Depression their enrollment was down, they happened to have a nurse on their staff, and after a moment's blinking said, "Why not?" The children were charmed with Claudia, and she with them. Not yet able to walk, bracing herself against a post or wall, she joined their games. A snapshot shows her plumply erect in plaid overalls, her fair hair blowing in the wind, a volleyball in her arms, while the six-year-old son of the Chinese ambassador beams paternally down on her.

Naiveté may have helped, too, at the office. With the unwariness of an Isadora Duncan walking into Rodin's Paris studio, I entered the offices of austere government officials and got interviews. Often these articles revealed startling information which, okayed by the eminent, could not be censored. Knowing nothing in so many areas I found every discovery exciting, and since I knew how to write for the multitude, I could put this excitement into consumer information.

We became expert at explaining the Depression: how the workers when laid off had to cut down on meat and milk and go without new shirts, causing more layoffs in the factories that made clothes, less income for the farmers who produced the meat and milk and cotton; these farmers would not be able to buy shoes or furniture or tractors; factory owners would lay off more and more workers, who would become unable to buy the food they needed; this pushed farm prices down so low that citrus growers let carloads of oranges rot, and milk flowed in ditches along the Iowa roads. Meanwhile factories went out of business, causing more unemployment, and so on and on.

We used this as preamble for telling how the Agricultural Adjustment Administration, along with the other New Deal agencies, would make the cycle start going up instead of down. Writing this caused us some misgivings. The AAA set out to raise farm prices by reducing surpluses, which at first meant destroying crops and killing young pigs. Wasting food, when millions hadn't enough to eat?

But that oversimplified the problem. Three hundred million bushels of wheat had gone unsold that year, even at prices lower than they had been for centuries. Henry Wallace, secretary of agriculture, remarked that our country had "the largest wheat surplus and the longest breadlines in its history." As it turned out, a terrible drought took care of that reduction problem.

We played up the good side, such as soil conservation. Every year seven hundred million tons of the richest topsoil blew away or washed into rivers that carried it to the Gulf of Mexico. When farmers were paid to take land out of production, they had to give soil-saving treatment to those acres. Roosevelt's favorite program called for planting bands of trees all over the country as windbreaks to prevent the terrible dust storms that were sweeping the West, dropping grit on the doorstep of the White House and on the decks of ships at sea.

We reported any salvaging we could learn about. If a group began to slaughter piglets and process them into usable meat we told the story. If the women in some town were making mattresses out of surplus cotton we explained the method. *Consumers' Guide* had a huge circulation, since we used every government mailing list we could find.

We worked out sly tricks to make the readers see the absurdities of the system without our censors catching on. The AAA chief of information became more and more vigilant. We had to seize times when he was out of the office to take our copy to the chief of information for the whole department.

Handsome and courteous, Milton Eisenhower treated my stories with respect. He made changes in the guise of teaching me correct government usage, but to my surprise the message came out clearer. I began to think that he was playing, very smoothly and discreetly, on our team.

One of the letters Mrs. Roosevelt sent over to us came from a sharecropper's young daughter. She told of planting a few rows of green beans around her family's cabin. They were almost ready to pick when the plantation's "riding boss" came on his horse and "tromped them all down."

Already the whole New Deal was outraged over the plight of southern tenant farmers, hopelessly trapped, Negro and white alike, in what amounted to slavery. They lived on the owner's plantation, tilled a segment of his land for a share of the value of the crop, and bought their supplies on credit at the plantation commissary, which might charge $4.00 for a $1.95 pair of overalls or 35¢ for a pound of salt pork sold in the local stores for 20¢. At the end of the year the tenant would get a glance at a tally that showed his share of what the crops he had cultivated had brought in, then what he owed, which always turned out to be more. Anyone who questioned the accounting automatically became a "troublemaker," subject to even harsher treatment.

The day that girl's letter came I had just written an article on nutrition, describing the terrible effects of pellagra, the plague of the South, caused by lack of the very vitamins found in green vegetables. I went fuming to Jerome Frank, general counsel of AAA. As he read the labored words on the tablet paper he shook his head and said that kid's writing to the White House would get her family thrown off the place.

"Why?" Weren't the tenants supposed to have garden space? Along with access to woodlots? If not, we had been been printing lies.

He said that question wasn't easy to answer. His young lawyers had struggled over the clauses, trying to keep the plantation owners from letting the AAA agreement, with its reduction of crops, become an excuse for putting people off the place. Naturally, the ones they wanted to get rid of were the "troublemakers." And even the mildest agreement about keeping tenants had to have the clause "insofar as possible" inserted to get the legislation through.

I knew what he meant. Our most senior southern senators, chairmen of powerful committees, owned some of the biggest plantations. Roosevelt had to keep them behind him or his whole program would be in trouble. That situation alone, I thought, was enough to make a revolutionary of anybody.

Jerome thanked me grimly for not having shown the letter to any of his young hotheads. One more letter like this, and he'd lose hold on their shirttails.

We knew about these lawyers who fought so daringly on our side. Too daringly, and too noisily, Mary thought. Everyone had heard about Lee Pressman's wild remark when he couldn't get a decent milk-marketing agreement. The lawyers for the middlemen were holding out for processors to get a spread that amounted to two-thirds of the price consumers paid for a quart of milk. That kind of bullheadedness, Pressman said, might result in the government taking over the sale of milk. The opposing lawyer said ironically that if they went that far they might as well take over all retail business. "Why not?" asked Pressman.

Later I wondered how he could have spoken so recklessly if he was a Party member then. The CP's first priority was career advancement. And only a year went by before our "Black Monday," when he would be fired.

The newspapers often accused us of "harboring subversives." And we weren't the only ones. As early as October I had written Claud that Hermann's fellow workers on the labor board of NRA took care how they greeted new recruits "because there are many real reds who knew one another as such in New York now working down here."

I went on to report what Hermann had told me of their methods of bringing industrial scandals into the open. "These labor board people are acting as cross-questioning attorneys on labor's side, grilling the bosses. A great deal of cleverness is being used to make some of those blustering hypocrites describe their own crimes. Then of course it's on the record."

Claud's use of the material I sent him was the only way I knew my letters had been received. I understood part of the reason for his silence. Once in speaking of his failure to write to Berta in Austria, he had said that the longer he put it off the less possible he found it. I assured him I had made a new life that was emotionally complete. Except, of course, for the sharing of Claudia with him.

Apart from this continuing pain my days seemed designed to satisfy. At work I was learning all the time, meeting new demands, using all my skills. If we lacked an illustration for an article, I ran up to the art department and drew one. I felt valued by a group of people I had come to care about. The rush and pressure of our hours at the office had the liveliness of social occasions, with the extra charge of working together for a cause important to us. And we could have spent all our evenings merrymaking. "It's lucky for the country that New Dealers are such hard workers," Hermann said once, "otherwise people would take jobs in Washington just for the parties."

We had slipped into domesticity with an ease that held a fillip of newness too. Neither of us had had anything like this experience. Together we could count on peace and reason, yet with a sexual tingle and glow.

Hermann had never lived with a woman before, though girls had started welcoming him into their beds when he was sixteen. In New York he shared an apartment near Columbia with his friend Ernst. But the only woman he had seriously considered marrying, Elsa, was still living with her husband.

Elsa was not the one who had a child that might possibly be Hermann's. That young mother, absurdly enough, never gave me any concern. To me there was something essentially unalarming about a dentist's wife. But Elsa — what Hermann told me about her — gave me sharp conflicting sensations. First, I had the shaky left-out feeling I had suffered as a new girl in fifth grade, in a new stepfamily that had not accepted me.

Elsa and her current husband, Bill, whom she preferred to call Clive, gave their local A & P market a French pronunciation, "Ah-

Pay." My New York friends went in for whimsy like this, but now I found it an odious affectation. And yet, absurdly, it made me feel inferior, left out.

Opposed was a feeling of superiority. Elsa, a singer, believed in total commitment to art — never to be deflected or even influenced by political urgencies. Police horses recently had ridden down a rally of unemployed in Union Square, only a few blocks from where Elsa lived. Shutting herself off to sing her scales put her in the class with my humorist friend on *Life*, who had written a comic piece from the point of view of the horses that had faced women defending themselves with hatpins.

As a Marxist, Hermann could not accept Elsa's position, and had given up the idea of marrying her. "Is politics *that* important to you?" I asked. He nodded, and I felt a little smug. A woman could take pride in meeting all a man's requirements.

Probably he and I had come together with the same need — to fill an emptiness, one we needn't be ashamed of but which had ached until we met. The first weeks had been tacitly conditional. But we kept finding more about each other to delight in, to depend on for satisfying deeper, unknown needs.

He was a ready, confident lover, with a talent for intimacy. His own natural savoring of sensation taught me to relax in a new, luxurious sureness. He seemed to savor everything about our life, from sex and food and drink to the lusciousness and comedy of Claudia. He found fun in small misadventures, like being roused in the night by the cat racing down the hall pulling a toy that rang bells when the wheels went around. But he took Claudia seriously, even trying to understand scientifically how her smile could carry such a charge of apparent love. Since from the first he had marveled at her clear resolve to become an upright walking person, he may have seen it as a greater triumph than even a "real" father would, when she celebrated her first birthday by walking across the room to him.

My apartment, high up in a large anonymous building, had had the feeling of a hideaway, which relieved my worry over our illicit status. After a time Hermann brought his things from New York. His books in stained and neatly stacked apple boxes formed walls of

French paperbacks and German philosophy, politics, and poetry. He found a neighborhood cabinet maker who built two heavy trestle tables of birch wood to his design, one for dining, one for his desk.

"The lines of our life have fallen, as the Bible says, in pleasant places," I wrote Claud, and heard from him for the first time in many months.

Guardedly he said the situation that had been "70% responsible" for his silence had "by a sad irony ended more or less disastrously" twelve hours before my letter arrived. He added that he had a drawer full of enthusiastic starts of plans for my joining him — plans that collapsed before he could finish describing them. He told of collecting money for my trip and having to spend it for a purpose I would have approved if I could have known about it. He ended with another reason for delay:

"The situation here, politically, gets tougher by the minute; what they have in Germany isn't anything like as far off as people might think, and in a situation like that I guess it's natural not to want the people you're fondest of to be in the firing line."

I supposed that was true, but the words sounded like a quotation. He loved the snapshots of Claudia, he said, then asked for more pictures of me. "The one I had when I left that I carry in my pocket case is so worn already." He cautioned me not to show his letter to anybody but Hermann, and closed with a sentence that might have echoed chapel services at school: "If you can think of any way I might make up to you for all those things I have left undone, you might let me know."

Neither Hermann nor I could. The magnolias bloomed on the Mall, Claudia had seen the new lion cubs in the zoo, and I still hadn't answered, when the call came that put an end to this whole period.

An accented male voice gave the name of Wiesner. "The friend of Claud, you remember. He calls me Berti."

Of course I remembered. When I first heard of him I had been confused by Claud's two most important political influences having

49

almost the same name. This Berti, an internationally known biologist, did research at Edinburgh University on female sexuality. He had once offered to write for my magazine, but we couldn't figure out how to put his kind of knowledge into language understandable to my readers without shocking them and breaking publishing taboos.

Now in New York at a scientific conference, Berti said he must see me about a matter of life-and-death importance. It had to do with Claud, and he could not discuss it over the phone. I must take the first train. Hermann agreed that I had no choice but to go.

Berti was a handsome, red-cheeked Austrian in his early thirties. Not much taller than I, he had an almost childlike quality due partly to his simplified English. But what he said had to be heeded. He was deeply concerned about Claud, whose present way of life he thought reckless and irresponsible. Without giving details he seemed to despise the company Claud was keeping.

I had heard disquieting reports from another friend of Claud's, Ernestine Evans, the journalist who had got him the contract with Lippincott for his book *High Low Washington*. She had said something about "orgies of young men." I had put it out of my mind, and now resisted Berti's hints.

But he persisted. Then he said he had been impressed last year at the change in Claud after his stay in America. He had seemed a much stronger character, more reliable and mature. From suggestions Claud let fall, Berti was sure it was due to his relationship with me.

Incredulous, I said the influence was the other way around. But Berti said all evidence supported him. And I had a duty to go to England, he insisted. Claud must be saved for his future. His ability to attract and disarm people, to win friends and neutralize enemies, combined with his political shrewdness and creativity, made him indispensable to the movement.

I brought up the same arguments I had used with Pat Jackson. How could I go over uninvited? And Berti, for his different reasons, responded much as Pat Jackson had: it was no time to think of such small things.

But what influence did I have now, if I ever had any? And would it be fair to Hermann? His attachment to Claudia had been deepening all these months, and hers to him.

Hermann answered that question himself, when Berti went back with me to Washington. Feeling immediate rapport with Berti, he explained that he had been thinking for some time that our situation should be "stabilized." He could deal with the indeterminate in philosophy but not in life. He wanted to know where he stood — or rather where I stood. To know this I must see Claud again.

With Mary's support — the journey appealed to her romantic fantasies — I was given two-months leave. I cabled Claud. His delighted answer made me wonder at my resistance last year to Pat's urging. But going to him then would have been a violation of all my principles.

By this time Berti had returned to London. His letters were filled with practical advice about the quality of English nannies, the publications I could write for. One ended with a paragraph that shocks me now:

"As to civil war I think it would break out all right if only a sufficient number of people were told that it was going to, and were told so for a long time in a loud voice. *The Week,* alas, is not yet equipped with a voice loud enough for the purpose. It does its best, though."

Reading this then, I felt only a surge of excitement.

CHAPTER 7

"If I had known how it would be to leave you," I wrote to Hermann that first night in May of 1934 aboard the USS *American Farmer,* "I never would have made the decision." I kept seeing that endearing curve of his mouth, the indentation below. "A philosopher with a dimple in his chin," I had called him. He preferred that I leave philosophy out of it. He did not want to be loved for his mind, he said with such emphasis that I laughed, not knowing how seriously he meant it, much less how I would ponder this seriousness, trying to search in it for a clue to the mystery I couldn't have imagined, that night, ever having to confront.

Lying in my bunk I relived our last weekend together, the excursion down the Potomac to Chesapeake Bay — in my memory all sunshine and clarity. What waited for me at the end of this voyage now seemed just the opposite.

When Claud had sailed for England he had given me an address on a famous London square. The "old chum" from Oxford who lived there had a wife now, and even an extramarital girlfriend — a mediocre one, Claud wrote, saying he had tried her out.

Like other boys of his class he had spent his adolescence in a boarding school, where students hardly dared admit they had sisters. Claud himself had told me that this system tended to replace the living young male heart with one of wood. Not his, I had told him. But what about those tales of Berti's and Ernestine's?

Claud's cousin, Alec Waugh, had exposed upper-class school life in his best-seller, *The Loom of Youth.* He wrote it on his way to

World War I, and never went to Oxford. If he had, he might have written about the literary clique there, to which his younger brother Evelyn and Claud belonged. Dressing like dandies, their Edwardian doeskin trousers pulled down skintight by straps under their shoes, they put on an air of weary sybaritic cynicism, scorning all family-style virtues. "Womanizers" were beneath contempt. Not until Claud had taken his honors degree and won the award that made it possible for him to travel abroad did he meet Berta and have his revelation. After that, he told me, he could never go back. "It was just so much *better*." But now people worried over the way he lived. What way? The unknown is always frightening.

I thought of Hermann, his easy candor, his steadiness, his undemanding calm and humor. I remembered the torn feeling I had had as I watched him, trim and erect, walking away from me, down the gangplank with his friend Ernst.

Courage returned in the morning. I couldn't resist adventure — and crossing the ocean to meet it.

Traveling on this modest ship with a baby was different from sailing on fast liners full of potential romance. Entranced as Claudia was by the doings of passengers and crew, she kept me within hand's reach at all times. And her bliss when I pushed her around the deck in her own stroller made me write to Hermann, "This proves the experts are right about a child's security depending on familiarity." This set me up for a surprise.

We were due to land on a Monday morning. Since it was Whitsun, a bank holiday, with no London dockworkers on the job, we must put in at Tilbury, twenty-three miles downriver. Supposing anyone would want to come that far to meet us, how would they find out where to go?

On the last day I packed early and had Claudia with me on deck an hour before landing time. A stir at the starboard rail caught my glance. And as I watched, astonished, a head appeared — Claud's. He had hired a motorboat to come out to us in midstream. And then, the least athletic of men, he had climbed up the side of the ship on a rope ladder.

For over a year I had imagined the scene of Claud's first sight of his daughter. Now, almost in a daze, I was seeing it happen. On his knees facing her, he spoke her name softly. I made a move, from habit, to reassure her. But she paid me no attention. Gazing into his face, taking a deep breath, she gave him both her hands.

In all these ten days she had put strangers to severe and lengthy tests before accepting their friendship. But now, her hands in Claud's, she turned to me and smiled, as if in some sort of mutual congratulation.

Claud had turned to me, too, and suddenly, after all those night-time fears, I saw him exactly as I had known him — unsinister, warmly eager, familiar, and dear. And with the extra shared delight in Claudia.

Claud had a taxi waiting to take us to London. He was lifting Claudia into it when I was called back to identify a trunk. I reached for her hand, assuming she would insist on going with me. Ignoring it, she hardly noticed me leave. When I returned she glanced up only briefly from her game — handing a match box to Claud and receiving it again from him with an ecstatic smile.

The day went on that way — an idyll. Claud had taken a room for us at a hotel on the Bayswater Road, and that afternoon we fed the swans in Kensington Garden. When Claud told her that the seven little brown baby birds were cygnets, she listened as if she had been waiting all her life for this information from her father.

When he had done his first paternal reading of bedtime stories and tucked his daughter in, we went down to the little bar, where the idyll came to an end. During the first half hour as we drank our scotch, it seemed like old times. I realized only gradually that we were both trying to make conversation, trying rather hard.

Until then, between his attentions to Claudia, Claud had filled every minute with politics. Even more sanguine than Berti about the prospects of civil war, he thought a big bloc of the middle class was so fed up with Britain's pandering to Hitler that they could be led to join the desperate working class against the Tory government. Stammering with eagerness, his brown eyes bright, he told about the intellectual and religious eminences he had brought together in organized protests. He spoke excitedly as he had in New

York, but with an important difference. Now he described what he was actually doing, not just planning to do. My cheeks burned with fervor. I couldn't wait to get into the fight.

The doubts of those nights on the ship had vaporized. True, he had cultivated all sorts of people, for political purposes, though it might have looked like choice. He had not been able to explain this to anyone. "My status is different, these last few months. That is to say, even Berti can't know what I'm up to nowadays."

This meant, of course, that he had joined the Party. I felt moved and honored to be taken into his confidence, and into his plans, on our first day together.

But that night as we sat side by side at the bar we made small talk. I gave him entertaining tidbits from the voyage, telling about Claudia's Eurasian admirers, the Urquharts, how Mr. Urquhart made a point of dressing for dinner even when in rough weather. "Ah yes," Claud said, "you won't find anyone more pukka any-where than a semi-Chinaman with the name of Urquhart or Mac-Tavish."

All I noted then was the absent way he said this. Only later did I wonder at the condescension in his tone. Was his abstraction so deep that he had forgotten his Marxism?

We were trying to talk through the same preoccupation — the night ahead. A sort of final silence fell at last, and he asked if I was tired. At that moment I could have said yes; I felt my exhaustion suddenly. But how could I rest in this situation? I remembered how scornfully he had dismissed women who delayed and teased. And we were married, after all. We had parted at the height of our pas-sion, and had met again with the joy of sharing our child for the first time. He had confided momentous news. Surely he would not ex-pect such a day to end by my cutting myself off from him. So, when he asked, "Shall I come up with you?" I nodded.

In the room where we lay hearing Claudia's breathing nearby, the test came that we did not pass. In loving simulation we each gave what we thought the other expected. Only after further whiskies at a different bar could we find words to admit, reluc-tantly, that something was missing, some essential had gone.

I could hardly have expected those months with Hermann to leave me unchanged. For himself Claud had worked out a theory based on his early erotic tastes. When he first met me in New York, with my hair cut short and sleek, he had seen me as a sort of boy-girl, dashing and reckless. Now he saw me as a mother, responsible. My hair, falling almost to my shoulders, symbolized the difference. He took a different pleasure in seeing me this way; it intensified our sharing of Claudia. But. . . .

He made his theory convincing, and so acceptable that I hardly noticed its contradictions, which should have become obvious when I met the women in his life.

On our second evening he took me to see a journalist who lived in one of the seventeenth-century cottages built by an early Prince of Wales for his mistresses, far out on a pier where the ships passed by to dock. Claud had suggested that she could help me find markets for my writing. But I sensed a sadness about her hospitality and guessed that Claud was using my arrival to make a tactful break with her. I found it easy to feel sorry for someone so frangibly feminine.

This began a period of irony, with Claud showing off his wife and child everywhere. Among the passengers on the bus to the Whipsnade Zoo he must have looked like any proud young father taking his child to see the animals roaming in the wild. But we lunched at the director's residence, and one of the other guests was Kingsley Martin, editor of the *New Statesman*. On the way home Claud told me that Martin had congratulated him in terms even more enthusiastic than he had expected. "And that is excellent," he said significantly, "in the circumstances."

Seeing that Claud valued this friendship, I was glad Kingsley Martin liked to come to dinner at the little house we had found in Chelsea. But not till the night we met him at the Cafe Royal could I realize how much importance Claud gave that friendship.

Until then, the idea of Claud telling me how to behave on a social occasion would have made both of us laugh. However much I might need instruction, he would not have dreamed of giving it. But that night he warned me that Martin was a restless type, and I should agree instantly to any change of scene. Since Claud himself liked to linger — in fact he often spent the whole day here meeting people — I guessed he was warning himself as well. And so calculatingly! He had a natural talent for pleasing; for him to please by careful plan seemed wildly out of character.

The *New Statesman,* like the *New Republic* and the *Nation* in America, effectively guided the political thinking of liberals. At the moment Martin could boast of a great coup: H.G. Wells had promised to let the *Statesman* publish verbatim his coming interview with Stalin in Moscow. It would naturally cause a sensation; but neither Claud nor Kingsley Martin anticipated the kind of sensation it would create.

I loved the excitement of all this, but longed for Hermann. Mail came five times a day; until ten at night I could hope for a letter to drop on the hall floor. Hermann wrote often, but tried to make his letters cool and objective. Only one began with "Dearest." In order to avoid influencing me he usually left off the salutation altogether. "I think you should not come back to the U.S. — or at least not to me and new possibilities — before you have cleared the slate." He was frank about having wanted to test a return to bachelordom — the independence he had always thought important for a thinker — but admitted it was "getting pretty awful." He wanted my candid reports of the crucial phases of my "experiment." "That is one of the reasons I love you. Because one can *talk* with you, too." But his control would sometimes slip: "I do wish we could just go to bed — it would be so good, I do love you. . . ."

"I know now what it means to 'pine,'" I told him. I felt physically ill, had lost weight. But we agreed that I should give the experiment a full six weeks.

Berti had found a new kind of nanny — young, slim, college-trained, who set off every Sunday for a fox hunt. Weekdays I worked. A piece of New Deal reportage (informal title "Wising up the Suckers") came out as "The Way of the Consumer" in *Time & Tide.* Lady Rhondda had founded this liberal magazine to expiate her guilt over inheriting a Welsh coal-mine fortune. For my friends on *Radio Fanfare* I reported the wireless broadcast of a crucial cricket game that calmly left a half hour's silence on the air while the teams interrupted their passionate contest to have tea.

At the first taste of domesticity Claud had become addicted. Politically it was practical, of course, with someone at home whom Claud could trust to take his mysterious messages. And the "chaps" who turned up unexpectedly seemed to find it easier to give him their secrets over a bowl of stew. What I found surprising was Claud's need for our chaste nights in the big double bed upstairs. They seemed to provide a sense of safety and affection important to him, and maybe also — in my loneliness — to me.

French doors in the dining room opened on a small garden; when Claud came home he hurried out there to toss a balloon or play horse with Claudia. One day he took us to Kew Gardens, even buying a camera to record the trip. When he called a taxi I protested that we could easily have gone by Underground. "If you get the habit now, what will you do when the revolution comes?" "Ah," he said, "the big shots will have cars and drivers."

Why should I remember this more clearly than the political analysis to which I listened so intently? Why can't I recall the articles in the British *Daily Worker* as well as I remember my first look at the advertising? The paper was having a proud period; with the best racing handicapper in the business, its circulation boomed. But as a consumer advocate I found the advertisements shocking. Claud said it was these or none; they had to take what they could get to keep going.

"But you expect the working class to trust you!" I cried. How could they offer a woman a contraceptive that was worthless? What if she counted on it, and then had to get a dangerous abortion — maybe even died? Wasn't that criminal?

Claud hadn't given the business end much thought, he said, but agreed that cheating the readers didn't make political sense. He comforted me by saying he might be in a position one day to do something about it.

Meantime he was working long hours at high pitch, often meeting with union leaders, some of them former Party members, whose cooperation he wanted for Popular Front actions. With these men alert to any sign of Communist maneuvers, he had to keep his guard up every minute.

He had an easier time with the intellectuals. Their own thinking had brought them to the need for action, and in their political naiveté they didn't question the leadership. A dazzling array came together in the Council for Civil Liberties to protest the new Sedition Act. E. M. Forster was president, and on the membership blank that I saved I see listed thirty-five stellar vice presidents. They include — besides Kingsley Martin — H.G. Wells, Bertrand Russell, Julian Huxley, Aneurin Bevan, Vera Brittain, author of *Testament of Youth,* Havelock Ellis, R. W. Tawney, (author of *The Acquisitive Society*), Harold Laski, A. P. Herbert, and the Rt. Hon. Lord Marley.

Gazing at Lord Russell on the platform at some meeting, I remembered the New Deal party where Griffin Barry had showed me pictures of two little Christopher Robin figures — his children, whose mother was Mrs. Russell. He received their school reports, he said, "Just like any parent." If we had used the phrase "open marriage" then, I might have said the Russells' was even more open than my sister's. Or, it appeared, mine.

I don't know why I've waited so long to tell about Jean Ross, whom I met within the first few days. "This afternoon the beautiful girl came into the garden," I wrote Hermann. "She represents in Claud's life what you do in mine." (This was no more accurate than other assumptions of mine.)

A snapshot I took shows Jean in the garden with Claudia. Decades later W. H. Auden put his big finger beside Jean's pictured face and said, "That's her. That's Miss Sally Bowles." And during the hours Jean sat in our garden Christopher Isherwood may well have been writing his *Berlin Stories.* The touching tale about Jean would be dramatized by Van Druten as *I Am A Camera* with Julie Harris a luminous Sally, and still later the musical and film *Cabaret,* with Liza Minelli, who could hardly have contrasted more with the real-life Jean.

In London during the sixties I walked with Jean past a theatre where *Cabaret* was playing. "Have you seen it?" I asked. She answered merely "No," with genuine indifference. She had given her permission and wished Isherwood well in his use of his memories of her. "I was the only girl Chris had ever known."

Meeting Claud had made an almost incredible change in her. Though she probably had seen him seldom in the decades since their daughter was an infant, her concerns were those he had taught her. That night in the sixties she worried about the rise in Underground fares, which made it hard to get workers together for demonstrations.

In 1934 Jean might have thrilled to the idea of herself as heroine of plays and musicals. Only twenty-two, she had come back fairly recently from Berlin, where she had "had over two hundred lovers," I wrote Hermann. Her proper upper-class accent describing those shocking Berlin vices made her seem curiously innocent. And all her spare time from writing film scenarios, I told Hermann, was spent in "concrete activity." By which I meant the Communist Party work we did together in the neighborhood. I liked her, I said, and admired her.

Jean had the even patrician features that should have stirred discomfort in a round-cheeked young midwesterner with a turned-up nose. But for some reason this did not happen.

"I am feeling nothing but the most intense sympathy and pain for these gals of Claud's," I wrote Hermann. "It may be that I can be quite unjealous of anyone I really know and know for a good person. The girls who suffer at Claud's hands — the cream of the crop, each one — really gain more than they suffer and frequently the better ones become infinitely more valuable people both to themselves and society."

Amazingly I wrote Hermann that Jean was "direct and forthright." Claud had told me in a wondering tone about her delay in going to bed with him. This puzzled me; he had always scorned women who kept men dangling. I gathered from his tender, amused smile that she represented something new in his life. She did, but as usual I saw things too simply.

If I could have read Isherwood's story then I might have been prepared for what Jean told me, describing her campaign to capture the man who was still my husband. "I had to put him off for almost a month," she confided. "Because, you see, I had told Eric I was pregnant and I had to wait to see if he would marry me."

I think now that she had become obsessed with having a child. When she told me, as ingenuous as Sally Bowles, how she had planned her campaign, I didn't know what to do. Shouldn't Claud be warned? But this was against my code. ("Tattle tale tit! / Your tongue shall be slit / And all the cats and dogs around / Shall have a little bit!") Pride entered into it too.

The problem became part of a larger one. Everyone kept urging me to stay in England; they said the movement needed what I could do. I wrote Hermann, "I am ready to fly to you at any minute of the day. My heart is definitely with you but should I let it be boss? Never before have I been confronted with a crossroads, knowing that either way I will have real reason for regret. Unless, that is, I can be sure of a chance at work as significant over there with you as is in prospect here."

I see that letter now as the beginning of the pressure I put on him, pressure that may have had more power than I realized.

I wrote that I had become a member of the Committee Against Malnutrition, one of Claud's best Popular Front projects. I sent clippings telling of events like the rally of Mosley's fascist Blackshirts, which the Communists systematically interrupted, taking terrible beatings. By great luck Claud escaped with minor bruises.

Berti now hoped for an appointment as "Director of Research of the College of Obstetricians and Gynecologists of Great Britain." He would be given "a terrific laboratory," I wrote Hermann, "and lots of money, and he intends to do things with it that the C of O & G would not expect, including the publication of what I would write. He has definitely offered me the job of collaborator with him which if any of it goes through hands me an unexampled future." The laboratory connection would take care of finances, I wrote, "and all the wonderful places I can work into usefulness with Claud would be on the side."

One night I rode in Berti's yellow-leather-seated sports car to see Katherine Hepburn in *Little Women*. Afterward, as we made our way down the theatre stairs, he asked me to marry him.

Claud had once accused Berti of being in love with me when he persuaded me to come to England. Berti had admitted it — I thought for political purposes. But now he seemed convincingly serious. Male unreason could always astonish me.

"He of course recognizes two obstacles," I wrote Hermann: "Claud and you. Maybe even a third: that I have no wish to marry him."

Berti might have been holding himself "in abeyance," as he said, to anchor me in London. He knew about Claud's affair with Jean, but couldn't predict how long it would last. Meanwhile he thought his bringing me overseas had had the effect he wanted. "Claud trusts me," I wrote Hermann, "depends on me, respects my opinion and uses me definitely for a stabilizer. And he has a responsible kind of love for Claudia that you'd hardly believe could blossom instantly the way it seemed to. All this makes it so difficult. I don't like to come along stirring up commitments like that and snatch them away again at the moment when they might begin to do some good."

Claud was still sure that I would stay. But he sympathized with Hermann and wished that he could come to England too. "I know how impossible it is," I wrote him, "but need it be? Everything is so much more advanced and clear-cut here. You get the chance to throw your weight where just that much weight might mean all the difference." I hinted too at the question of whether I should take the "big step" now. "Claud is delighted that I intend to do it and would be glad to have me do it now but apparently it is not necessary to do actually *that* in order to be a recognized cooperator in a useful direction." I think in my guarded language I was telling him that if I went back I could take that step later in America.

The work I could do in England attracted me strongly. And Claud had convinced me that he wanted not only my work but myself, too, "as his closest confidante and deepest emotional commitment." Yet as the weeks passed I knew this could not win against the appeal of a partnership based on constancy and warmed by what Hermann and I had called our "fortifying flame." I had to go back, I decided; we would work together in our own country. And once I had made up my mind, Claud felt he had no right to press me any more to stay. Nor did the others, sad as we all felt at parting.

I would sail from Southampton, across the bay from the Isle of Wight, where Claud's mother lived. Continuing to do things in reverse, we visited her for the first time then, that last weekend. She was charmed with Claudia, and desolate at losing her. For years afterward traditional letters would come from "Granny," mystified but pathetically grateful for the snapshots and reports I sent her, month after month.

The ship did not arrive from Cherbourg till nearly midnight. We spent our last hours together as a family, we three, in a dockside pub. With no sleep since early morning, Claudia should have whined or wilted. Instead she spun and whirled, rushing from one of us to the other, laughing and shouting all the words she knew, in random order. "Precisely like her father in a state of exhaustion," Claud said.

When at last we could tuck her into her bunk, he wept. He would not see her again for twenty-four years.

CHAPTER 8

I had been back in Washington a week or two before the issue of the *New Statesman* came out with the dialogue between H.G. Wells and Stalin. Hermann's response worried me.

All through the long interview Wells had held out for his liberal position against strong Marxist logic. He had even suggested that something like Roosevelt's New Deal might do as well for the people and still preserve precious freedoms that he thought were being sacrificed in the Soviet Union. "He really stood up to Stalin," Hermann said. "Even his illusory stuff about the New Deal might sound convincing."

I wondered how Claud had taken that. But even if he could bring himself to write me he could hardly discuss this. Meanwhile we had political problems of our own.

I had come home hot for action. But just now John Donovan, who wanted to recruit us, was at the center of a storm. He had been fired for starting to organize a union in the very office charged with legalizing and protecting labor unions. The irony put the story on the front pages of the papers. Pickets from progressive groups all over the area marched up and down outside the Commerce Building.

John used section 7a of the new law to appeal his case. I went with Mary to the hearing to see a friend of hers in action — John Finerty, a liberal lawyer who was also Master of the Foxhounds of the Fairfax hunt. Abe Fortas from the AAA counsel's office assisted him. He was only twenty-two, but his passionately reasoned argument probably won the case. If anyone that day had predicted his appointment to the Supreme Court we could easily have believed it. John got his reinstatement, and the blustery drunken administrator of NRA had to resign. But all this made John a marked man, forcing his Party connections into deep secrecy and changing his plans for us.

Hermann had been giving John documents from the Labor Board that the Party would find useful to the unions on the waterfront. "So far," Hermann told me, "stuff that would be available to anyone who knew what to look for. But now...."

"Now he wants the unavailable?"

Hermann nodded, adding that this would be just the beginning. "Once you get involved like that you're a dead duck."

I let it pass as a German's misuse of our slang. But I knew he was too American. And I think his own words bothered him, for he went on, saying that the Party, in order to accomplish anything, had to be able to count on members coming through with what was required.

"So?" I expected him to act on the theories that he was teaching me.

But he had said he needed time. John had teased him: "You must have imbibed the great American dream in Plainfield, New Jersey."

Hermann admitted it was true. And for him (though he may not have said so) an essential part of that dream was freedom to be a scholar, to explore, to follow trails, to reflect, to shift his focus or change direction according to his own thinking.

For a time John stopped pressing him, and this period became a sort of breathing spell in which we could give ourselves to enjoying our life together.

Sometimes when a lover yearns as I had in England the reunion doesn't live up to all the hopes. But ours had, overwhelmingly. In those first moments in the stateroom on the train, after Claudia had settled for her nap, we turned to each other with a hunger so intense that for me it was a throbbing physical pain, yet delicious too with the promise of fulfillment in the long night ahead.

During the time before my trip our only lack had been security. Now we had that — or so I thought. I had sent a hundred dollars to a lawyer in Juarez, Mexico. Soon it would be time to send the other hundred, and receive the document which, however dubious legally, would let us start a true and solid marriage.

In November the *New Statesman* published a reply by Bernard Shaw to the Stalin interview. Shaw had turned the keenest edge of his wit on Wells, jeering not only at his politics but at his person.

The slashing attack delighted me. A game player from childhood, I loved to win. During my time in advertising I had relished the sport of it. But Hermann had doubts about the tactic. In reasoning, Stalin had bested Wells. This could have been shown point by point, objectively, and far more educationally. Personal ridicule, he thought, was hitting below the belt.

Hermann was still responding with what we would soon learn were obsolete bourgeois ideas of honor and fair play, which in my usual inconsistency I shared. I began to hope Claud hadn't had anything to do with Shaw's attack. And I had put it out of my mind long before John started working on Hermann again.

Finally he called on us late at night — so late we could hear the roar of lions in the zoo — to tell us he was glad that Hermann had held off before. The Party had an underground organization where we could work more effectively.

I had assumed all along that we would join. The New Deal seemed to Hermann more and more a patchwork of palliatives, some of them regressive. In our office we had made an explosive discovery: by computing the acreage that would be needed to produce the food called for in the cheapest of the four diets recommended by the Nutrition Section of the Department of Agriculture, we had learned that giving this minimal diet to every American would require more land than had ever been tilled before. Meanwhile the AAA was taking thousands of acres out of production.

When I wrote the story I made it as dry and factual as I could. To give it a hope of being approved, I larded it with quotations from the most respectable authorities, beginning with the original statement about AAA from our leading agency economist: "We seek to shape an agricultural program to meet the needs not only of the rural population but the whole country." But Mary's best scheming could never get the story published.

It may have been then, when I told of our final failure, that Hermann quoted Lewis Mumford: "Before we can become sane we must remove the greatest of all hallucinations — the belief that our society is sane now."

Whatever the cumulative reasons for Hermann's changed response, that late night, as we heard the roar of lions, he told John we would join the Party. John said at once that Charles Kramer would make contact with me in the office. Hermann gave him a wry grin. "Okay. And from now on we do whatever we're told by whoever happens to run some branch of the CP."

"Ah," said John, "but this guy's not just any whoever. Wait till you meet him."

Hermann shrugged that off, resisting the idea of a leader. He knew well what the word *Führer* was doing to Germany. And the adulation of Stalin had to be explained away by the history of czarist Russia. Anyone knowing Hermann would have thought he was immune.

We set out for our first Party meeting on a mild winter evening. To passersby we must have appeared as we were meant to — just one more strolling pair of lovers. "Act as if you're visiting us socially," Charles had murmured, bending over my desk with his finger on a line of milk-price figures.

As we walked I must have said it felt strange to go to a meeting on the very Euclid Street where at age eighteen I had lived with my mother in a "light housekeeping" room. Refusing to go to Iowa university as a poor "town girl" I wanted to be "independent." But Mother had come with me to Washington.

The Kramer apartment was not in one of those row houses, where everyone sees who comes and goes. In a modern building, with an unusual entrance at the back, it seemed almost too obviously suited for conspiratorial purposes. There was no lobby, just a bare, open stairway, where we found Charles leaning over the fourth-floor railing. As we reached the top he greeted us with a warm smile I had never seen before.

68

In the office I had first met him as a morose man named Krevisky. The change to Kramer had not caused much comment, perhaps because he never took part in the camaraderie of the staff. Among all these vocal New Dealers his silence had made me curious. When I came to know him better I would realize that he had to keep his lips shut tight to hold in his rage and scorn.

Inside the apartment his wife Mildred was waiting, a shy southern girl with ash-blond hair and the pallor of the Appalachian children whose pictures we had been publishing in our articles about how Subsistence Homesteads would better their lot. Beyond her, in the light of a bridge lamp, a boy knelt trying to untie a bundle wrapped in brown paper. He looked up distractedly, biting his lip and brushing back his hair, when Charles spoke his name, Victor Perlo. A mathematical prodigy, he had been at City College in New York with Charles. Now at age twenty-one he was a full-fledged statistician. The other member of the unit, Marion Bachrach, looked small and hunched in a deep canvas sling chair. But her face was fine-featured, with intelligent brown eyes and smiling, receptive lips.

Charles began talking in an assured voice I hardly recognized as his. He explained that though there might be changes — a comrade had already been drawn away to head another unit — we would try to limit our knowledge of other members, in case of interrogation, possible torture. Such an idea, he admitted, might seem rather remote in the radical Washington climate, but climates could change fast. In most places members of units knew each other only by their Party pseudonyms, so as not to be able to give real names if questioned. But here in Washington, where the New Dealers were always meeting one another socially, we'd run the opposite risk, of using the Party name at the wrong time. But though they would be used only on official records, we should each choose one now.

I listed myself as Mary MacFarland, after my strong-willed, talented musician aunt who had died in Mother's arms at the age of twenty. To me she was a romantic figure; for exactly the opposite reasons Hermann chose the unremarkable name, Walter Becker.

Continuing about precautions, Charles warned us that Marion's husband, who as a nonmember must be kept in ignorance, caused practical problems. Marion had made every effort to bring him close enough to recruit, but though sympathetic he had the typical liberal's fear of committing himself. Charles turned to Marion. "Is that a fair statement?"

"Let's just put it," Marion said, "that he's a wise old bird."

Charles smiled, but in a strained way. Even I, new to the Party, felt a slight shock. It would take a while to learn that under Marion's mischief was a dedication deeper than that of many comrades who religiously parroted the official line. She would rise to the next-to-highest national rank in the Party, be indicted under the Smith Act, and escape trial only by death. Charles went on to say that Marion was a writer who had published in *Atlantic Monthly*. We would hear later about her project.

But first came collection of dues. Basically they would be ten percent of our salary, plus occasional extras. We had been warned of this. It had given Hermann some concern, since he sent a regular stipend to his friend Ernst, who was on the last lap of his doctorate in chemistry. But we could manage, I was sure. Mary and I had proposed a consumer column to *McCall's* magazine which they seemed about to take. And in free-lancing I had ranged from *Snappy Stories* to the *New Yorker*.

Charles was explaining that more was expected of us as a privileged group. Our salaries — even in the Depression — were far above the average comrade's. We were permitted — in fact, urged — to win career advancement, usually impossible for open activists. Extra assessments from us would help support comrades who could not make public appeals for funds. While rallies in Madison Square Garden could collect money for such causes as the Scottsboro Boys, there were unknown comrades in the South living on almost nothing — eating with the sharecroppers they were trying to organize — alone and always in danger of being beaten up or shot. We could think of our money going to help them.

I hardly needed his persuasion — any more, I suppose, than my mother had needed the minister's persuasion to find somehow an extra quarter or half dollar for a foreign missionary. And Party dues of ten percent — thirty dollars out of my three hundred a month —

seemed quite normal to one whose mother tithed. She had given to the Lord's work ten percent of an income that was sometimes as low as fifteen dollars a month, even including what my oldest brother earned by chopping wood for neighbors.

Hermann was taking out his penknife; he cut the cord that Victor Perlo had been struggling to untie. (When he told me later that he had seen the address — John Smith on Third Street northeast — I had visions of a murky cellarway over beyond the Capitol. A dark figure was emerging with this bundle, hurrying across the sidewalk, glancing over his shoulder, tossing his burden into a shabby black coupe and speeding away. One day I would take my turn at being that dark figure.)

On the floor were stacks of the *Daily Worker,* the thick red *Communist,* the red and white *Communist International,* the violent black and white *New Masses,* and the mimeographed agitprop bulletin.

Hermann declined *New Masses,* saying he had bought it at the newsstand on Pennsylvania Avenue. Charles told him sharply never to go there again. We must keep away from any place where leftists might gather. We must avoid, as far as possible, associating with radicals, difficult as that would be in Washington. Even liberals, outspoken ones such as Gardner Jackson, Charles said, looking my way, were out of bounds. This saddened me. Pat had been so kind a friend.

Obviously, Charles added, we couldn't go near any public protests or rallies.

This disappointed me, remembering Trafalgar Square, feeling part of a huge crowd unified in the same uplifting urgency. But these directives carried their own charge, setting our group apart, preparing us to face our own hard challenges.

The literature we had to buy cost almost ten dollars. This, plus the dues, almost exactly equalled the wages I paid Mamie, the cheerful woman who now brought Claudia home for lunch and put her to bed. Hermann had insisted on hiring her after going once with me to pick up Claudia after work. Sitting on the nurse's lap she had seemed quite contented, but at her first sight of me large round tears had spurted from her eyes, splashing on the floor. Mamie must stay, whatever else we gave up to the Party.

When Victor Perlo had bundled up the leftover literature, he gave a report on the national news, starting with Roosevelt's appointment of Joseph P. Kennedy as chairman of the new Stock Exchange Commission. He called it a capitulation to the most vicious political elements. A Wall Street operator himself, Kennedy had made his millions in bootlegging. Such facts were probably a fraction of the truth, Vic said; but enough to rid us of the illusion that FDR was "any better than a glorified ward heeler."

These words were painful to hear. I knew Roosevelt was a politician, but nothing I learned about his compromises could keep his voice from stirring me physically. Sometimes I spent a night in erotic, idolatrous contact with him, waking to a sense of privilege which might stay with me for days. When I told Hermann about my dream he did not laugh. He envied me in a way; he himself could not remember ever having dreamed. Because I was a posthumous child, he said, I was even more vulnerable than most, but the whole population right now felt a childlike need of a father figure. I resisted this. I had no wish to share that private intimacy with 120 million people.

Marion reported that she was writing a profile of a typical American teacher, one lucky enough to be still employed. A quarter of a million teachers had no job, and a huge number worked without pay. In eighteen states they were paid in IOU vouchers called scrip, for which they could never get the stated value. Low as salaries already were, they were constantly being cut. Even so, Chicago owed back salaries amounting to $28 million.

Marion's figures showed that at least 200,000 children couldn't go to school for lack of clothes. And there would be many more, she said, but for the teachers themselves. In New York City alone they had given over $3 million to buy hot lunches, shoes and so on, for the children who otherwise wouldn't be able to come to school.

Marion planned to show the teacher in her everyday life, handing out her own lunch to hungry-eyed kids around her desk, slipping a sweater or a pair of socks to a cold child in the cloakroom.

72

If teachers hadn't made these sacrifices the country's educational system would have fallen apart totally in the past five years.

Charles asked dubiously where she planned to publish this. In the *Atlantic,* Marion hoped, or *Scribner's.* Vic waved his hand urgently. When he got the floor he asked why she should glorify a group of fuzzy-minded liberals who were only postponing the moment when the workers would seize the means of education. He moved that the comrade point this out, showing how piecemeal charity was reactionary reformism; that these inequities could not be corrected under capitalism.

"But if she put that in," I asked before I could stop myself, "where could she publish her piece?"

"Exactly." Marion's grateful glance may have begun the collaboration that would bind us so close. She said that what Vic had outlined would fit into the *Sunday Worker* but would come as no surprise to its readers. Whereas she could reach a wider audience, one less political. And mightn't such readers one day become important to us? Having them friendly — or at least not hostile — could make a crucial difference when the chips were down.

Charles thought she had a point there. The Party needed to "neutralize" potential class enemies. But Vic insisted that any valuable material we had must be used to strengthen the voice of the Party.

Hermann said in his reflective way that he was struck by how often the *Times* quoted quite radical statements by New Dealers. Didn't that suggest that the middle class at the moment was more ready to listen than we might assume? He proposed that our comrade use her material doubly. She could first follow her strong impulse, then afterward put her facts into form for Party publication.

"That's the second Gordian knot he's cut tonight," Marion cried.

The group agreed on a plan to have editorials ready to go into Party publications when Marion's article was published, calling attention to it and making any points that seemed strategically desirable.

It was the sort of consensus that Hermann often brought about during the next few months. Soon he would be put in charge of a new unit of high-powered, neurotic economists.

73

Charles reported on foreign events, pointing out the continuity of our state department's reactionary policy through all the changes of administration, how the thirty warships sent last summer to stand off the coast of Cuba continued the line taken by President Hoover at the time he sent our Marines into Nicaragua. When Charles turned to Austria, predicting a civil war that would make it possible for our Party to win leadership of all revolutionary elements, I listened with special care. He was getting into a problem Hermann and I had worried over, without a clear conclusion.

Charles reminded us that liberals had made snide remarks about our German comrades' refusal to make common cause with the social democratic trade unionists. The Comintern had correctly stated that a counter-revolutionary was far more dangerous than an open fascist. Sometimes it was necessary, and certainly safer, to work with the Nazis in specific situations, such as in Prussia, where the comrades had first condemned the plebiscite, then realized their error and voted with the Nazis. We must remember, Charles said, that even though this tactic might have had the effect of bringing Nazis to power, their party by its very nature was a temporary threat; because of "inexorable economics" Hitler could not maintain control much longer. Meanwhile our comrades there were continuing to "advance toward the inevitable victory of the real proletariat."

I felt a wonderful relief. I hadn't expected to see a confusing issue like this set into a coherent and hopeful pattern.

Mildred reported on tenant farmers, in a nervous, self-conscious monotone that took me back to Christian Endeavor young people's meetings in church. I was by this time nervous myself. Charles had said that he would be calling on the new members to tell about their work.

I saw my role as apparently innocent passer-on of consumer information that to the reader — or listener — might come as a shock. For example, on one radio program I had my clubwoman ask if it was true, as she had heard, that white bread was poison. My boss then answered, "Well, I wouldn't say it's exactly *poison* . . ." Leaving the word poison fixed in the listener's mind, he went on to explain why the Food and Drug Administration hadn't yet acted on its doubts about the safety of the bleaching agents used for flour, or also on the chemicals used to puff up the bread with air that at the same time hold a high percentage of water to add to its weight. I had my chief add thoughtfully, "It does seem a bit odd, though, that the bakers should cut down on the amount of flour in a loaf, just at a time when farmers are getting less for their wheat than in the days of Shakespeare."

Vic asked if I had the facts on the bakery process — names of chemicals, formulas, figures, etc. I told him they were in a letter from an engineer who designed baking machinery intended for just such purposes. He was so disgusted that he had to tell about it.

Charles took sudden interest in that engineer; he asked me to turn over to him a copy of the letter. Then, saying that he would give Hermann his assignment separately, he adjourned the general meeting.

On the way home Hermann was silent at first. I wondered what Charles had asked him to do. But from now on we would have to have secrets from each other.

I couldn't hold back my relief at the prediction of Hitler's downfall. And I remember the doubtful way Hermann said he hoped they were right. But ever since 1924 he had heard the line, "Hitler can't last."

I suggested the Party might know things that we didn't know. There was Claud's dispatch in *The Week* about the illegal publications that kept appearing, in spite of Hitler. Sometimes a folded mimeograph would have "Horoscope" outside, and inside would be items of world news that had been suppressed in the newspapers.

Hermann agreed that this sort of mass operation was encouraging, and the great reason for working in the Party. But it may have been then that he spoke worriedly about the engineer's letter. What would happen if it landed in the hands of someone with poor judgment? Suppose this comrade met the engineer and thought from something he said that he was ready to be recruited. Whereas in fact the engineer was a Trotskyist, say, rabid against the Party. Wouldn't he betray the Consumers' Counsel rather than miss a chance to damage the Party? Our office was already suspect because of vocal liberals like Howe and Jackson. If it got out that a letter to the Consumers' Counsel had been given to the CP, the fat would be in the fire. A lot of powerful people were looking for just such an excuse to get rid of the whole group and put in their own puppets.

That was frightening. But surely, I said, the Party would understand the danger and be careful. Hermann hoped they would, but they were human, with built-in fallibility. I refused to let my spirits be damped. "We've joined," I said, "so we've got to trust them." And he agreed.

After a silent step or two, I suddenly stopped short on the sidewalk. The letter had not even been addressed to us. It had been passed on by the Consumer Board of NRA. Hermann laughed, saying that NRA might as well be hung for a lamb as a sheep. He had been talking out of fatigue, he said. The meeting, like all meetings, had been tiring.

Tiring? In my mood the word was unthinkable.

Arthur Koestler's memoir, *Arrow in the Blue,* describes his first meeting with a group of comrades as "one of those rare moments when intellectual conviction is in complete harmony with feeling, when your reason approves of your euphoria, and your emotion is as lover to your thought." It was true for me that night, though I couldn't have analyzed it if I had tried — though I wish I had. I just told Hermann that I'd never been so stimulated in my life.

That delighted him. We hurried home newly elated toward another night together.

CHAPTER 9

"The political state is a very difficult institution," Dr. Howe wrote in his farewell letter to his staff, "but not as inefficient, wasteful and dishonest an institution as many people believe." He even added that his experience with us had greatly heightened his belief and confidence in democracy. How could he say this, we asked each other, when he had been dismissed for no other reason than that he had tried to protect the consumer, as the law required? He was not even involved in the case that caused the "purge."

While the administrator was out of town, the office of the general counsel had issued an interpretation of the law that required plantation owners, when they reduced acreage and received payments from the government, to keep not only the same number of tenants but the same ones. Alger Hiss had done the actual writing of it, but he was so quiet and unobtrusive that the administrator apparently thought he had just been misled by those loud, vociferous defenders of the underdog. The axe had been hovering over these "trouble-makers," and now it fell not only on the young lawyers in Frank's office but on Jerome himself and a few others including Dr. Howe and Gardner Jackson.

Everyone loved Pat Jackson, and angry groups gathered around him. I bade him only a brief goodbye; his dismissal had proved the Party's warning correct. But Mary passed along what she heard. When the men received their notices they had met in Jerome Frank's office to plan. Alger Hiss had threatened to resign if they were not reinstated. But he had not resigned. Mary said he had known two weeks before, and never alerted anyone. From what Pat had learned, it seemed Hiss had hoped to take Frank's place as general counsel. Since Pat never spoke a malicious word, Mary took his allegation seriously.

Roosevelt, who at the time "hadn't known what it was all about," according to Pat, but "felt sorry" when he heard about it, made sure that decent jobs elsewhere were found for those with enough standing to cause political trouble. Dr. Howe simply vanished.

Black Monday became the text for Vic's Marxist analysis at our next unit meeting. That this could happen to Dr. Howe and Jerome Frank — neither of them Communists, both insisting on the American kind of liberty — confirmed what we knew: no amount of high purpose and integrity could stand a chance against ruthless class power. The only way to oppose it was with the same weapon, the ruthless power of another class, a far larger one.

At the office we concentrated on learning how to manage our new chief, a slow, colorless type of economist, well meaning in a mild way, and obtuse enough so that he could often be maneuvered into positions on our side without his knowing what battle lines he had crossed. The Information Office knew, of course. But outward respect had to be shown the new Consumers' Counsel. It must not appear that the position of Consumers' Counsel was just impossible. Less direct ways of sabotaging our work had to be found. We thought we were prepared, but the first one caught us by surprise. Not even Mary suspected that they would stoop to anything so low.

Our office had a continuing project, the National Milk Survey, with Charles Kramer in charge. He did his job, though he saw it as attacking the symptom instead of the disease. Still, getting the facts about a scandalous situation seemed a necessary first step toward cleaning it up. Our figures might show, for instance, that the dairy farmer would get three or four cents for a quart of milk and it would cost only a cent and a half to pasteurize and distribute it, yet the consumer would pay twelve cents for that bottle of milk. Meantime millions of children (many crippled from rickets) were going without milk, while farmers were dumping tanks of it along country roads.

Letters to us and to the White House mostly cried out for help. But sometimes people wrote about a community doing something on their own. A woman in Michigan told how consumers had organized a cooperative to buy and process milk they could sell for six cents a quart. In her neighborhood milk consumption had tripled. She enclosed a snapshot in her letter.

To get the story past the censor we gave it some such title as "Local Experiment in Marketing," and made it dull and factual. We counted on pictures to catch the reader's attention. The article went to the Information Office with two illustrations. It came back okayed, but with only one picture in the envelope. This was a glossy photograph of Claudia at a sunny window happily drinking from a large glass of milk, with our prettiest stenographer and a handsome economist as fond parents beaming in satisfaction. It had been made in the upstairs cafeteria by one of the department's professionals. The missing one had been taken with a Kodak Brownie by some unknown housewife. Half of the blurred snapshot was occupied by the blank wall of a roadside stand; the other half showed two Negro children, aged about five and three. The five-year-old's thin little hand extended from the rolled-up sleeve of a man's jacket, reaching for a bottle of milk a woman was handing across a makeshift counter.

The contrast had been meant to draw attention. Now without the snapshot we would seem to be suggesting that all American children were sunny-haired and blooming like Claudia. The Information Office insisted that only the department photo had come to them with the manuscript.

"Can't you get another copy?" Hermann naturally asked. But we had tried. The woman who had sent it in had signed her name and failed to give her address. No phone was listed in the town under the name, Etty Brown, and no Brown with a phone knew any Etty. We assumed she lived in a poor Negro settlement like Hall's Hill in Virginia where Mimi's maid lived, without running water or electricity.

Couldn't we make contact with the cooperative? We had tried, but these small groups seldom had real offices, usually meeting in some borrowed room. And we had to have this in the next issue. Speed was our best weapon, getting facts out before the powerful forces of an industry had time to wheel up their big guns. But why should the Information Office resort to such a trick when they had complete power? Because they didn't want to show their hand. If they killed the story outright we'd have had a case we could appeal over their heads. Mary was sure they actually preferred underhanded methods.

Like Mary herself, Hermann said. She wouldn't be happy, he thought, unless she was sniffing out plots. I probably sprang to Mary's defense, as I often did when he accused her of loving intrigue for its own sake. Seeing conspiracies everywhere, he said, clouded one's thinking. (His firmness about this makes what happened to him later even stranger, almost incredible.)

I conceded that Mary had a taste for detecting plots. Her eyes would shine like topaz through the curtain of blue smoke when she leaned across the desk to describe such devious plans as the ones for getting a Catholic cardinal's support for her radical friend who needed the help of the Mexican religious hierarchy in putting through land reforms. But in this case we weren't just imagining a plot; it really existed. We had learned that the men fired on Black Monday had been precisely the ones who were on the Dairy Association's secret list of "enemies."

I was shocked, seeing it through the eyes of a mother: How could these men act in such a conscienceless way, denying food to hungry children? But Hermann said calmly that this was the way the system operated. He actually took satisfaction, I think, in seeing Marxist theory confirmed. Perhaps it reinforced his feeling that he had had no choice but to join the Party. And learning to accept such conflicts as inescapable, ordained by an inexorable set of laws, relieved my own helpless anger. It also added another exciting political element to the office drama.

The snapshot never turned up. As in other emergencies I made a quick drawing, sketching the milk kiosk and the children from memory. It wasn't as effective as a real child's thin arm reaching out for milk, but the article brought good response, and several other communities were inspired to start milk cooperatives.

It was about this time that Will Geer was kidnapped out on the west coast. I could tell from the talk at our unit meeting that he meant something to the Party. He had been directing a Clifford Odets double bill in Los Angeles — *Waiting for Lefty* and *Till the Day I Die* — when in walked some members of Friends of New Germany. They dragged him out and gave him a fearful beating because of a scene in which Hitler's picture is torn from the wall.

The comrades seemed shaken by this revelation of how far the Führer's power reached. On the way home Hermann said he had expected and rather hoped it might lead to a discussion of the Party's assumption that Hitler's hold was tenuous. But nobody had brought it up. This may have been partly due to the crowded agenda. One of the items was the announcement that my divorce had come through; when they saw us next we would be a properly married couple.

The warmth of the response surprised me. I knew the Party wanted our lives to be outwardly respectable. And now that the Popular Front had begun, with Browder proclaiming that Communism was twentieth-century Americanism, Party members must be essentially bourgeois. So we had expected political approval. What we got was much more, and not only from Marion Bachrach, to whom I had become personally close. I realized for the first time how deeply we all were involved with each other as comrades.

Hermann had been spending many weekends on missions to the New York waterfront. He never talked about what he did there, but I guessed that he was giving information from the Shipping Board and perhaps turning over secret documents. The cloak-and-dagger aspects of these trips excited me, but Hermann called it playacting, with a shrug of distaste. Still, he conceded that the Party had to train people in conspiratorial techniques. "Then we might as well get some fun out of it," I said, and he murmured "Crazy," in that tone of loving wonder that was half incredulous.

Later I would see other meanings, far more complex, in such exchanges between us, see the important differences in not only our vocabularies but our temperaments. He took seriously whatever he did, weighing its value, its implications, and possible consequences; while I, once having made my commitment, accepted blithely whatever went with it. Mother's secure faith in Providence had become in me a faith in the Party — a faith truly reckless. I didn't reck, or reckon. But Hermann did. Perhaps that was partly why — though he never said so — he wanted to join a research project his Columbia professor, Carter Goodrich, had started organizing in Washington. Hermann's taking a leave of absence from the job at NRA would require permission from the Party, which valued those waterfront trips. But now as a unit leader he was meeting each week with Hal Ware, who directed the Washington undergound. Hal, he thought, would give him a fair hearing.

In their long interview Hermann argued that his career would be advanced by the study; the results would be published by Columbia University Press, his part under his own name. Goodrich had said that this would serve as his dissertation, all he lacked for his doctorate. The Party wanted us to rise fast in our professions, to be ready for the "next stage." These arguments apparently won Hal over. But he may have seen how well the project would fit into other plans for Hermann.

On a June weekend we set out for Maryland in my 1931 Ford roadster. A former contributor who had followed me into the New Deal took charge of Claudia, having plans for her. ("She must have a raspberry linen dress, and a white hat.")

I think it was on the way to the courthouse in that Maryland town that Hermann told me about his mother's marriage. While very young she had fallen in love with a handsome officer who had escorted her to the great balls given before Lent each year in German towns. Whirling in a waltz they had come to an "understanding." But his family did not think her's grand enough for an alliance. When the young baron gave her up, she desperately applied for a post in a Romanian school. There at the age of seventeen she taught German to Carpathian princesses, and between classes combed lice from their hair.

Coming back with no taste for a traditional life with an old-fashioned husband, she waited for that rare German male who would treat his wife as a partner. She found him, and Hermann thought his parents had built a solid marriage. But he suspected that she had never recovered, that she might never have been in love the same way with his father.

Months afterward I remembered Hermann's thoughtful tone and wondered if he had been thinking of my feeling for Claud, and perhaps his own for Elsa. And of the possibility that we were both making a choice very like his mother's. But at the moment I was just surprised at his phrasing; I had never heard him use the words "in love" before.

Once we had the license we drove until we came to a church; it was only after we had turned in and rung the parsonage bell that I noticed it was Methodist. The door was opened instantly by a large red-faced man I took to be the janitor. Hermann explained that we were looking for the minister.

"You're looking *at* him," he said in a booming voice, beckoning us in. "I don't need to ask what you folks want. And let me tell you, you won't find anybody can tie the knot tighter than yours truly, Reverend J. Stanley Aub."

The parsonage parlor was dark, its shades drawn against the heat. As my eyes adjusted, I stepped back, startled. On a bookcase beside my shoulder, poised as if to leap, was a large bird with razor-sharp beak. Then I saw that it was made of pine cones. Beside it a turtle glared morosely from a shell with the painted words: "Roses are red, Violets are blue, God's love in Jesus Is Perfect and true. Souvenir of Glens Falls, 1915."

The Reverend Aub cleared a chair, snatching up a half-empty box of chocolates, sending frilled candy-wrapper cups through the air like a flight of butterflies. Taking our documents from Hermann he held out the box. "They'll steady your nerves." It was the wrong prescription for me, but Hermann politely took one, then held it partway to his mouth as he watched the minister read.

The Reverend Aub's genial smile slowly faded; he hadn't, he said, figured on a divorce. With a severe glance at me he said he hoped that at least I was not the guilty party. I disclaimed this in a tone of such horror that Hermann looked at me in surprise.

"But Mexican." The Reverend Aub frowned dubiously at the paper. My throat was too dry to answer. And what could I say about a piece of paper bought the way my mother sent for lamp wicks and winter underwear from Montgomery Ward?

The minister put on his glasses, but could still see nothing to cheer him. "There's no guilty party here. I'm afraid . . ."

"But isn't that better?" Finding my voice I asked if it wasn't more civilized that way.

He repeated the word "civilized" as if in pain. I hurried to state my view that if a man and woman could not go on living together it was better that they separate without the anger and accusations that might poison their feelings and the child's.

He stopped me on that last word. Hearing that I had a daughter he shook his head, pronouncing it the duty of parents, regardless of their whims and fancies, to make a home for their child.

I believed this too, I told him, and that was what I was trying to do. "I want to give her a *real* home."

Hermann made some slight movement, and I added quickly that for both my child and myself this marriage promised a future with someone we could trust, utterly, always. The minister turned a long measuring look on Hermann, who bore the inspection, his eyes steady.

But the minister came back to me, asking how he could be sure I wouldn't take a notion to leave him too? "Maybe you thought the same thing before, with this. . . ." He consulted the paper. "This Cock-burn fellow."

I must have said something innocuous about our growing apart, for Hermann asked helpfully if it hadn't just been a friendly agreement to separate.

I saw the danger there, but too late; already the Reverend Aub was scowling. "That has the smell of incompatibility to me. *If* not collusion." His soft mouth had become a hard tight seam as he went on to say that scriptural law recognized only one reason for dissolution of the bonds of matrimony.

Rather falteringly, for by now I was really shaken, afraid that with this Mexican divorce no one would marry us, I said that I had hoped not to have to mention it, but that I did have those grounds. To my surprise, I felt my cheeks wet with tears.

"Ah!" Reverend Aub waited for me to go on. I said that in speaking of Claud's temperament I meant an inability. . . . As I paused here for words, I was given them:

"To keep to the bed of one woman?"

I nodded. This was certainly true.

"Ah . . ." Again the deep satisfaction. "That's a horse of a different color." The Reverend Aub strode over to a corner cupboard. Searching among a pile of Sunday school leaflets and a heap of apple peelings, he drew out a small worn book. As he righted a misplaced china rabbit eating a carrot he discovered a cellophane bag, which he held out to me. Under the circumstances I had no choice but to risk a jelly bean. When Hermann had taken his, our host tossed the rest into his mouth, explaining that he had a kind of sweet tooth. His happy tone and the welcoming gesture of his arms, bidding us to rise, made me know that he too had felt suspense, if not to be compared with ours.

We took our places before him, and his round face stiffened to formality. He wiped his hands on the shining mohair of his thighs, then lifted a jacket from the doorknob and put it on. It hung to the right and left of his paunch like vestments, giving him a certain majesty. Standing erect, he touched my upper arms with two fingers of each hand, adjusting my position beside Hermann so that we faced him precisely. Then, with amazing speed, still chewing, he dispatched the marriage ceremony and pronounced us man and wife.

Perhaps simple relief can take the place of music and flowers and champagne. For years I carried a clear memory of the place where we spent our wedding night. The window of our bedroom, I recalled, looked out over a rushing stream, with meadows and blue foothills beyond. When after a decade, for sentiment's sake, I drove back to visit the town, I discovered that the hotel where we had experienced such exquisite release, such a genuine sense of consummation and fulfilment, was beside a railroad cutting. Our room had a view of small-town stores and a factory.

We circled home by way of the new Skyline Drive, which was still unfinished. Holding the light car steady on loose pebbles I felt my muscles losing the bruised, beatific consciousness of the night. Hermann, sensing this, wished he had not postponed learning to drive. Even after all our other good nights together this one had left us marveling. Hermann explained it as the survival of the primitive in us. "Maybe we're still susceptible to the magic of ritual."

The spell returned whenever we stopped to rest. Walking back and forth along the rim of the world, we looked out over receding ridges, each a paler blue, until the farthest faded into a faintly gilded haze presaging rain. The downpour caught us on the Lee Highway just outside Fairfax. I drove through opaque curtains, rain drumming on the canvas roof and threatening to drown the motor. I was able to save it each time till the moment when Hermann distracted me with a shout of laughter. He had seen a sign on our left: ROSEDERE CATTERY. As we sat waiting for the rain to let up, I saw another sign across the road: FOR RENT.

The house was white clapboard, apparently just remodeled, with a blank brick terrace where a porch had been. Pools of water stood in the bare clay of the yard. "Look," Hermann said. "A decapitated ivory tower." The house looked sad, I thought, with its one claim to architectural distinction cut off abruptly at the second story. In the rain the long windows stared out at us, as if in some sort of appeal.

When the rain stopped I picked my way among the bricks and puddles. The front door had two vertical panels of glass etched with leaves and flowers. Through them I could see an open door at the back of the hall leading to a room with windows looking out over misty meadows to a distant grove. And in the corner was a fireplace. I had always dreamed of having breakfast by a fire. Hermann had come to stand beside me, noting that the ceilings were probably four meters high.

Peering in one of the long front windows, we saw what must have been the parlor, which opened with double doors on another room with the same tall windows at the back. Both of these had fireplaces. I turned and clutched Hermann's arm. He murmured, "Crazy!" But I was already running ahead down the steep slope to the back. Looking in a basement window we saw another fireplace. In all, there were seven, we discovered the next week when we inspected the house.

We hadn't thought of living in the country, and we worried at first about the busy highway. But we saw how we could make Claudia safe by fencing in the backyard. I could have a vegetable garden in the sunny acre beyond. Hermann may have been lured more by the prospect of looking out over that garden from the large bright room that would be his study.

Falls Church even had a nursery school, only half a mile away. But we would soon find that redundant. With the kind of luck that I had now begun to think the gods kept on hand for us, we found Cora. Meeting Claudia she said, "Being she so young, do she need to spend the summer days at school?"

Cora was tall and broad-shouldered, with walnut-colored skin and features that showed her Cherokee genes. At our first interview she held herself, unsmiling, with an air of reserve that I was afraid might turn out sometimes to be sullen. In this I was wrong; she had pride, but she also had a sense of humor, and was kind. We paid her eight dollars a week, feeling that six dollars, the going rate for a live-in maid, was just too low. I also bought her uniforms, which some maids had to provide for themselves. The ones I chose were light yellow; though they became her I felt dimly (too dimly) that she made them look absurd.

Cora had spent much of her childhood with her Indian father in the Carolina forests. Now we could watch her, large and dark, marching along the road with Claudia, small and fair, pulling a cart to the woods. For cool nights they kept the hearths stocked with oak and hickory, and in June when we held our housewarming they filled the fireplaces with Queen Anne's Lace and tawny roadside lilies.

CHAPTER 10

Our first entertaining was meant to demonstrate the kind of life we were expected to live. Carrying conventional mores to an extreme, I ordered towels embroidered with my new monogram and hung them in the bathroom for the occasion. Not drawing too definite a line between the past and present, this became our wedding announcement. Knowing how people liked to explore houses, I was sure it would suffice.

Our invitation list, extending as far upward as possible, included all our chiefs. When I introduced Mary to Carter Goodrich, the director of Hermann's new project, she suddenly cried, "The colt in the snow, I believe!" I was mystified, but he answered, unsurprised, "Maybe, once upon a time." She had been at Mount Holyoke when he was at Amherst, where he was one of Robert Frost's poet-students. Frost, she explained, had him in mind when he wrote "The Runaway," about a foal bewildered by his first snowfall.

Carter was a big man, dark, with a curious cast in one eye, giving his smile a glint of mischief, engaging but deceptive: he was anything but mischievous. Though only in his late thirties he had a look of solidity I trusted even at first glance. I found it hard to imagine him as the slim, vulnerable youth who had inspired a poem ending: "Whoever it is that leaves him out so late / Ought to be told to come and take him in."

The party made a good occasion for a visit from Hermann's friend Ernst Volkmann. He was taller than Hermann, with the Celtic combination of dark hair and blue eyes that north Germans sometimes have. His speech was less easily American than Hermann's, his manner more formal; he spoke to me in a tone of deference I liked. He exclaimed gratifyingly over each fireplace and congratulated us on the bargains we'd acquired by placing low bids at an auction house on Tenth Street: a piano for fifteen dollars, a set of Philippine straw chairs for twelve dollars, and a sofa for a dollar. But he shook his head, speechless, over Hermann's new tool chest, its compartments filled with exactly the right equipment for domestic chores. As he surveyed Hermann's fence enclosing Claudia's play yard he found words for his wonder: *"Bist du nun ganz Haushalter?"*

I wanted to answer: No! Not only householder, Hermann was intellectual, revolutionary, husband, lover.

When I led Ernst over to Mary at the party she was telling about listening to Huey Long talk away the days in a filibuster to delay the passage of the social security bill. "He lifts his head and gallantly kisses his hand to the ladies in the Senate gallery whenever he utters something especially obscene." To keep his recipe for Roquefort salad dressing she had saved that issue of the *Congressional Record*. Ernst listened, entranced.

Could a woman with freckles and protruding teeth be a femme fatale? Yes, literally, as all Washington would one day learn in sadness. But at that moment the phrase came lightly to my mind, remembering my first party at Mary's. Larry Todd, correspondent of the Soviet news agency, Tass, had stayed close by me, perhaps because he knew I was close to Mary. Gazing at her, he murmured something that might have disconcerted a woman less happily situated than I: "No female in the eastern United States," he said, "can match her for sexual allure."

Carter Goodrich had seemed unentranced, perhaps distracted by planning the proposal he would make to Hermann. For at some point in the evening he presented Hermann with a choice at first glance difficult and ultimately disastrous. But all this happened in an atmosphere of gaiety, with the high decibel count that meant success.

I woke next day to the lazy pulse of insects in the heat, and at a little distance the click and whir of mowing. The breeze brought fragrance of cut clover and honeysuckle. Through a half-dream came Claudia's voice, clear and high in a question, Cora's low murmur answering, then Claudia again, moving off diminuendo down the road. They were setting out to replace the lilies, I thought. And then the music began. Beethoven's Ninth was filling the house from the living room where Ernst had started the victrola, an Orthophonic with full and glorious sound. Hermann turned to me.

Making love in the morning is not always irresistible to women. Observant and logical, we tend to suspect such male ardor as rising not solely from response to our unique, incomparable attraction. But that morning, relaxed in languor after our happy partnership the night before, I had no doubt, as Rosa Ponselle's voice came up to us in the *Ode to Joy,* that we were reaching together for our highest moment of appreciation of each other, of our home, our life.

It was not until long afterward that I wondered if Ernst, in sending music up to us, had sent more than music. I wondered if the house that weekend might have held hidden emotions strangely intensifying our passion — tangled emotions, perhaps not even conscious, that would have troubled me if I had known about them. But even in pondering the memory I couldn't make sense of my own mixed gropings. If such crosscurrents existed they would present problems too complex for me — or probably anyone — to understand.

In the afternoon when Claudia was asleep and Cora had gone to town the men went for a walk. I had my reading to do — seven issues of the *Daily Worker,* like the week's seven make-up chapters of the Bible I had had to read on Sundays as a child. In those days I had learned to let the sentences flow through my mind without registering; now I was finding this habit a handicap in my study of Marxism.

At the sound of the men's voices I stuffed the stack of papers into the blanket chest and went downstairs to be found with the *New Masses,* the literary magazine meant to attract liberals. But the Party required us to read it, just as Mother had required me to read not only the Bible but the *Christian Herald*. (She marked the articles at ten or fifteen cents, by which I earned my meager spending money.)

Hermann was telling Ernst that Carter wanted to suggest him for an assistant professorship at the new women's college, Sarah Lawrence. Ernst congratulated him, recalling how the academic life had always attracted him. Hermann agreed, but his voice held a doubt that Ernst caught at once. Was he put off, Ernst asked, by the prospect of teaching at a progressive college?

On the contrary, Hermann said. He went to the wall and put his finger on the light switch, his eyes brightening. "In teaching about public utilities, for instance, I'd start like this, and trace the wire all the way back." He sounded so eager that Ernst asked what kept him from jumping at the chance.

Hermann started winding the victrola. He felt hampered, I thought, by not being able to mention the Party. I said that maybe it was a question of alternatives. The Labor Board wanted Hermann back, with a good promotion. And the Wagner Act would give the board actual power to help the trade unions.

Hermann smiled and said that the real reason he hesitated was my low opinion of professors. Before I could protest that this would never apply to him, he had put the record on. Against the loud preliminary hiss he told me that Ernst had brought the Furtwängler *Lucia*.

I went back to the article by Henri Barbusse, trying to concentrate on the effect of science on literature in its progress from romanticism to realism and then to the naturalism of Zola. But after a time the high soprano voice defeated me. Ernst caught my wrist as I started to leave. "Don't go." He drew me to the sofa beside him.

"Yes, try one last scene." Hermann slipped the next record out of its sheath and handed me the album. I scanned the synopsis, all about how Lucia is rescued from a mad bull by the young man who, by killing her father, had become the deadly enemy of her brother. Laughing at the idea of characters named Edgardo and Enrico bellowing about ancient Scottish feuds, I handed the album back. "It's just too absurd."

Hermann said that Italian operas used Italian names. But the story showed truly what happened in Scotland at that time. "And

92

for opera they choose the high moments," Ernst said, "the extremes of life."

"It makes sense," Hermann agreed, "to sing about what's too intense for — say, a letter to the *Times*."

And as the music began Ernst begged me to think of the voice as an instrument.

"In this aria particularly," Hermann said.

The high sweet voice began, not tremulous but with an effect of faltering, and Ernst murmured to me softly, "Imagine Lucia coming down the stone stairway of the castle after she has killed her husband. She is wearing a flowing white robe, and her hair is falling loose around her shoulders. . . ."

"It's her wedding night, remember. She's groping, feeling her way blindly. . . ." Hermann's voice was dreamy, as if he could see her. "She's hardly aware of where she is, but still feels guilt, afraid she's committed some terrible act."

Then the flute began to answer the bewildered girl, with the other instruments fading until there were only the two voices, the silver one reaching out toward the human's poignant loneliness. In a moment of unison the flute condoled, soothed, and then in exquisite reply gave pity in answer to the searching, the questioning, the increasing desperation, agreeing ecstatically with the rejection of life, the certitude of loss, and of renunciation finally through death.

I was listening in a way I had never listened before. When it came to an end I could only sigh, not even trying to say what this hour had taught me.

"Now we'll let you read," Ernst said, and the men went into Hermann's study. Almost reluctantly I picked up my magazine.

It was necessary in these days, Barbusse said, to take the step beyond naturalism. "Today we must enter into the collective drama. It is even more stirring than the drama of the individual, and it does not end with death. We must raise on the stage a new protagonist, the most imposing of all: the masses. . . ."

I looked up and saw the amber curtains lifting lightly in the breeze, revealing the sunshine on the meadow outside, and what I was reading seemed to continue the music, respond to it, with a passionate cry against the narrowing and diminishing of life.

93

"When one has climbed to a certain height," Barbusse said, "one no longer sees a man isolated, nor a house by itself; one sees a multitude. From that height a city consists of people having a new and unified form. One sees the outline of the world no longer as it is abstractly reproduced on a map, but rather the geographical configuration of countries in flesh and bone . . ."

I sat bemused by a sense of revelation, filled with gratitude to Barbusse, and to Hermann and Ernst, whose voices I half heard as they spoke and laughed together in the study.

Even though I only half heard them then, I could later remember a vague uneasiness beginning to flow beneath my exultation. I wasn't trying to understand the German, but the tone of intimacy I could not miss. And in that later recalling I thought of the way they had revealed the opera to me — their two voices as true a duet as the one in the music, perfectly attuned to each other, in long-established harmony.

All this came to full consciousness only months later, but within the next hour I had specific reason for concern. I had turned to another article, about the lung disease of marble workers in Vermont, a form of slow suffocation called silicosis. The worker would breathe stone or metal dust until it so irritated his lungs that they filled up with scar tissue and he could no longer breathe enough to work. Within a short time he caught pneumonia or tuberculosis and died.

Hermann was coming out of the study, Ernst behind him telling a story sprinkled with English words, "subway," "Fifth Avenue Cinema," "Clive." I wondered what could be so funny — except maybe the fact that Elsa chose to call her husband Bill by the classy name of Clive. I shamed the thought away. That jealous, left-out feeling belonged to my childhood, to the time after my mother remarried, a time that justified it.

When a worker died from silicosis the company paid the family $500. "In the cost of operating the quarries it is necessary to budget $1 out of every $5 to cover disability claims."

Bending over my shoulder to study the captions Ernst said he had thought potter's rot was a thing of the past. I told him that granite workers die of TB at a higher rate than the rest of the community

94

from all diseases put together. His response made me love him suddenly. "Why, that's criminal!" he almost shouted. "Those quarry owners ought to be guillotined!"

Hermann asked dryly — Ernst now worked for Koppers Coal & Coke — if he really thought businessmen should be guillotined for keeping costs down. Ernst looked somewhat perplexed, but still insisted that nobody should be allowed to get away with this.

"That's just about the conclusion we've reached," Hermann said quietly, and came to stand behind me. Catching his significant tone, Ernst looked from one of us to the other. "But what can be done?"

"The quarries can be run to get the granite out," Hermann said, "not to keep some idiot loafing on the Riviera. It would be cheaper, even if...."

"Just a minute," Ernst broke in. "The New Deal can't do what you're talking about."

Hermann agreed. In fact Roosevelt was trying to save the very system that made it profitable to let workers die. Ernst saw then what was coming. He asked slowly, as if dreading the answer, "Have you committed yourself?"

"Yes." Hermann laid his hands on my shoulders.

"You've joined?" Ernst seemed still to hope it wasn't true. But Hermann said it was. His fingers pressed my shoulders, as if sharing with me the seriousness of his admission. Membership in the underground was a secret not to be revealed even to a fellow-traveling husband or wife.

Ernst said uncomfortably, "I suppose you know what you're doing."

Hermann told him we did.

Ernst said he had not guessed that Hermann was so close. "At Florence Powdermaker's dinner just last month you sounded like, ah, *Le Bourgeois Gentilhomme*."

He had been in New York on Party business, Hermann said, and Ernst winced. So did I, almost, for a different reason. Hermann had told so much. But clearly Ernst understood. He said, "Then this is very confidential." Hermann nodded.

"No marching in parades and handing out leaflets and so?"

"No. We're in a different line of work."

Ernst was quiet for a moment, then made one last protest. "You always said this was not for you."

Hermann nodded. "But now. . . ." He shrugged, as if unable himself to explain the change. In the silence I heard the words, "Lord, it is time." They were the first words of a Rilke stanza Hermann had taught me in German. Translated into English, the last lines had given me a strange shiver:

> Lord it is time.
> The summer was very great.
> Let thy shadows fall on the sundial
> And on the open fields let loose the winds.

CHAPTER 11

Falls Church was a lazy Virginia village in 1935, not yet the vast suburb it would become. We had farmers for neighbors, and one of them turned over the soil of the sunny area beyond Claudia's play yard. My first radishes, eaten for breakfast European style, seemed in some absurdly charming way to symbolize our life.

But one morning we found a wood tick in Claudia's hair, unaccountably missed the night before. Then came three days of suspense: Rocky Mountain spotted fever was deadly in those days. When she stayed rosy-tan, playing as usual with the baby goats at the Rosedere Cattery, I took it as another symbol of our luck.

Hermann with his Leica, circling, kneeling, climbing a ladder, recorded our days. There I am with Claudia in her little wading pool, our bodies sleek and gleaming. And riding: Claudia on a fat pony, with me beside her on a high-flying mare named Blackbird. Hermann would not ride; he had had enough of it in the German army, sitting to the trot, Wehrmacht style. He used the hour to work on the report of his research for Carter Goodrich's project.

He wanted to make the English of his first publication in America not only correct but vivid and readable. Impressed by the way our *Guide* livened up statistical facts, he asked my help with this. I found it no easy task, changing the passive voice to the active. When he had written "It can be assumed," or "The service industries are expected to," I asked who had done the assuming and expecting. But scholars didn't like to say. Their augustly impersonal tone suggested magisterial knowledge. "They're just playing it safe," I told Hermann. Together we found solutions. Carter called the result an eye-opener; he asked me to write a memo to help his staff spark up and simplify their prose.

During weather hot enough to make us selective, we couldn't decline Mary's annual *fête champêtre*. The dinner would be cooked by an old New York friend whose name she clearly expected me to recognize. From habit I nodded wisely, but then forgot it. Thus Hermann was unprepared when she introduced the white-crested man stirring the spaghetti sauce. "This is Carlo Tresca," she told us, "the greatest revolutionary of them all."

After a few minutes Hermann drew me aside, saying I looked ill; probably the heat was too much for me. I stared at him, puzzled, but at that moment he could hardly explain about the Party's deep hatred of Carlo Tresca. (A few years later someone would murder Tresca, with nobody ever sure whether the killer had acted for Mussolini or for Stalin.)

By the time I caught on that Hermann wanted to leave, he had changed his mind. I might have resisted anyway. Lumbering toward Tresca was the enormous bearlike figure of Heywood Broun, every liberal's favorite columnist. Jerome Frank hailed me from one corner, and from another Maury Maverick, an exciting young Texas congressman whose family name had been given to creatures who refused to stay with the herd.

"The situation with Tresca was tricky," Hermann said on the way home. Since we pretended to be ordinary mild liberals ("sailing under false colors," he called it), we couldn't suddenly leave at the sight of an enemy of the CP. "But I can just imagine Steve's face if he learns we've been breathing the same air with Carlo Tresca."

"Steve" was J. Peters, in charge of the Communist underground nationally. On one of his visits to Washington about fifteen of us — a sort of chosen elite, mostly unit leaders, some with their wives — had gathered at Lee Pressman's new house in the suburbs. Marion Bachrach had come with her brother, John Abt, a handsome brown-eyed lawyer, already important in a quiet way.

Steve had made the trip to give us authoritative answers to our larger questions. When Hermann's turn came he mentioned reviews in Party publications of a recent book by the philosopher

Sidney Hook. Wouldn't Party critics have a more convincing effect, he asked, by analyzing and demolishing the book's arguments on philosophical grounds rather than using the space for invective?

Steve's heavy brows had knotted furiously. "This kind of stupid talk I never expected tonight!" he shouted. "To call by the name philosophy the filth that renegade spews out!"

After a moment John rather hesitantly reminded Steve that Hermann, though a new comrade, had faithfully followed Party directives, and was successfully handling a difficult unit. Steve calmed down, probably remembering the material Hermann had carried to the New York waterfront; still, the comrades asked only cautious questions after that.

Driving home I cried out against Steve's unfairness. Hermann explained that Sydney Hook was a former Communist, and his turning against the Party's policies made him seem a traitor. "Just forget what happened tonight." (I couldn't forget it, but I failed to take in its full significance.)

Hermann went on to say that we members of the lower ranks couldn't keep questioning policies. The Party's strength lay in its unity. Any attempt to change the agreed-on position would lead to fragmentation, breaking up into weak and ineffectual splinter groups. I loved Hermann for this ability to be objective even about what he might well have resented as a personal insult. It showed an inner assurance that attracted me strongly. And that night, in a state the Party would have called "confused," I needed his instruction. My memory was still warm with Tresca's charm, his intentness on giving us a superlative meal, his refusal to act the prima donna. Why did the Party hate him so? Was he a Trotskyite? I knew that the very name of the Red Army leader Stalin had exiled after Lenin's death was anathema to the Party.

Tresca was an anarchist, Hermann said. Quite close to the Party until a few years ago, he had suddenly turned against us. When that happened, the Party had to expose him, show the consequences of what he was doing.

But Jerome Frank had told me that Tresca did courageous work against Mussolini among the Italians in this country, and had great influence. Hermann agreed about his bravery in fighting fascists.

But the more effective he became, the more he undercut us in organizations we should naturally have led — must lead. In my midwestern simplemindedness I resisted. It still seemed terribly wasteful to fight against people who were battling the same evils.

They were against some of the same evils, but they are also against us, Hermann said. And they were not *for* what we were for. To bring that about the Communists all over the world had to work together, indivisibly linked to the Soviet Union. Men like Tresca made our leadership in day-to-day struggles infinitely more difficult. Could we afford to let that go on?

Hermann was lying back in the open car, the moon shadows shifting on his face. "In politics, even if we admire someone, we can't let that blind us. We can't separate things out the way you do, things like personality." If we could, he admitted, he would say he found Tresca appealing. In the abstract Tresca would seem exactly the kind of radical he had imagined as a student — who lived what he believed, never hesitated to speak and write what he thought, regardless of dogma or doctrine or expediency. But we couldn't judge this abstractly.

Recalling this scene I feel that Hermann denied his own intuitive wisdom. For he respected intuition; it developed, he had told me, from a sense of *gestalt,* the sum of one's actual observations. What he accused me of doing — separating out personality — he himself did when he denied Tresca's personality its weight in his judgment of the man. I wonder how soon he would have come to realize this — or whether perhaps he did, finally. But that night I accepted his analysis, listening intently and loving him for his teaching, though probably I remembered it so clearly because of my resistance.

Besides his weekly unit meeting, Hermann had to give up an evening to a session with the other unit leaders. One Thursday in July they met at our house. It was Cora's night off, and I whisked Claudia upstairs early. After her bedtime stories I settled myself to read *Fatherland,* an account of the torture endured by members of the German anti-Nazi underground. (We comrades, so excited about the book, could not know that the author, whose real name was Massing, would later become disillusioned and try to leave the Party. An appeal from a woman would lure him to a lonely road in Switzerland where he would be murdered.) In the middle of the evening, the male rumble continuing, I crept down to the kitchen for a glass of milk. As I poured it a voice in the doorway asked if there was more where that came from.

When I handed over the cold dewy glass I had to concentrate on not letting it slip. Seeing this man as the leader of our underground came almost as a shock. I had expected a dour alien type like Steve. But Hal Ware, with his tanned lean face, his rolled-up blue shirt-sleeves showing the muscles in his forearms, might have been a farmer neighbor out in Iowa. Hal had in fact worked in the Bureau of Agricultural Economics, and now he ran a news agency for farmers as his cover in Washington. In 1929 he had led a delegation of experts helping set up farm collectives in the Soviet Union.

Hermann told me this when the men had gone home. By that time, I had news of my own. Hal had invited us to a Sunday picnic.

It started as a sort of idyll. There we were, the three of us, lying on a grassy hilltop in the June breeze, looking out over the white-fenced pastures and orchards of summertime Virginia, talking about my garden. Hermann and I had expected to join a group of comrades, like the time we ate hot dogs with Hal's mother, the red-hot revolutionary Mother Bloor. But he had arrived at our house with only his teenage daughter and six-year-old son, David. He asked to leave his car in our garage and ride in my Ford roadster, with his children in the rumble seat. "They'll have all they can do, holding their hair on," he said. "They won't hear a thing."

This suggested that we would discuss Party matters, but on the way he talked mostly about the apple orchards whose rows whirled in diagonal patterns as we passed. We all had lunch from the hamper together like a family, and I was sorry Hal hadn't suggested bringing Claudia. She greatly admired boys David's age. She would have given him the breathless attention that he clearly wanted for his chatter about trolls and elves.

At one of Mary's parties I had met David's mother, Jessica Smith; someone had called her a "golden goddess." She worked at the Soviet Embassy, but kept her distance from our underground organization. The dark-haired sixteen-year-old, Judy, Hal's daughter by an earlier wife, struck me as unusually restrained for her age. Sometimes she gave her father a quick look, perhaps wistful. Did she have few chances to see him? But soon she took David off to explore in the woods. And here is where the scene begins that moved us with its intimacy. Now I wonder if this was part of a careful plan.

Half-lying on the grass, Hal talked about my vegetable garden. I watch the muscles move under the brown skin of his arm as he rubs a sprig of pennyroyal between his fingers. Its pungent scent stirs me with the memory of family picnics during the August week when Chautauqua came to our little Iowa town. Hal is telling me that with the first frost I should have someone bring a load of manure and spread it over my garden. "Let it stay there all winter," he says. "Let the rains soak in, and then the snow, and the rain in the spring." Hal's voice, always easy sounding, unlike the staccato of most Party men, slows now, describing how the nutrients enrich the soil. "Then when the time comes to plant again, have it gone over with a disk harrow before you plant your seeds."

I ask why he skips plowing. He says we should forget these old-fashioned chores and keep the topsoil where its richness goes into the roots.

Hermann speaks of the difficulty of getting rid of rituals, even in engineering. Hal laughs. "You should have seen the ones we came up against in the Soviet Union." His wry tone surprises me, but Hermann simply asks if the problem was sabotage by the kulaks. Hal says he thinks one of them tried to kill him. When we gasp he tells us about a tractor accident. For five minutes, until help came, he had to thrust up with his feet against the full weight of the overturned machine. Only the strength of his legs saved him from being crushed to death as he lay on his back in the field.

"It was no cinch over there." The surprising calmness of his voice makes me remember the next words, the same ones heard from my great-grandfather Bent: "They've got a long row to hoe."

Hermann starts to pursue this; the Party statistics have puzzled him when they showed the Soviet Union to be ahead in everything agricultural. But just then the children come back, talking excitedly about the thunder that we hadn't realized we were hearing. If we're to get them home dry we have to hurry.

We had hardly reached the highway before Hal asked casually if Hermann ever went to the German Embassy. Surprised, Hermann said he didn't. Hal asked whether he knew anyone who did. The answer to that had to be yes; I'd heard Hermann speak unhappily of his friend Dr. Corell's willingness to appear at embassy functions.

Then Hal came out with the direct question: "How about wangling an invitation for yourself?" As Hermann hesitated he went on to say he had heard that the ambassador resented the snubs the embassy was getting from local Germans. This might be a good moment to become persona grata there. The task was essential, and Hermann was uniquely qualified.

I was driving fast because the sky was dark and the wind was tearing at the canvas top of the car. Soon the rumble seat would be a wild place to ride. But I was tensely aware of waiting for Hermann's answer. Finally he said he thought he could arrange an invitation. In a neutral voice he asked what Hal had in mind, how he saw things going on from this beginning.

The farther things went, naturally, the better. Then Hal made a promise we would soon have reason to recall in pain. He would always be around, he said, to talk over developments. "We will work out tactics together as you go along."

What I noticed at the time was the change in Hal's verbs. Not "we would" or "we could" but "we will." Hermann must have noticed it too, for he said dryly that this meant giving up any idea of teaching at Sarah Lawrence. Hal asked if he had received a formal offer. When Hermann said no, I probably spoke up and said it would come as soon as Carter Goodrich could tell the college Hermann was interested.

Hal asked if it wouldn't seem perfectly understandable to Goodrich if Hermann decided he wanted another year here, on the new Labor Relations Board. Hermann agreed. Of course, and nobody would think ill of his choice of work. But what about his frequenting the Nazi embassy? Respect from those he respected meant a lot to Hermann.

It was then that Hal said quietly that such a decision wasn't likely to be easy. Without putting it into explicit words he was reminding us that in joining the Party we had accepted the fact that great changes in the world would involve great sacrifices on the part of many people. Hermann must have heard what was not spoken. With a smile he told Hal that I had been against his teaching anyway; I had seen too much of professors.

I protested. "But he could never have been like *them*." And realized how much my own verb form had revealed. Hermann caught it too, and turned to me. "So we should accept the directive?"

Hal denied at once that he had put it as a directive. If he had, perhaps it would have been easier to argue about. But against those unspoken words, carrying the force of centuries of struggle, what choice had we?

As we approached Falls Church, Hal went on to speak of the role I would play in this project. I would be an ideal partner, he said, at the embassy affairs. I took this as a compliment then, but now I understand better what qualities of mine Hal saw as "ideal."

We reached the house before the rain began, and heard Claudia's high voice from the lower yard. When the others had greeted her and taken their leave, we stood for a minute beside the fence. I told Hermann that the assignment sounded exciting. "You talk as if you really look forward to it," he said with a smile that was half incredulous.

I admitted that the word "underground" had suggested something like this when I first heard of it. An adventure, I suppose I really meant.

His smile, with his head tilted in that familiar marveling look that seemed partly envious, faded after a moment. Was he looking ahead, wondering where this first step might lead, what repellent and even dangerous assignments would follow, once he had become persona grata with the Nazis?

Cora was waiting to be driven to the Old Dominion Station — she had already missed one church service — and Hermann didn't speak of the new assignment again until the first engraved invitation came from the embassy.

CHAPTER 12

Two weeks later Hermann and I were entering the German Embassy to attend a reception for Leni Riefenstahl. Her great film, *The White Hell of Pitz Palu,* had made her famous for innocent scenes of climbing in the high Alps. But now her fans all over the world were troubled; she had gone on working under Hitler. We couldn't know that she would help turn the 1936 Berlin Olympics into a Nazi festival, but already we had seen her shots of cheering hordes gathered to hear the Führer.

The embassy entrance was jammed with people. Pushed by those behind us we were almost against the slender young woman in the inner doorway before we recognized her. I think it was the intensity of her eyes that made us know it was Leni Riefenstahl. Yet her smile of welcome was becoming strained; trapped there with the receiving line held up inside, she was almost in physical danger from the crowd pushing behind us.

Hermann braced himself with his hands on the wall behind her to give her breathing space, asking casually if such a number had been expected in this heat. No, she said modestly, they had not thought so many would come. The conversation went on in German, perhaps about her lighting effects; Hermann had been a lighting engineer. As the line began to move past Riefenstahl she asked his name. I gave it, for by that time he was too far ahead to hear. Or so I thought. But driving home he spoke rather wryly about being so well identified.

I said something naive about her interest showing he had been a success. "And if you're going to be persona grata there, you have to be a persona, don't you?"

I remember his shrug, conceding. "You make everything so simple and easy."

The next week something happened that could not seem so simple and easy. On one of Hal's trips among the Pennsylvania mines his car crashed into a coal truck and he was killed. We never got a detailed report. Someone said Hal had been trying to avoid a school bus. And we all knew he would have been driving too fast. "As if the devil was after him," Hermann said. I wonder now at his choosing those words.

Each comrade probably felt a personal devastation. I know Hermann did; but also he was left without Hal's guidance on the German Embassy assignment.

Mary made my own sorrow even worse. Adding what she called an "ironic footnote" to Hal's death, she named a certain poet Jessica had brought to dinner at Mary's. This "chap," a lover of Jessica's, she said, had declaimed a so-called poem ridiculing one of Germany's greatest socialists. Mary had protested; he had jeered at her protest, and Rodney had thrown the fellow out.

The story troubled me in many ways. I had read the poem in *New Masses,* accepting its contempt for socialists. The Party must know best, I assumed, though each day I saw Mary, a socialist, working hard for the same goals as mine. Her intrigues for great causes fascinated me, but now her savoring voice made me squirm. Mother must have planted deep in me a scorn of gossip; I listened uncomfortably, telling myself it was my duty to pick up anything politically useful.

The story assumed, to begin with, that Hal's wife was unfaithful to him. And Mary added that Hal had been "no mean Don Juan himself." But recently, afraid Jessica might leave him and marry the poet, Hal had decided to put his house in order. Bringing together his "sundry kids" on a Maryland farm, he had told Jessica to stay put or depart. When the chips were down, according to Mary, Jessica had "opted for home and husband." The poet, piqued, had then married someone else. "And now," Mary ended in a tone almost of relish, "Poor Jessica, having settled for the bed she had made, finds it suddenly empty."

Normally I enjoyed Mary's irony, but this hurt. I hated discovering faults in people I loved. And I couldn't fight back with denials. Even if I had dared try, I had no proof. Mary's most complex accounts usually turned out to be true. Remembering Hal's way of looking at me (was this part of every leader's hold on people?) I couldn't be sure Mary wasn't right about his tendency to stray. His mother had had a series of husbands and lovers, and showed no signs of changing her ways.

Journalists clearly knew Hal's pedigree. When the papers reported that at age seventy-two, Mother Bloor was in a West Coast jail, Mary spoke of Hal's being the son of this "fiery old Red who could stir up any crowd." I asked in a tone of naive surprise if he hadn't come out of our own stodgy Bureau of Agricultural Economics. "Yes," she said, "but a lot of water has flowed under the bridge since then. And blood into the Russian soil."

My report that week disturbed the unit leaders, who had met to plan strategy as we waited for Hal to be replaced. (Our temporary leader turned out to be John Herrmann, the husband of Josephine Herbst.) When I quoted those ominous words of Mary's, several comrades said I should have asked what she meant, and learned how much she knew. But I hadn't dared; I couldn't trust my face. Its open look of honesty worked well normally but it could betray me when caught by surprise. I had turned away quickly and started typing.

Hermann tried to calm the group. He said Mary probably knew only what all Hal's acquaintances knew — that he had gone to Russia in the twenties to help organize collectives. The little news sheet he had been running recently would hardly cause a ripple in the leftist Washington current.

But Jessica, someone pointed out, did publicity for the Soviet Embassy, producing a news bulletin. Hermann said that connection had always seemed asking for trouble. "How come it was allowed?" This didn't go down well with the others. Their voices reminded me of Steve's that night at Lee Pressman's. It was hardly our place, they made cuttingly clear, to question such upper-echelon decisions.

Hermann had earned such respect that their bluster surprised me. It may have masked their own worry, and their grief. But in that first moment Hermann's mouth tightened as if he'd taken a blow.

Someone pointed out — I think it was John Abt, who would later marry her — that Jessica used her own name in her work. But we knew that most of the journalists, like Rodney Dutcher, Mary's own husband, were quite aware of who she was.

The press, so far, had simply reported Hal's death. How much else might come out we couldn't foresee. What if there had been some loose talk? Lee Pressman's had led to his being fired from AAA. He was working now on a project with Dutcher — a newspaper with mass circulation that would give the worker's side of current events. Hundreds of thousands were swallowing what Hearst and the other reactionary publishers fed them. And probably as many listened to Father Coughlin, the Roosevelt-hating radio priest. Maybe the most dangerous demagogue was Huey Long, campaigning all over the country on the slogan "Every man a king!" He drew huge crowds. It looked as if he might even win some of the state primaries against Roosevelt.

For the newspaper Lee was counting on financial backing from Pat Jackson, and was getting it. (Not enough, as it turned out, though the Party would later be accused of bleeding him.) Because Pat's boundless sympathy for the underdog made him so generous, Lee was exempted from the taboo against associating with liberals; but he might let something out that Pat in his enthusiasm would pass on to his friends, not guessing the sinister significance a Trotskyite or experienced Socialist would see in it.

Hermann spoke as objectively as if he hadn't been reproved. This did seem a danger, he agreed. Even though Dutcher talked a good Marxist position, he was a newspaperman. Could any reporter be counted on to to resist a sensational story if it fell into his hands?

Vic laid out the precautions the Party prescribed for emergencies: no meetings, no unnecessary contact with other members. If we had to communicate we must use the conspiratorial techniques we had learned, such as pay phones at preplanned hours and intervals, and so forth. I expected Hermann to make some joking protest at these unwieldy methods. We had so many natural ways of exchanging messages. But Hal's death had left nobody in a mood for jokes. And on the way home Hermann said the hiatus would let him concentrate on finishing his report.

I knew he was having trouble with the conclusion, and I understood part of the reason. This would be his first publication as an economist, and would mean his doctorate. Still, he had written the rest of the report with surprising ease, and seemed to enjoy our revising. Now with all his facts and figures and tables ready, knowing what they proved, he had only to sketch this out before we put the report into final form. But he somehow found it hard to do the sketching out.

We had promised ourselves — and Claudia and Cora — a week at the Delaware seashore when he had finished. I kept reserving cottages and canceling them, writing radio programs ahead, then having to use them and plan new ones. "You look like the last run of shad," Mary told me. "Vamoose."

Our weather-beaten cottage in Rehoboth belonged to the family of an old suffragette. On the walls were photographs of pompadoured women in high-collared shirtwaists, speaking from soapboxes or chained by their wrists to the White House fence. Instead of a backyard we had the ocean. Claudia raced into the waves; Cora, looking like a goddess carved in walnut guarding a golden cherub, bravely followed her, though salt water was new to her. Meanwhile Hermann and I let the surf sweep our sorrow away. Or seem to. For we talked of other things, reminded of scenes in the past, right for confiding to a seaside lover.

Warmed by sand beneath me and sun on my back, I told Hermann I had been lying like this on Jones Beach when I first felt "life," the baby moving in me. It was October, and three of us — Ellen Kerkhoff and her husband Jack and I — were alone on those miles of Long Island shore, bare then with only fireplace grills like pencil marks on a watercolor. Jack was one of Hearst's highest paid writers, a big man who put on a show of male invincibility so convincing that I could hardly believe Ellen when later she revealed how perilously false was that show of strength.

How much I said now about Jack I can't be sure. I know I spoke of his special attraction to pregnancy, quoting him: "All women," he said, "should be with child, always." My figure had not changed yet, but he knew, and was as excited as I was by what was happening inside me that day.

"I didn't recognize it at first," I told Hermann. "It felt like a little fish flipping."

"That's just about what it was," Hermann said. "The fish stage of evolution." He spoke in the neutral tone that I knew concealed emotion. And suddenly I heard in it the promise I had hoped for. I turned to him, "Let's start our baby here."

We were full of desire all day long, and at night our lovemaking with the salt breeze blowing over us would have begun a new life gloriously. But we must wait, he said; this period after Hal's death was full of risks.

He went on to recall a saltwater memory of his own; though a sort of triumph too, not such a happy one. During a weekend at a friend's summer home, he made a long swim from one point of land to another across the bay. In the midst of congratulations his friend Howard Selsam had laughed at his European breaststroke. "He was just jealous," I said, indignant.

Hermann shrugged off my anger at the swimming story, making light of the whole incident. Yet why had it stayed in his memory? This question came to me later, but at the time I simply matched it with a moment of my own.

It was soon after Mother's remarriage; I was ten, not accepted either at school or home. One day I was impersonating a doughty steed and rider prancing across the lawn when my stepsister and her high school chum arrived. They were only fifteen-year-old girls, I told Hermann, but looking back I still saw them as two stylish young ladies standing there laughing at me. And I could still burn with shame.

Hermann listened with the interest he always took in a childhood so different from his. He knew how I had to wring the necks of chickens and see the headless body dance crazily around before it finally allowed itself to die. And how I had to let Mother scold me for mud tracked in by my stepbrother — one of her pathetic strategies in a hostile household.

Hermann told of a Christmas holiday when his mother had tried to keep him back from a skiing trip. But his father, home on leave from the war, had intervened to let him go. I would hear this story again, from Ernst, with frightening suggestions that were missing in Hermann's telling. And I would see significance in his questioning me about my early ordeals.

But as I lay on the sunny beach in Rehoboth I was only listening to my mother's cries and moans in Iowa darkness. The first night I heard them, when I was twelve and had moved to the room above the one where my mother slept with my stepfather, I rushed downstairs in panic. Whatever he was doing to her had to be stopped. But there was a puzzling richness to her weeping. It was wild, imploring, yet full-throated like a singer's — voluptuous, as I hear it now.

I reached their door, had my hand on the knob, but the voice was different. It was my stepfather's now, low and coaxing as I had never heard it, and then there was only breathing. I suddenly felt uneasy at being there, I didn't know why, and hurried back up the stairs. But every night for months I lay tense for hours listening to cries that were sometimes imagined and sometimes real.

Hermann asked if I had ever talked to my mother about it. I hadn't, as a child. Children don't dare; they sense dark mysteries. But years later, my stepfather long dead, Mother told me why she cried out to him in the night. As a doctor he regularly found emergencies to keep him from going to church. This added to her terrible burden of guilt. She had married him, she confessed, because of physical attraction. To atone for the sin of lust she must bring him to Christ. She had to use whatever power she had, "so long as it accomplished God's purpose."

Hermann was shocked. But I doubt if either of us heard a Marxist echo: the end justified the means.

We came back from Delaware on the day Huey Long was shot. Cora reported this that night, standing in the study door in her bathrobe. They said on the radio that he was still alive, but the young doctor who had done it had been killed by dozens of bullets from the bodyguards' guns. She asked how we felt about it, how a person ought to feel.

It was the first time she had looked to us for political guidance. But without showing surprise Hermann said that terrorist acts by individuals were always wrong, even though the danger of dictatorship had been real. I added that once when somebody asked Huey if he could imagine fascism in this country he had answered, "Sure, but under the name of antifascism."

Cora thought about this a minute. "Then no call to pray for Huey," she decided. "Only for the family of that doctor his body full of lead."

When she had gone upstairs Hermann said regretfully, "I was all wound up to give her the works on terrorism."

"And I had to butt in." Still, I said, he couldn't really wish Huey hadn't been shot. Wouldn't he be glad if he heard right now that Hitler had been assassinated?

Probably it was then that Hermann remembered the embassy smoker for exofficers of the *Wehrmacht*. It would coincide with a celebration in Nuremburg, where Hitler was having himself awarded a replica of the sword of Charlemagne. German embassies all over the world were using this way of stirring up support for rearmament. Their new war college was due to open soon, in violation of the Versailles treaty. In spite of their secret fear that France and England might get together to stop it, the scheme succeeded; the Allies did nothing, and in that crucial autumn of 1935, the embassy announced a celebration of the opening of the war college. Anyone invited to this was being brought close to the inner circle.

When I picked him up from work the day after that invitation came, he told me he had been asked by the Labor Board to make a tour of the Great Lakes ports, ending with Chicago. This conflicted with the embassy affair. But he could get out of the trip, I said, with the excuse of the unfinished conclusion of his research. To my surprise he said he had agreed to go. He had already cleared it with Carter. I guessed that the Party had some work for him to do along the way. Normally he disliked meeting furtively with comrades, but he showed no sign of it when Claudia and I saw him off. He had always thought there should be more commercial air travel in America, and now that it was happening he took every chance to fly. The blue-green of his eyes looked bright under the lights of the little airport that would one day become a hub of world travel but in this October dusk was almost deserted.

What really exhilarated him may have been the sense of escape. True, he had the lake port assignment to carry out, but he was getting away from the worst. Or what he thought was worst.

CHAPTER 13

While Hermann was away the research staff invited me to a party for Carter: he was returning to Columbia and would be coming to Washington only once a month. As I drove to their house on Foxhall Road I was tense with apprehension. What place had I at a tableful of economists? But after only a few minutes I felt at home with them, though I suspected several were socialists. Afterward Carter walked with me to the car, saying how sorry he was that Hermann had been away. On a sudden daring impulse I asked him to come to dinner the only night they would both be here.

When Hermann stepped off the plane he looked tired. I wondered how he would take the news. His favorite English proverb was "Forewarned is forearmed."

To my surprise, he seemed pleased, even looked less tired. We stopped at the new state liquor store, where he found a spicy Alsatian wine to go with Cora's chicken-and-peas version of Hopping John. He'd make cocktails of FFV (the finest fruit of Virginia) apple brandy.

At the second swallow Carter's speech became less measured. Not every sentence began with his judicious "Well." When I spoke enthusiastically of Sinclair Lewis's antifascist novel, *It Can't Happen Here,* he didn't hesitate to question my taste. An author weakened his case, he said, by making things too simple, presenting evil as an outside force embodied by the bad guys, so the good guys had only to fight them.

A bit dashed, I waited for Hermann to defend the book, which the Party press took as a triumph of the Popular Front. But he turned the talk discreetly to the research project, a study now formally titled *Migration and Economic Opportunity*. Carter saw it as a "distinct success," even though most of the staff's reports were running late. "I wish you'd all remember," he said benignly, "that you needn't find a remedy for every evil under the sun."

But they had to arrive somewhere, Hermann protested. Didn't the last words of the title promise some sort of predictions?

Sipping gewürtztraminer, I dared to quote my radio chief, who said economists were like birds that could fly only backward. Carter made some rueful remark about this old saw having some truth to it. Hermann didn't see why it had to be true. If they missed the implications for the future, it must mean that they hadn't spotted what was significant in the present and past.

This startled me. He was actually taking issue with Carter. I tried to listen as I did when interviewing. Carter was naming important economists that Hermann's statement seemed to dismiss. "If their theories don't hold up," Hermann answered, deferential but still firm, "they deserve to go." A theory had to take account of what was happening in order to read the signs of where it would lead.

I wondered how his chief would react to being challenged this way by a staff member who was still a student. But Carter smiled, asking if he was being pushed into a corner. "I notice you didn't throw Marx out with the bathwater. Am I expected to concede that he was the one true prophet?"

Here I held my breath. How much would Hermann admit?

He didn't answer directly. But when he spoke, his tone was not evasive. Looking from one of us to the other, his lips quivering, he said that something seemed to be developing that wasn't part of classic capitalism as Marx had been able to observe it. "And if this should keep on the way it's going, I have a hunch we're going to show that we can bypass certain rigid relationships." I think he mentioned wages and gross national product (a phrase I always found depressing). He thought this change had begun, whether we knew it or not.

Carter asked quickly for examples; I could tell from his voice that we were hearing something important. Herman cited an article in the morning *Times* reporting that the Works Progress Administration had allotted $27 million to a theatre project. It would benefit the people who saw the plays and the people who put them on. There was no such limit to this, he said, as there was on how much in goods and services the country could produce and use. "There's no limit to the possibilities," he ended, his cheeks flushed, "everywhere — art, music, science — with society always gaining."

I had never seen him so animated; I felt our reunion upstairs couldn't come soon enough. But Carter was saying dubiously that the WPA was just a temporary expedient to give employment and build up purchasing power.

"Why does it have to be temporary?" Hermann asked. The trend could go on, maybe had to. Their study had shown that mechanization was taking place faster than anyone had foreseen. Even Marx, who had been in on the beginning of it, couldn't guess how few people would be needed to produce enough for everybody if automation went as fast as our technology now made possible.

"Will the labor chiefs let it?" Carter asked, and Hermann agreed there was a problem. But he hoped the new industrial unions would take a more progressive stand than the craft brotherhoods had. They might see that their members, if the right adjustments were made, would profit more as people, as citizens. New tools and techniques could turn running factories into a sort of maintenance job, just keeping the raw materials going in and coming out. The saved man-hours could go into more satisfying activities — sports and arts and scientific research.

I tried to think what the catch could be. "How would you get big business to cooperate?"

"And just when they glimpse a bonanza in automation?" Shaking his head, Carter reminded us how Detroit had let years of research go down the drain because it would mean cars that would not be replaced so often. I remembered a scandal about their suppression of a formula for cheap motor fuel. Hermann agreed that it wouldn't be simple. And even getting the corporations and unions to make concessions wouldn't solve the whole problem. "To take care of the unemployment caused by automation, the savings would have to be funneled into education. There'll be fewer and fewer well-paid jobs, of course, for the uneducated."

I said naively that we could tax the corporations and give it to the colleges. Hermann answered seriously that the corporations and government were already giving grants for research. "Projecting the present figures along the curves they've started, education may get most of its support that way."

"We'd fight that in the universities," Carter said, "if it meant we lost control."

"Sure." Hermann grinned at him. "Isn't that fight part of democracy?" He talked cheerfully of the shifting pressures, all sorts, that would push from above and below, and in new directions. "It would have to work itself out — and I think it can — in a pluralistic and fairly competitive way."

He spoke in a jubilant tone I had never heard before. He carried me with him, of course. But Carter stared silently into his coffee cup as if formulating some major flaw in Hermann's thinking. Recalling that moment, I breathe the scent of burning candles, see melted blue wax sliding down silver, and feel my muscles taut with such suspense that I can't move to save the tablecloth.

Carter spoke at last. "I confess I thought your picture utopian, but now I'm not so sure."

Hermann said utopian dreams were based on wishes, or ethical judgments on how people *should* behave. "This grows out of the facts we've learned about what's actually happening."

"You've got your conclusion!" I cried.

"And then some!" Carter started nodding, each nod more vigorous then the one before. "Yes, I think you've hit on something."

"That sounds as if he'd been throwing dice!" I protested.

"All right, Hope." Carter smiled at me in a new way. "All right, would it satisfy you if I said that even though the depression has led to some fairly fertile soul-searching, your husband seems to have done some thinking of a distinctly higher order?"

Hermann strode to the kitchen door, as if to escape, but when he came back he brought another tall bottle.

After Carter's toast (formal, professorial) the talk was leas heady. A long-range forecast like this was bound to have thorny problems. But Carter thought they might turn out to be "relatively amenable."

In the study, as I lay back on the chaise longue listening, their voices blurred, and dreamlike figures moved before me "husbanding a circulatory flux of natural forces."

It was late when Carter left, but Hermann said he must make notes on their talk. By the time he climbed the stairs I was asleep. I blamed his methodical habits for our missing the the kind of night I had counted on. It was nearly a year before I learned the real reason.

At the height of our morning rush Hermann came out of the bathroom after starting to shave. With his face half-lathered he told me he had stopped off in New York to see Florence Powdermaker. "Oh, your adorer?" I began, but he said he had consulted her about his problem with his report. I remembered then that she was a psychoanalyst.

I stood silent, puzzled. In those days psychotherapy wasn't taken for granted as a recourse for normal people. And the Party was against psychoanalysis. Once we had corrected the large social problems, the small personal ones would disappear. In the Soviet Union, according to the only Party-approved psychiatrist, Dr. Frankwood Williams, this had already happened.

But Florence was a friend; that made it less startling. She had told him that the problem went back to his childhood. "To my mother's perfectionism, the way she always expected me to be at the top of my class, and so on."

I laughed that off. "If she thinks your mother was a perfectionist she ought to know mine! If I got 95 in an examination, she would ask why it wasn't 100."

"And look at you!"

I reminded him that he needn't worry about his conclusion any more, and he returned to his shaving. Soon Claudia came running to show me her face covered with lather.

At breakfast Hermann said this October weather was good for riding; had I made an appointment at the stables this week? When I said I had, he told me to make it for three — he had been missing too much. And maybe we should start planning for the future. How about a real pool that we could all swim in? We could design it ourselves, free-form. The neighbor with the plow also had a backhoe.

I was amazed. If I had suggested a pool, he, the practical one, would have reminded me that we didn't even own this place. (But it was for sale.) On the way to work I couldn't help telling him what I had thought he meant when he had spoken of planning for the future. Wasn't it time to start our baby?

"I had it in mind," he said, and quoted some of the Rilke poem he had murmured to me on one of our first wakings together in the cabin. It begins with an anemone opening to the sun, and ends with a wondering, doubtful question:

> But when, in which of all our lives,
> shall we be at last open and receivers?

He had thought I was like the anemone, while he was less open to experience. But no longer; as soon as I reached the office I made an appointment with Dr. Heiligman, a refugee doctor who lived across the street from Mary.

Two days later Dr. Heiligman told me he wanted only a basal metabolism test before giving me the green light. We set a date for it. Mary was jealous; she still hadn't convinced Rodney that he needed more than the one son he had by his first wife. I tried not to show how lucky I felt.

Perhaps I didn't try hard enough, and the gods heard. Or it could have been another conversation, with Charles Kramer. When he caught up with me in the hall I thought he had a political message; we had resumed our normal contacts after these weeks passed without any threat. But his first words were about Mildred. She was obsessed, he said, with having a child. She wouldn't listen to rational argument.

I was in no mood to give him support; I said these instincts were too strong to fight.

"But how anyone can conceive of having a child now, when . . ."

"You have to conceive to have one," I told him.

He looked blank — humor was not his strong point — and went on about the madness of bringing a child into the world now. When I had Claudia, I said, the times had been worse, but we had not let it stop us. We wanted to have a child of the revolution.

That made him frown in thought. Then he asked how we had planned to look out for her, with our lives so committed.

"Claud said it would be no problem. While things went on the way they were, we could hire a nanny. When the revolution came, he would be in some high-up spot, with perquisites."

I spoke lightly, as Claud had. Under Charles's sober questioning glance I tried to think how to explain Claud's blithe statement. But Charles was saying that Mildred seemed fixated on our backyard with its sandpile and canvas wading pool.

"That's only the beginning," I told him. "Hermann's planning to build a real swimming pool."

"*Hermann* is?" Charles was incredulous. He said Mildred better not expect anything like that from him. I told him children made changes in a man. That was what he was afraid of, he said as we reached the office.

I found a note in my typewriter: "Call Hermann imejit." Before I could pick up my phone it rang. Hermann's voice was brusque. "How soon can you meet me?"

I started to tell him I couldn't have lunch till I had revised my radio script and started the typist on it. But he broke in. "I have to see you at once."

His peremptory tone startled me. I promised I'd get away as soon as I could. He said it had to be right now, "Something terrible has happened."

I cried out, *"Claudia?"*

"No, no! Nothing like that. How soon can you come?"

Across the desk Mary was waving me away, signaling that she would take over; I told Hermann I'd be there in ten minutes.

Hurrying out to the parking lot I tried to imagine what sort of crisis this was. The secrecy of the underground depended on the discretion of many people — how many was not clear. Most of the men I had met in the Party at first were now unit leaders. Each unit represented five or six members, most of whom I didn't know. And ours was not the only group in Washington. We knew that some units were part of legislative groups over at the Capitol, and guessed others were outside government, in unions. Maybe there had been a leak somewhere.

As I drove down Fourteenth Street I realized that this guesswork was off the track. Hermann would never have spoken about Party matters in a way that would make my response give Mary a sense of urgency. When a group of us gathered after Hal's death he had been the one calm person in the room. This crisis must be quite different. About someone close to him? But wouldn't he have told me? "My father's had a stroke." Or "There's been an explosion at the plant where Ernst works."

Maybe it was an outside disaster, like the burning of the *Morro Castle* off the Jersey coast last year. He had had to go to New York with the commission investigating it, seeing all the horrors. His shoes covered with ashes, he had come back to the hotel and told me about the charred corpses and the company's neglect of safety rules. His anger had stirred me, but he had spoken straightforwardly; it wasn't his style to make a mystery of anything. As I came in sight of Lafayette Park I saw his tautly poised figure at the curb. He got in the car as if with effort, and leaned back heavily against the seat. I asked, "Where to?" but he only shrugged and said it didn't matter.

"Don't we have to do something about — whatever it is?"

"There's nothing we can do. It's too late."

His bleak tone was worrying. Not knowing what to be worried about made it worse. I begged him to tell me.

He said it would be hard to make me understand. I told him I could try. The car was moving slowly along K Street; I asked again where we should go. "Some place where it's safe to talk." That sounded political. I headed for Rock Creek Park. But his silence seemed strange. To fill it I told him Mary had taken over my script, so I was free. When did he have to be back in his office?

He said, "I won't be going back."

I tried not to hear the note of finality in his voice. "Not all afternoon?"

"Not ever."

Bewildered, I tried to find a good explanation. "You mean your report is finished? I thought it was just a rough draft. Is that all they need?"

"It's certainly all they'll need." His lips curled away from his teeth, differently from when he drew the first smoke from a cigarette. "And they didn't need that, to know."

"To know *what*?"

"The truth about me."

Horns began a clamor behind us. I sent the car forward. "What truth? I don't understand!" I felt like a baited child. "Don't talk in riddles!"

"It won't be easy to make you see. You have your notions about my intellect."

I cried out that they weren't notions. He told me I would have to give them up, whatever they were. Still in the dark I tried to argue, citing Carter Goodrich.

"Don't speak of him!" Hermann's hostile tone shocked me into silence. I drove into the park and stopped. He sat staring up at a tree as if studying the top branches. I took a breath and tried to speak calmly. "Hermann, please tell me what this is all about."

"It's about the fraud I've perpetrated."

"Fraud! That's fantastic."

"Yes, it is fantastic. That I've got away with it so long." He added, "Of course I don't really know how long. They may have begun to suspect quite early. Sooner or later they were bound to find me out."

These melodramatic words for some reason made me angry. When I told him sharply that it was absurd he said I might as well face the facts now before they become public knowledge. "Soon everyone will know me for what I am."

"But what you are is fine! That's what everyone knows. Wherever you've worked you've given more than you were expected to. Remember what Carter said about your conclusion — 'and then some!'"

Hermann turned in the seat to face me. "Didn't it strike you that he overdid it?"

"No! You'd made him excited, and with good reason."

Hermann kept his eyes on my face. "You really think so?"

"I know so."

"You don't think his reaction was — extravagant?"

"Of course not! Remember, he raised objections. Then even after he was convinced — he only said you had 'hit on something.'"

"Exactly!" Hermann seized on this. "He slipped there. What he meant was that it would have to be an accident if I produced anything. Then he tried to cover up, and went too far."

I reminded him of their long talk afterward, dealing with specific points. He seemed to want to believe me, but just when I thought I had him persuaded he pounced on some chance phrase that stirred his doubts. I tried hard to keep my voice calm. Why on earth, I asked, would Carter want to tell him anything but the truth?

"He has to," Hermann said quietly, almost sadly. "He has to play along with the others, keep me on the hook till they can land me, so to speak."

"But what others?" My voice was rising again.

"The rest of the staff. They probably laughed when he gave me the key assignment, on which the whole project would stand or fall. Will fall, of course. But now they see it endangers their own careers, and they have to act."

"Are you talking about people I know?" I asked. "Dan Creamer, for instance?"

Dan was a shy, slight man with an abnormally high forehead above a beaky nose and teeth that protruded like a skeleton's. At the staff dinner I had been fascinated by the way his kind smile could make his extraordinary homeliness attractive. Now the mention of his name seemed to give Hermann pause. "But the others — "

"Wolf Ladejinsky?" He had been assistant cook at the dinner. Asking instructions in his simple English he had seemed touchingly childlike. "These people couldn't be enemies! They aren't the kind to pretend."

Hermann frowned doubtfully, then shook his head. "You haven't seen the way they are now — their smiles, the sly phrasing, the double entendre." He studied the treetops again. "The whole staff is watching me now, and waiting."

"Waiting for what?"

"For me to give myself away."

"But how?" My voice rose and I forced it down. "You've done your job." I tried to say this was already proved by the first draft of his conclusion.

"That's precisely the point." He sat up and drew a shuddering breath. "I can't fool them any longer."

I straightened too, and started the motor. "Look. We can clear this up. Let's go back this minute and talk to Carter."

"He's not here. He doesn't come till the weekend."

I had forgotten. Nervously I followed Hermann's gaze up to the top of the poplar tree. Its yellow leaves, the few that were left, were turning and flickering in the wind. I started to say we could consult Dan, but something stopped me. Already without conscious thought I resisted telling anyone. "Besides," I said, "we both know what Carter would say. And remember what Wesley Mitchell said about you? The head of the department? That you were the best graduate student he'd ever had?"

"He's probably written words to that effect dozens of times. Professors have to give so many recommendations they develop formulas."

"They couldn't use that formula very often. Anyway I *know* how Carter feels about you. I can tell by the way he looks at you."

"You can?" Hermann turned again and studied my face as if trying to believe.

"Yes, I can."

He sighed. "You're always so sure." He said it in almost the old way, a smile trembling at the corner of his mouth. But he turned before it could come, looking up into the tree. The withes at the top were straining in the wind, blowing out horizontally and then springing back upright. I had to break the silence. "Have you had lunch?"

"Lunch?" He shook his head. "I don't think so."

This shocked me almost more than the other things he had said. He was a man of habit. I swung the car around swiftly, glad to get away from the tree and its writhing fronds. "Where shall we eat?"

"Eat?" He had forgotten already. "Anywhere."

Near Twentieth and K, I parked outside a hotel coffee shop. With its bright lights and white tile it seemed like a refuge of matter-of-fact reality. But when we were seated in our solid chairs Hermann hardly seemed to see the waitress who hovered over us. I ordered omelets and tried to break into his preoccupation.

I told him Mimi had invited us to dinner again. She had accused me of having no time for my family. Party obligations made this a problem. Now I suddenly felt we must go there. "We can take Claudia," I said.

"Claudia," Hermann murmured, as if waking from his daze.

"Yes. It's her chance for social life."

I started to get up. "I must call her back. I waited, thinking you might have to. . . ."

Before I could say the word "work" he checked me, shaking his head. "No." He had started to eat, but now he put down his fork. "I can't get out of the trap that way."

I accused him of being melodramatic. "No one is trying to trap you."

"Who is the better judge?" he asked in a strange stern voice. "You, or the one for whom the trap is being set?"

I asked ironically just who might be setting this trap.

He answered with patience that was worse than his anger. "Carter Goodrich and the others are trying to trick me into an attempt to get away with fraud. Then they'll have me where they want me."

"Hermann, no!" I couldn't understand. After all our argument we were back where we started. "The Carter Goodrich I know would never play a dirty trick on anyone!"

"Maybe you don't know him as well as you think you do." His cold, suspicious tone made him a stranger.

I pounded the table with my two fists. "I won't have you saying these things about Carter!"

This seemed to shake his certainty; he said Carter too might have been trapped, forced into playing their game. I hurried to take advantage of his doubt. "But Carter's a professor. If he found something wrong with your work wouldn't he discuss it with you first?"

Hermann conceded that this would fit the usual case. So why not his? It took him a moment to find the answer: "Because it wasn't just faulty work. Fraud is a criminal act."

Almost moaning, I gave all my arguments again, about his being hired for his ability, the Labor Board eager to have him back. He waited, as if for more convincing. I told him he was just tired; he had worked too hard. He had gone stale on his report, and now he couldn't see how good it was.

"*Is* it good?"

"Of course it is." But if he didn't think I was qualified to judge, Carter was. "He's in New York right now, reading your rough draft. When he comes back he'll tell you, and you can believe him." Hermann's head tipped, weighing this. I gripped his hand. "Promise me you'll wait, and believe him."

At last he nodded. I let my breath go and stood up. It seemed the right moment. He rose and started away, leaving the bill for our meal lying on the table. That lapse, so unlike him, really frightened me. Friday seemed terribly far away.

CHAPTER 14

When I tried to reach Carter on Friday I was told he would not be coming that week. He would be in Ohio, representing Columbia at the installation of a university president. I couldn't believe it. I'd been able to get through the days only by counting on him. During our work hours I didn't know what went on at Hermann's office, but at home he hadn't let me out of his sight.

Desperate, I asked to speak to Dan Creamer. When his gentle voice came on the line I seemed to see his smile light up his kind, ugly face. "Tell me!" I wanted to cry out, "What in the world is wrong?" Instead I asked if the switchboard operator could be mistaken. But he said "No, alas. Carter's away just at the moment when we need him most."

I was speaking from a booth in Woodward & Lothrop's, where I had persuaded Hermann to stop with me to buy a snowsuit for Claudia. Passing through the book department he had paused where we had often lingered. I had once told him of the days I worked there, how the buyer, patrician old Mr. Woodward, used to come up personally to the correspondence office to dictate his letters to me. I murmured something about letting Mary know I'd be late, and rushed away.

Dan was saying they needed Carter to tell them how counterproductive it was to drive themselves too hard. Was he talking about Hermann? But I couldn't ask. "I suppose you all drive yourselves?"

"We tend to." He paused, as if he would say more. Or did I imagine it? I hesitated, then saw Hermann glance my way.

"Why did you have to call?" he asked as I came back. "You could have bought the snowsuit by now." I admitted it, smiling; he was his logical self. But in the elevator he looked around at the other shoppers suspiciously. When he peered over an old lady's shoulder to read her list, she jerked it away with an angry glare. "Did you see what she had written?" he asked when we got off. "China silk, white. Yarn, Prussian blue and crimson. Needles, *steel*."

"Knitting needles, silly. She's making Christmas sweaters for her grandchildren."

"But those colors . . ."

A saleswoman asked if she could help us, and I saw baby cribs all around us. This scene a week before would have set me tingling with excitement. Now I felt a sudden sense of loss that deepened as Hermann stood absently watching me buy the snowsuit. His silence lasted as I drove toward his office.

In Lafayette Park a gaunt figure sat on a bench. Still childishly hopeful, I quoted Mary's jingle:

> Morning's at eleven,
> The park is dew-pearled,
> Baruch's at his post,
> All's wrong with the world.

He didn't respond. I tried again. "Mary says he'll wait there indefinitely until FDR appoints him to something, with those sixty congressmen in his pocket."

If Hermann really believed that his colleagues thought him a fraud, he must be dreading the hours among them. But his look of concentration made me wonder. Was he planning something? What should I do? After leaving him I felt a strong urge to talk to Mary. But I was held back by a resistance that should have told me what I couldn't face. I had gone as far as suggesting that Hermann phone Florence Powdermaker. He had refused, even though he had consulted her before. He made me promise not to call her.

Passing the State, War and Navy Building I glanced up at the flag and gulped with nausea: the colors on the old lady's shopping list.

That was just too bizarre. I knew then I had to do something. I couldn't break my promise. I thought of Ernst. But wouldn't it be disloyal? Still, they had been partners all this time; if one was in trouble, the other had a right to know.

Back at the office I called him, simply asking him to telegraph inviting himself for the weekend, giving whatever excuse occurred to him. Without a moment's hesitation he agreed.

At two o'clock on Sunday afternoon I was pouring coffee when a car door slammed outside. Hermann was taking a final hearty bite of Cora's chocolate cake. He had been teasing Ernst for consulting an economist about a problem in a laboratory. Ernst said it was mostly a matter of personnel. "And you're so good with people."

That scared me. I waited for a violent response. But Hermann just shrugged off the compliment and listened. I think he was even about to give advice when we heard pounding footsteps on the patio.

The weekend had been outwardly normal. The two men had taken walks and stayed up late in the study. All these hours they had talked, and I could not know what they were saying.

As the knocking started I ran to the hall, peered though the glass. Two inches from mine was the face of Hermann's most difficult unit member.

This was highly irregular. Comrades saw each other socially when it would have looked odd not to, but dropping in on one another was totally against the rules. I shook my head. He yelled, "Let me in!" Hermann came up behind me and opened the door. The man burst in, waving a briefcase, shouting: "Wait'll you see what's in this. Figures that'll screw yours into a . . ."

Hermann had pushed him into the front parlor. But from the dining room Ernst must have seen the wild-haired comrade. "He's one of the most brilliant men in the administration," I said, "but a little erratic."

Ernst seemed preoccupied. As the loud voice went on, he suggested we take our coffee outdoors. And in the sunlight of Claudia's yard I was able to ask how Hermann seemed to him.

133

"Tired."

"Only tired?"

"And under a strain." he added, seeing my worry. "But this has happened before."

"It has?" I felt a surge of relief. It might pass quickly, be over already. I asked about the earlier times. Ernst called them "sieges of doubt, doubt of his own ability." But he and Hermann had always helped each other. Once when they were students at the Technische Hochschule he had made a drawing Hermann needed for a paper he had just time to finish overnight.

Ernst must have noticed my shock — I had been brought up to scorn cheating. He said quickly that Hermann could have made the drawing if he'd had time. And they had always done these things for each other. Once when he had needed a certain table of values Hermann had gone around in the middle of the night to all the boarding-houses, waking up students until he found one with the right reference book.

It wasn't quite the same. But now Ernst had started speaking in a different, careful way. "Hermann thinks," he said, "that he is not satisfying you."

I stared at him. Could he mean sexually? But that would be unbelievable, after all our nights together. Yet Ernst did mean that, for he went on, "He thinks you are still in love with Claud."

I sank down on Claudia's swing. Looking back at my two years with Hermann, I searched for any possible basis of Hermann's doubt. His interest in Claud had stirred his interest in Claudia and me. Like his relationship with Elsa, mine with Claud had been a "given." But we had discovered each other. And when I came back from England we had decisively left the past behind us. Or so I had thought. I said haltingly that I couldn't see how he could have failed to know how happy he had made me.

"And you have made him so. He has seemed more content than I have ever known him to be."

"But still . . . ?"

Ernst shrugged. "I tried, but I could not convince him." He came round behind and gave the swing a gentle push. As I glided out over the bed of cosmos he asked softly, "Have you thought of getting in touch with Florence Powdermaker?"

That gave me another shock. Reminding myself once more that she was their friend, I told him about Hermann's consulting her in New York. "But now he's made me promise not to call her." We had just time to agree that I should keep my promise, at least until Carter came back. A car door had slammed and an engine roared.

When Hermann came out we were talking about the dark clouds in the southwest. I hated our social voices, so brightly different from before. Yet I went on, asking why the leaves of the poplar tree looked so much lighter now than the sky. Hermann explained, just as he might at any time, how the air currents struck the leaves from below, revealing their lighter underside before a storm.

Ernst was looking at his watch. *"Es ist zeit . . ."*

"Yes, it's time to get going." Hermann spoke as a helpful host to a departing guest. He didn't seem to feel my need to implore Ernst not to leave, not ever to leave.

In the next few days I realized that whatever we say or do is based on premises. Mostly we don't think about them. But now I had to fight consciously for my own. I could not let Hermann's stand, for they grew more fantastic day by day. Even comrades came under suspicion; he ruled out Party contacts for either of us. To excuse us from meetings (much as I hated deceiving a comrade) I said "Hermann's parents will be with us." By Mother's rule it wasn't a falsehood — we had talked of their coming for Christmas. At the office I thought Charles gave me dubious looks, but that was his nature.

What Silverman had gathered about Hermann's state that Sunday afternoon in the study I couldn't be sure. But by crashing in, refusing to be snubbed, he must have learned more than any of the other comrades knew. ("Whole careers," Hermann once said, "have been built on insensitivity.")

Silverman's own customary behavior was so bizarre that he might not have seen anything amiss. But he probably would have reported the attack I had heard him begin against Hermann's research conclusions. In a way I hoped he had; it worried me to be out of touch with the Party.

When Hermann let me accept Marion Bachrach's invitation to dinner I felt sudden hope. Artie was away, she said, and we could talk freely. Her experience with his neurosis should make her judgment valuable. In the midst of his career as a successful trial lawyer, Artie had suddenly become unable to appear in court.

Our route took us past Dr. Heiligman's street. The last time I had driven down this block Hermann had been tearing up a prescription; the scraps were flying around us like confetti. Seeing him scatter paper on the street had shocked me more than his rejection of the medicine. Hermann must have remembered too; he asked why I had wanted him to see that doctor. "Because you were run-down," I said, "and I happened to have an appointment you could take." He then wanted to know why I hadn't kept it myself.

I hated to think he had forgotten, but he clearly had. I said only that I had been scheduled for a basal metabolism test, which I was only too glad to escape. When he asked why, I decided to tell the truth. It might be good for him to know that other people did not always feel so secure. I described my sense of panic when lying flat on a table with my hands strapped and my mouth and nose covered.

"So there are some things even you can't take in your stride," he said with the sweet smile that had become so rare. Perhaps I should have told him then about my plagues in the months of Mother's nighttime weeping. During the day at any moment I would begin to hear a shrill and menacing ringing noise, meanwhile seeing visions of a stark white grublike body (which I somehow knew was my father's), that would rhythmically change from white to the shriveled brown of an Egyptian mummy. This persisted, inexorably, an hour or more at a time, for perhaps a year, then stopped, perhaps when I earned acceptance in my stepfamily. But as I drove through Washington on this night in 1935, I thought only of my hopes for the evening ahead.

At the top of the long stairway from the street, Marion met us, smiling like any happy hostess, her little hunched figure dressed with the élan of a Marlene Dietrich. But when she pushed Hermann toward the bar to make our drinks and hurried me upstairs to her study, I was sure he would think she had more in mind than our agitprop pamphlet.

In her room, scrabbling among the papers on her desk, she asked how I was getting on with my chapter. I hadn't begun it, and I was tempted to tell her why. At that moment she found her folder and began talking gleefully of how she would blast the Party's medieval metaphors.

"Like running dogs of imperialism?" I asked nervously. Hermann was coming up the stairs. "Where," I asked him, "did the running dogs run, and why?"

"Beside the coaches of the nobility," he said, handing us our drinks. "To give protection, which would have been needed." He seemed himself, the teaching self I loved. But Marion, bending over her desk, spoke of the bombshell she was about to land on the ninth floor; that meant Steve's office at Party headquarters. Hermann turned quickly. "You too?"

She was reading aloud her scathing critique of the Party press. Luckily the maid called us just then to dinner.

Marion's meals were more sophisticated than Cora's. Tonight I was impressed by the toasted almonds on the string beans. Hermann ate appreciatively, giving the maid a smile as she served the dessert — Bavarian cream, planned in his honor. Only his mother was Bavarian, Hermann said. His father, who was Prussian, was the one with the so-called southern nature. "While my mother, who was born in Munich, is rather —" He paused, as if startled that he had said so much.

"She's rather Prussian?" Marion asked, and he nodded, but I noticed that he had stopped eating. Just then the doorbell rang. "That will be Vic, the early bird," Marion said, and added casually that she had asked some comrades to drop by for coffee.

As he rose Hermann reached for the bottle, poured the last of the wine into his glass and drank it off. This was so unlike him that I noted it even while worrying about the portent of the comrades' coming.

My first glimpse of Vic in the living room made me worry more. I loved Vic, and he had begun to accept me as a comrade; now his mouth was set as if for a distasteful task. I was babbling about the original Braque on the wall when Charles arrived, and Marion kept up the art talk. One picture, she said, her father would not have traded for twenty Braques. It showed a little girl, apparently herself, costumed circa 1910, sitting on the grassy shore of a lake. Her hair ribbon obscured all but the poop deck of the sailboat on the lake beyond.

Hermann said absently that it had a certain genre charm. Marion laughed. "My magazine salesman should have thought of that line." Charles asked sardonically if she had her own magazine salesman. I think he, like some of the others, felt uneasy about her background. Her brother John lived with their mother nearby in what was really a mansion.

Marion, unabashed, told about the day in Chicago when a new maid let in a "neighborhood boy" selling subscriptions. When Marion came downstairs she found him studying this painting. "Madam," he had said, "do you know this is a genuine Katzman?" She said she did, and he asked if she realized how lucky she was to have one of his pictures. "I ought to," she answered. "He is my aunt."

Hermann laughed with the others. But when I murmured that Marion had been a bit mean to the boy, and she answered, "I can't abide people sailing under false colors," he jerked upright and was just able to keep his cup from going over. No one noticed, for Lee Pressman was coming in then with Henry Collins.

Henry was the treasurer of the whole group of units. A bland-featured WASP type, he stood out from the other members in many ways. If I hadn't known he was a comrade I might have thought him conceited, his manner pompous. But I knew he was useful to the Party for entrée into certain rich social circles. His arrival must have struck Hermann as just too much. "I see you've wheeled up the big guns," he said bitterly. "I suppose I should have expected it."

Lee started to bluster; Charles said quickly that as comrades we must work together. "We have ways of dealing with any problem that —"

"You obviously know about mine," Hermann broke in. But then he seemed to pull back, gather himself and begin again in an objective tone, as if he had planned his speech. The problem, he said, was in two parts. The first was fairly innocuous, he thought, amounting to a miscalculation of the results of his research. Though perhaps not so simple in its connotations. "That will be for you, my comrades —" he was losing his calm now, "— or rather, my comrades pro tem — to judge, along with my other, more heinous culpability."

His words came brokenly, as if forced out with pain. When Marion protested gently at his language he told her that no language could be too extreme.

I had been trying to intervene, deny, defend him against his own abject confession, but he insisted on his guilt. He had failed to accept Marxist criticism, had given way to his unconscious bourgeois inclinations, his craven inner weakness . . .

He was interrupted by Nat Witt, a lawyer who had come up the hard way but unlike most self-made men had a warm sympathy for others. "Comrade," he told Hermann, "I don't think the Party hangs anyone for unconscious motives. So why don't we just assume that it was an honest mistake?"

Standing up beside him, I cried out that it wasn't even a mistake, but Hermann waved my words away. A qualified member of his unit had said his report was not only dubious statistically but counterrevolutionary. I insisted that this wasn't true. In my hearing the comrade had gloated over how he had screwed up Hermann's figures. What did that say about his own unconscious motivations?

Hermann told them to pay no attention. Wives traditionally "stood by" their criminal husbands. Marion had come to his other side, taking his hand. If his problem was so serious, she said, it should be discussed with Steve. The men agreed. As Hermann paused, considering, Marion seized the moment, telling him that a good movie was great for refreshing one's decision-making powers. A hilarious film was playing nearby. To my amazement Hermann asked her the name of the theatre and we took our departure like any guests, thanking our hostess for her hospitality.

It was the W. C. Fields picture where he arrives in town with his theatrical troupe, pursued by dunning telegrams from sheriffs. Unless he can find a new backer, this one-night stand will be their last. With his high hat and low intentions he woos a wealthy spinster, promising her star billing in his play. The rehearsal scene, in the lady's parlor, is classic Fields, his aplomb unshakable as he sits upon a burning cigar with the lady on his lap.

Hermann gave himself up to laughter, breathing in gasps and sobs. By the light of the screen I could see the gleam of tears. But at the film's most crucial moment he stood up, saying we must go.

Driving through Georgetown I tried to break the silence by talking about "East Lynne," the play within the play. The hackneyed plot had worked with this sophisticated audience as well as it had with its first ones, decades ago. Such observations usually interested Hermann, but now he shook his head distractedly, saying he was trying to think.

At home he leaped out of the car with sudden vigor. Bringing the FFV bottle and two liqueur glasses up to our bedroom, he lighted the fire. "Toss this off," he said, handing me mine, "and we'll go for a walk."

The moon, a few days past the full, was directly ahead of us as we started down the woods road. Hermann tucked my hand in his pocket, as he often did on winter walks. In a musing tone he began talking about the constellations. Those seen below the equator, he said, were different, though even down there people saw the same side of the moon we saw here. Talking about the Southern Cross he broke off to ask if I'd like to go to South America. "Why, sure." I said, "I love to travel." Then he halted on the road and turned to face me, putting his hands on my shoulders and asking if I would really go, with him. The moon was behind him and his eyes were shadowed, but I felt his fingers pressing through the cloth of my coat.

When I said "Yes, of course," he seemed still to wait. Then with the moon full on my face so that he could not doubt me I gave him the answer he wanted: I would go with him anywhere. His hands

140

came round behind me then, bringing my body close against his until my breasts were hurting. I felt a kind of exaltation. He had given me a chance to disprove his doubts, and he had believed me.

We started walking again, and he said that during this past week he had thought everything was lost, that there was no way out. All was lost for this country, but tonight the idea had come to him of making a new life far away. Even if he was no economist his engineering qualifications would probably rate him high enough in South America for a decent job. As soon as he learned the vocabulary — he was quick at languages — he could support me and Claudia. Living was cheap down there. Sounding calm and practical he said he thought from my progress in German that I would enjoy learning Spanish. Or Portuguese; I might prefer Rio, for the beaches and its exotic quality, though Buenos Aires had a more European culture. At either place it would mean an adventure, which he knew I liked.

As we turned back toward home he outlined the plans he must have been making in the car. We would travel on a freighter with his parents. His father, whose abilities complemented his own, had always wanted to go to South America, and had dreamed of their working together. This partnership would also atone for Hermann's decision to desert his father's profession.

I had not known he had ever felt guilt over this, and even now he spoke of it matter-of-factly. But as we came into the yard he suddenly lowered his voice, asking me not to talk about this in the house. "If you want to discuss it we can take a walk." The sudden disappointment had no time to penetrate; he had put his arm around me, and that made all the difference.

He half lifted me up the stairs, and as soon as our door was closed he seized me hungrily. Then letting me go he turned to toss more logs on the fire, turned again to start unbuttoning my jacket. We undressed there with the firelight flickering up and down our bodies. And almost before I could believe it — so often I had tried to tempt him to make love in odd places, the woods or even the water, and he had said that bed was good enough — he spread a blanket on the floor and drew me down with him, moving swiftly, as if he could not wait to seal our agreement physically, finally.

As a lover he was himself that night, more than himself; almost with violence he gave me more than the pain that is the edge of pleasure, rather pain experienced for itself, enjoyed unmistakably. I did not know I was weeping until I felt our faces sliding wet on each other and heard my sobs ebbing with his as we lay exhausted.

I went to sleep that night so deeply under his spell that later, when I heard the term *folie à deux,* I knew how real it could be, how powerful.

CHAPTER 15

I woke up to see Hermann by the fireplace, running his hand around the joining to the wall. When he saw me watching he put his finger on his lips. He thought the house was wired.

I had had a plan for this day, Friday. But Hermann's high mood last night had made me hope it wouldn't be needed. Now I knew his euphoria had not been a good omen; far from it. But how could I carry out the plan when he was so suspicious?

I would never have expected to welcome a phone call from Silverman. Yet as soon as I heard his voice it became what Mother would call providential. I told him what had to be done. And he agreed as tersely.

At breakfast Hermann asked who had called. "Larry at the garage," I said, "about lubrication." It was the safest subject, since Hermann regarded the car as my department. But I had never lied to him; even Cora tipped her head in question, which turned his suspicion on her. Clearly she had been placed in our house as a spy, he said on the way to town.

He could only have meant the Party. Years later when Cora was a CP functionary in Harlem the idea would not have seemed fantastic. But that morning I tried to laugh and almost wept.

This exchange may somehow have prompted Hermann to stop at Woodward & Lothrop's. The store had probably become involved in his obsessions. But I could use it in my scheme. Saying I had shopping to do I went in with him. When he paused at the book department I rushed to the phone booth. Silverman had kept his promise to wait at his office for my call. I told him where Hermann was and that I would keep him there as long as I could.

"Give me five minutes and I'll be on his tail." His imitation of a tough private eye was strangely comforting.

Hermann was making notes, which he put quickly into his pocket when I asked him to help me find a Spanish language text. He looked puzzled; he had forgotten about South America. I picked up books and discarded them; he studied their titles as if trying to make out a code from their sequence. At last I saw Silverman.

With his bush of curls concealed by a black Homburg pulled down to his ears, his topcoat collar turned up to meet it, he was peering at us between raincoats on a sale rack.

Hermann was ripping a page from his notebook; he tore it into tiny pieces and put them in his pocket. When he started moving toward the G Street exit I told him I might not be back in my office till late in the afternoon because I had to get a lot of figures from the Census Bureau. He accepted this with a troubled frown. I hated to desert him if he felt a need of me, but my afternoon might make all the difference.

Behind the raincoats Silverman had hunched down out of sight. He gave Hermann a lead of forty feet, then fell in behind, moving with long, low, catlike strides. I was sure this Groucho Marx pursuit would startle the shoppers, but no heads turned. Hermann went out the door preoccupied.

Union Station, that afternoon, grew every hour more rawly cold. Under the great glass roof the train shed was exposed on the north to a sleety wind. Carter's secretary had said he could arrive any time from two o'clock on. As each New York train arrived I examined all the passengers coming through the gate.

Now my last best hope, the Colonial, had been expected for thirty minutes, which I had spent, cold and rigid, staring down the tracks through the drizzle. I dared not risk missing Carter. And for my

144

purposes he had to be on this train. When Hermann called my office I must be there, or almost there. I told myself that the results of today's wait could be worth all the tension and fear. But first Carter had to arrive, and then he had to agree to the plan.

I saw at last a soft blur begin to glow. It intensified, became a headlight, flinging toward the station two bright lines. Taking up my position by Gate 14, I concentrated on male passengers six feet tall with bulky shoulders. One of the first to come was so nearly right that my gaze stayed with him, as if by willpower I could make the slight changes needed. Then, fearful of having missed the real Carter, I jerked around and almost collided with him. He greeted me with a smile that faded quickly. "Is something wrong?"

I could gasp out only a few words, and he dropped his suitcase, gripping my elbow. "What *about* Hermann?"

I told him I wasn't sure, but if he would help me carry out my plan we could clear it all up. He tried to get me into the restaurant; my teeth were chattering. There was no time, I told him; they were waiting for him at his office; everything depended on his going there and seeing Hermann. But first I must tell him about Hermann's ideas, ideas that might shock him.

"Ideas don't usually shock me," he said, walking to the car. But as I told him more he made incredulous sounds. "Does he have these suspicions of *me*?"

"Not so firmly. Or at least I can usually make him see that he's wrong." But only temporarily; he always had to come back to Carter. His premise required a master strategist, waiting for the right moment to pounce.

When Carter groaned I told him that we could take advantage of the power this gave him; I explained my plan. First, Carter must act on the assumption that Hermann, simply from weariness, so doubted the value of his work that he couldn't bear to turn it in. Carter said this often happened with graduate students and their dissertations. So much hung on the results.

We would use that, I said. Carter could stress that the whole study hung on his part. But wouldn't that make it even harder, Carter wondered, to call his report finished?

"So you do it for him!" I cried. "*Call* it finished! Tell him you thought the draft was so good you handed it in to the committee and they approved it with flying colors."

Carter said quietly, "That's more or less what happened." He had been late because he had met with a key member of the committee who had already gone over the material. "He said — in fact we agreed — that Hermann's contribution was the highlight of the study."

I felt a curious letdown. After all the effort to convince Carter, this was like an implausible daydream. But it was wonderful, I told Carter, if only he could make Hermann believe it. Imagining that scene, his measured way of speaking, I urged him to play it strong. "Make it big news! Just blast his ideas away!"

"I'll do my best." Did he sound reproachful? Had my stage directing offended him? But I couldn't take it back. He *had* to do this. As I let him off I seemed to be praying.

Mary was working late, as usual. Some nameless character, she said, had left a message that my merchandise had been delivered safely at the normal address. A Census Bureau messenger had brought a batch of statistics. (What I had told Hermann was like one of Mother's careful not-quite-lies.) I opened the envelope, saying I'd get started on the piece while I waited for a call from Hermann. She kept looking at me. "Lamb," she said, "mayhap I could help?"

I shook my head. It was unfair to shut her out, but now was no time to start confiding. I needed all my self-control. And by tomorrow there might be no problem to confide. This was easier to believe while she was there. When she left to meet Rodney the silence grew more and more threatening. The phone's ring made me jump; it took a moment to answer. "I think I drove the quarry to cover," Silverman said. Should he continue keeping Hermann's building under surveillance? I said no, and he hung up before I could thank him or ask any questions.

Later I learned about the day from Hermann. He had only gone back to his office, he said, to get away from Silverman, who had accosted him at the Library of Congress just when he had almost persuaded the head librarian to get some important restricted material. He had not been able to pursue it; then Silverman had insisted on sharing his taxi.

At six, when Hermann finally phoned, he said Carter wanted us to have dinner with him. "It seems," he added in that neutral tone that concealed emotion, "some sort of celebration."

I was jubilant. "Didn't I tell you? I'll be there in ten minutes."

During the drive to his office I gave way to my best daydream. We are on a cruise boat, Hermann and I, lying back in our deck chairs in the sun. Or Claudia can be there too, and we're watching her play around us. But I could not make the scene real, not even as real as Hermann's picture of our voyage to South America with his parents.

Under a street lamp at the edge of Lafayette Square the two men stood talking. Hermann's face was in shadow, turned to Carter, who was smiling. It was a sweet, rather guileless smile. Perhaps he still had something of what Robert Frost had seen in his youth. But he needed guile tonight.

Carter did greet me as if after an absence, proposing that we eat at L'Escargot if that met with my approval. I said it was marvelous, then thought I sounded too enthusiastic. But wasn't that the way I always was? Maybe the role of oneself is the hardest to play.

The lights of the restaurant cast a glimmering path on the rainy pavement. The warmth inside washed over us with a rush of voices and winey food odors. People were smiling across red- and white-checked tablecloths, candlelight flashing on the silver moving in their hands. Hermann glanced around appreciatively. When I ordered escargots he smiled and said it wasn't *de rigueur.* This was so like his old self that my voice shook absurdly, telling him I really liked snails.

With the drinks Carter offered Hermann a toast of congratulations. Even in its academic phrasing it was as extreme as I could have wished. Hermann seemed embarrassed, as anyone might, and soon asked Carter about his trip to Ohio. The new university president was young, Carter said, and this was all to the good. In his opinion the best thinking was done by men under forty.

"Only men?" I asked. Carter's professorial manner always made me cheeky. "And how old may you be, by the way?"

He blinked. "Well. Thirty-eight, to be exact."

We all laughed. It was a wonderful sound.

"Speaking of female thinkers," Carter went on, "my partner in the procession was Margaret Mead." They had marched about midway between the callow young and the eminent graybeards bringing up the rear. Since their progress was slow, he said he could now "claim certain new areas of knowledge."

When I said he sounded ironic, he thrust out his lower lip judiciously. He rather enjoyed Mead. "And I'd say, on the whole, she's a fairly innocuous faker."

I bristled at his male superiority, which I thought misplaced. But I had to remember the purpose of the evening, and listened respectfully as the talk went on, coming round of course to Carter's appreciation of the research group. During his absence he had received progress bulletins from Foxhall Road. They were mostly humorous, describing domestic misadventures. From his report I thought the humor a bit elementary, but was glad to be able to laugh. I wanted the evening to go on and on. Then, just as I was thinking this, Hermann suggested that we skip dessert, since Carter had such a heavy day ahead. Carter agreed, saying that since he was staying at Foxhall Road they would probably want to start conferring tonight.

As we let him out he paused by the car, telling Hermann that tomorrow he would give him such suggestions as had been made about his report. They shouldn't take more than a day or two to deal with, he said, if he agreed with them. "And then off with you, for a long vacation."

I had driven a hundred yards when Hermann asked darkly, "What did he mean by that?"

The shock was sharp, but I tried to answer as if the festive evening still continued. "He meant just what he said. And you do need a vacation."

"He wants me to have a good long one. The longer the better." His voice was so grim that I tried to break in. But he was saying that he knew what they would "confer" about at Foxhall Road.

Obviously the staff would have plenty of questions waiting for Carter, I said. He agreed too quickly, adding that the kind of questions was also obvious, though apparently not to me. I tried reproaching him: hadn't he always said I was smart?

This gave him pause. "Yes, if you used your intelligence —" His lips worked as if trying to solve the problem. "How could you miss the meanings behind what he said tonight?"

"Tonight?" I had counted so much on the evening, and it had seemed what I hoped. It took me a moment to find my voice and protest that nobody listening from outside could possibly have heard anything suspicious in the conversation.

"It was not meant for someone outside. It was meant for me."

I think I began to see then that arguments were no use. I drove on silently, down the hill toward Chain Bridge. And Hermann must have had a moment's insight into my plight, for he put a hand on my knee in the old way. And kindly, as if explaining some political question, he asked if I agreed that communication had to depend on the listener understanding the language of the speaker.

I did, of course, but my answer was lost in the rattle and clank of chains and planks as we crossed above black rocks and cascading water. Tonight for the first time this scared me, and I drove faster than was safe on the narrow bridge. But reaching the other side was worse, the dirt road rising abruptly between steep clay banks, red now with rain, the roots and pebbles glinting bright in the car's lights. I had to concentrate, shifting gears, giving the motor just enough fuel to keep going, not enough to let the tires spin and slip in the mud. Hermann sat tense beside me as the tires caught hold and we went on climbing, up and up. At the top I would have a choice. Turning left I could be with Mimi and Rollo in five minutes.

"You haven't answered me," Hermann said. I brought my mind back to the question and told him I agreed. "But suppose the listener thinks he understands the language and really doesn't — the grammar's a little different — say, full of double negatives. Isn't he worse off than ever?"

Hermann seemed to give this the serious thought he had always given my ideas. Then he nodded, saying rather sadly that it could cause a breakdown in communication. He sounded so discouraged, yet so like himself, that I felt a loving sympathy. Perhaps that was why I drove straight across the intersection. Or maybe because I imagined us in Mimi's living room, the boys rushing to greet me, Rollo behind them with his little smile, and Mimi pleased but sardonic: "Well, at last you deign to favor us with your company."

I had to resist the vision. And I was glad they couldn't hear Hermann now, recalling Carter's words, "'Innocuous faker.' He meant me, of course. And he didn't mean 'innocuous.'"

I was still speechless when he went on. "And those postcards."

"But they were so banal! About putting salt in the cake instead of sugar."

He had been the salt, Hermann said, that spoiled their cake, and the bad egg in the dozen they got from their neighbors. "Do you realize there are exactly twelve people working on the project, counting clerical staff?"

He was almost convincing. It did seem extraordinary (it still does) that those postcards should have happened to report just those items. But I went on trying. When he again accused me of being obtuse, I reminded him that even Carter had once said I was perceptive.

"He had reasons for everything he said." Hermann's voice had taken on that ominous tone. For an hour or two I had thought I would never have to hear it again. Now it was clear that his ideas couldn't be changed by reasoning. But something had to be done.

My office was empty — few people worked on Saturday — and I immediately called Marion Bachrach. Almost before I could speak she asked how Hermann was. "Any new developments?"

The question scared me — what was she expecting? — but made it easier to tell about the dinner with Carter. Nothing I said seemed to surprise her. She asked questions in the matter-of-fact but serious tone of someone checking on a pneumonia patient's pulse and temperature.

Mary came in just as I was starting on the sinister meanings Hermann saw in Carter's anecdotes. After hearing only a few words she moved toward the door, her face concerned. I beckoned her back; she couldn't be shut out any longer. I went on answering questions, concealing nothing. "You'll have to get help in this," Marion finally said. "Do you know anyone?"

I had to face her meaning. Hermann had a psychoanalyst friend in New York, I said, and before I could speak of my promise she said, "Then get in touch PDQ."

I told Mary about the day of Hermann's urgent call. She listened intently, not shocked, as I expected. This came as a relief in the first moment. But her thoughtful frown told me that she, no more than Marion, would offer some simple, reassuring explanation. Not till I had brought her up to date did she speak. Then she asked, "Have you called Florence Powdermaker?"

I had forgotten that Florence was among her many New York friends. Telling of the early consultation I had to report my promise, which Ernst had thought should be kept. Mary shook her head: "There comes a time when all bets are off." This scared me into agreement. But how could we get Hermann to see her? Before I picked up the phone we worked out a scheme. Mary would invite us for drinks with her weekend guest.

It seemed the kind of best-laid plan that would surely go wrong. First of all, could Florence be summoned like this, at the last minute? She could, and that scared me more. She would cancel all her engagements. The next hurdle was getting Hermann to meet her. We decided not to give him a chance to decline.

Florence had already been met at the train when I picked him up at the office. "We're stopping by for what Mary calls a 'wee doch an' dorra,'" I told him, as planned, quickly adding as distraction, "Isn't that a Scottish expression?" I held my breath, but he only gave the tolerant shrug he usually gave Mary's whimsies.

Normally Hermann was a social being, going gladly to parties. Looking back I see him standing as if poised on the border between our real life and his own dark suspicions, waiting for some signal, some sign that would lead him the right way. The sign I had stage-set with Carter had almost persuaded him, at first, but the threatening voices had been too strong. Still, even that night when he desperately planned an escape after confronting the comrades, he had worked out a way of holding on to his real world by taking his parents as well as Claudia and me with him in his flight.

Hermann may have welcomed Mary's invitation as another chance to linger in our real world. We had taken advantage of this need. I wish now it had been only what he expected, an hour or two with friends. But I had consulted people who were knowledgeable; they had said we must not temporize. And my nature, too, demanded action. Yet I wish now that we had temporized.

CHAPTER 16

Mary's maid led us into the living room — a bad moment. Hermann had entered the house with almost his old air of easy anticipation. But in this emptiness he stopped as if sniffing danger, and started back. I caught hold of his hand. What would he do, though, when he saw Florence? I remembered his tone when he spoke of her, embarrassed at being pursued by a woman he found unattractive. He would have a right to be furious at our springing this surprise.

There were footsteps on the stairs. The voice I had heard this morning on the phone said something about Mary's adorable house. Hermann turned, looking incredulous.

Mary must have introduced me, but I was watching that other meeting.

As Florence approached Hermann and laid her hands on his shoulders I was afraid he would draw away from her pouter-pigeon bosom. But he was gazing into her eyes — eyes large and lustrous, as if they somehow secreted tenderness. I felt a surge of gratitude. He was asking her in the wondering tone of a child rescued from a nightmare, "Why did you come?"

"Because I'm your friend." Her voice was different, richly soft. "Because you need me."

He let go a deep breath, accepting this. She drew him to the sofa. "Then let us talk."

He seemed to search for a reason to resist, and his considerate habits helped him find it. He murmured something about not wanting to take her away from others. "I have come to be with you," Florence said in that soothing voice. "Let us talk."

Mary gave the Spanish formula about her casa being theirs, and I followed her out. The four-poster in Mary's room was broad and inviting. "Put your feet up," she ordered.

"But do you think he'll talk?"

"Listen."

The voices came up to us dimly, Hermann's effortful and halting, but always resumed after a few murmurs from Florence that even to me — hearing only their sound — brought comfort.

I woke to a different voice, brusque and urgent. Florence was at the bedside phone. Some words began to come through: "exploratory," "responsibility of advising," "choice of appropriate treatment." She mentioned a German name that meant nothing to me then, though this seems incredible now. "The case should interest her," Florence was going on. "A brilliant young professional . . . Yes, quite acute, with a definite paranoiac trend."

That word terrified me. Why should it have come as such a shock when I knew so well Hermann's "premises"? Was it innocence, or resistance? Maybe I made some sort of sound then; Florence looked over and with a hand covering the phone explained that an excellent German refugee analyst who had studied with Freud happened to be on the staff of a small private place in Maryland. "I think I can get Hermann admitted as her patient."

"Admitted" gave me another shock. But Florence said it was the only course, especially with a child involved; any other would be unsafe.

"Unsafe!" I couldn't take that in. But Florence nodded incisively. This pattern of symptoms was a clear danger signal. She added that she was trying to interest Fromm-Reichmann in Hermann's case enough to get a concession on rates.

She turned back to the phone, passing on my answers about insurance (we had none) and my earning power. "No other resources," she told them firmly. Hanging up she remarked that she had seen no reason to mention Hermann's parents or Ernst. "Those places charge what the traffic will bear, and you can't blame them. It's bound to be an expensive setup."

I didn't realize the grim meanings of those words then. "But surely it won't be for long?"

Her look rebuked me. "I hope you're not asking for any guarantees at this point."

Everything I heard sounded more and more portentous. I followed her dumbly down the stairs. That was all I could do now: just follow.

At breakfast I placed Florence where she could see both the fire and the sweep of beige-green meadow. Looking around, she said it was a pleasant dining room. That seemed to puzzle her.

I said it was mostly the light, and thought how often Hermann and I had enjoyed seeing the sun on Claudia's hair. This morning she had been fed earlier and taken off to gather wood.

I had not talked to Cora about this crisis until we brought Florence home for the night. Then she seemed to understand before I could explain. That bothered me vaguely, but at the moment Florence was drawing me with her into the bathroom. She would give Hermann a sedative, she whispered. "But you and I must still keep alert."

Now as I spoke of the light Florence looked critically at the curtains I had made from strips of sheer theatrical gauze in shades from pale yellow to terra-cotta. "I suppose you'll be putting up drapes for the winter."

This must be a cue to make small talk, I thought, and managed something about not being good at planning ahead.

"There's a place outside Baltimore where you can have drapes custom-made at wholesale," Florence said, and added that she hoped to order some slipcovers there. Hermann looked at her as if trying to decipher the code hidden in her words. In a way I was doing the same thing. The simplest meaning — that getting slip covers was part of her plan for this trip — did not occur to me. The

155

clue, I guessed, was geographic. The sanitarium was on the way to Baltimore. I said I could drive her there.

She gave me a reproachful look. "I think we have more important matters to take care of first." Then her voice softened. "Hermann, don't you agree?"

Gazing at her as if hypnotized, he nodded.

"And we shall find the way that is best. Right, Hermann?" Her eyes had that liquid look of tenderness.

He nodded again.

"Hast du eine cigarette, mein Freund?"

He took out his case and offered it. Seeming not to notice the bad accent that he and Ernst had laughed at, he followed her to the study. I took the chance to go up and pack his bag. I could hear their voices below, an apparently calm exchange. I wondered if she was letting him think she believed his statements, as I never could bring myself to do. Not only would it reinforce his ideas, I thought, but also insult him by not treating him as an equal. Still, Florence might have decided that getting him to the sanitarium justified any means.

I had packed shirts, handkerchiefs, socks, robe, slippers, pajamas, toilet things. What else? Books, paper, pens? No, he wouldn't be there long enough.

Downstairs I found Florence sitting on the chaise longue by the window. "We have been talking together." She spoke in that gentle, distinct way, looking up to where he stood by the fireplace. "Yes, we have been talking together about rest. And Hermann says that in these days he has felt a need of rest."

Hermann nodded, his eyes never leaving her face.

"And I have told him we can find a place where he can rest from all that has worried him. And we agree that to go there might be the thing that is best."

"You think," he asked, "that is the thing that is best?"

"Yes." Florence's voice and eyes were soft. "That is the thing that is best."

I expected her to act then, immediately, as I would have, to take advantage of his agreement. But she sat still. I saw that I had much to learn. Hermann dropped his cigarette into the fire. She was looking at me, and his glance followed hers, expectant. Was I meant to make some move? Imitating Florence's measured cadence, I told them I would take them when they were ready. Then I left, crept upstairs for the suitcase and slipped out to the car.

The air was chill with damp. Nervously I pressed the starter and heard what I had feared: only a shrill whine. I jerked the choke and tried again. At last the engine caught. I pumped the accelerator. Never had I done this with such urgency. Everything depended on keeping that motor going. In the midst of the roar I reached for maps, and by the time the house door opened I had found the tiny letters: Rockville. It was about twenty miles due north of Washington.

On high heels Florence was picking her way among the puddles. Hermann began to follow, but stopped short. She turned back with a coaxing smile. "You get in first and we'll make a sandwich."

I knew — and she probably did too — that gallantry would make him comply. Once inside he laid his arm along the seat behind me.

As I turned right on the highway we saw two figures coming along the side road, one large and one small. Hermann twisted around. "Wait . . ."

Florence signaled me to keep going. I did, telling Hermann, "You know how Claudia can stretch out a goodbye."

He frowned, unsatisfied, and sank into silence. If Florence talked I didn't hear her. Trying to visualize the scene ahead of us, I suddenly faced a problem. How much should I tell the doctor? There was one essential fact that I was sure Hermann would not reveal. Yet it must be involved with his dreads and fears. To treat him intelligently a doctor would need to know. But I was bound to secrecy.

At the top of the long hill above Chain Bridge, Florence looked down the narrow road between high banks of red earth and tangled roots, exclaiming that it was a scene right out of a fairy tale. A frightening one, I thought, remembering our climb in the rain after the dinner with Carter.

As I turned north at last on the main road, I felt Hermann's hand pressing my shoulder. He said that when he had spoken of solving the problem by getting out of our life he hadn't meant this way.

"No?" Florence was answering for me. "You had some other way in mind?"

His voice became reserved. "There were several possibilities."

"Yes." With her face close to his Florence said there were always a number of possibilities, but some were more viable.

He seemed to ponder this. Then, "This way is viable, you think?"

"Yes, Hermann. I am sure."

He leaned back and I could feel his body relax. But after a few miles he tensed again, glancing out one side and then the other. At a traffic light in Maryland he reached across Florence to the door. She caught his hand and laid it against her cheek, and they sat that way for a few minutes. Then he cried suddenly, "Florence, do you think I'm crazy?"

Florence seemed to give it judicious consideration before she said no.

"No! I'm not, Florence! I'm not crazy!" He was breathing hard. "Believe me!"

Before she could answer he rushed on. "But what kind of place are you taking me to? If I go *there* — " He was gasping. "Florence, I don't know — I can't answer for what — "

"You don't have to answer for anything," Florence said in her soothing voice. "Just leave it all to us."

His plea had been irresistible, and I had slowed the car. But she gave me an abrupt forward jerk of her head, at the same time speaking to him with that contrasting softness. "Remember what we said we would do? How we would find a place to rest, to forget all the worries? Remember how good it will be, just to rest?"

In spite of all she must have known, she made this convincing. Hermann became calm again, listening to her gentle syllables. We were in the village now, moving beside the interurban tracks. After a moment I saw on the left an arch of trees over two stone columns, one marked "Chestnut" and the other "Lodge."

A heavily shaded drive led to a circle overhung by the porte cochere of a Victorian mansion. Under the trees it was dark as dusk. Florence got out and gave a tug to an old-fashioned bellpull beside the massive door. Hermann's body was taut beside me, and I laid a hand on his knee. Florence was pulling the bell again. When there was no response she tried to turn the knob but it did not give. She pulled again. Hermann's hand reached for the car door, and I caught it. He drew it away and jumped out of the car. Just as I reached him the door of the house opened.

A tall, strongly built man in a tweed suit stood there smiling. "Greetings!" His voice was hearty. "I'm Dexter Bullard. Come in out of the cold!"

Hermann held back, probably feeling it was his last chance. But in her magic voice Florence reminded him that this was the thing that was best. And with one of us on each side he let us draw him in.

I hung my coat beside Florence's on the antler of a stag. Dr Bullard said, "No hurry," when Hermann shook his head, and went on to say that he had kept this house exactly as his parents had left it. We followed him through bead portieres to a parlor crowded with heavily carved old furniture. Bidding us make ourselves at home, he excused himself. We heard a key turning in a lock, a door opening and closing, then another click of a lock. As Florence murmured about the wonderful atmosphere of old houses Hermann broke in. "Is this the place — I can't — "

"Dr. Bullard is the owner," Florence told him. "You will soon meet Dr. Fromm-Reichmann."

The key clicked once more and Dr. Bullard came back with a small, plainly dressed woman of middle age. As he introduced her she glanced at each of us, pausing at Hermann, inspecting his face openly and intently. After a moment he lowered his eyes.

Florence reminded her that she shared a common language with Hermann, giving the title of doctor. He tried to correct her, but she went on to tell Dr. Fromm-Reichmann how brilliant he was, that he was an outstanding student at Columbia. Dr. Fromm-Reichmann smiled approvingly at him: *"Wie alt sind Sie?"*

Hermann looked as if he hadn't understood. I knew it was not the meaning of the words that puzzled him, but of the situation, in which he could be asked so bluntly, as if he were a little child, "How old are you?"

159

"He may yet not be ready to speak with me German." Dr. Fromm-Reichmann addressed Florence as if he were not present. In such cases, she said, one must work slowly to achieve the necessary confidence. Then she turned back to study Hermann again.

When the silence had lasted some minutes Dr. Bullard made a formal speech about Chestnut Lodge, how with a staff like a small family it had all the advantages of a home but could provide the quality required by a great city and the needs of highly placed professionals. Florence said she was sure Hermann would fit in, once this initial resistance was overcome, which Dr. Fromm-Reichmann said was only natural in this type problem.

"Oh sure," said Dr. Bullard. "After all, our friend here's hardly met us. He doesn't know what tricks we may be up to. Right, old man?" He winked at Hermann, who turned uneasily to Florence. She patted his hand, and again a silence fell.

Dr. Fromm-Reichmann continued to study Hermann. I felt confused. I hadn't known what to expect, but surely not this strained silence. It would make anyone nervous, even someone who had come in feeling calm and secure. I waited for what must be the normal procedures. But nothing happened. Hermann sat biting his lip and gripping the chair arms, his tension growing with every long minute. I wanted to say something, as one would in any awkward social situation. But I was among professionals; they must know better.

The room was stiflingly warm. I suggested to Hermann that he take off his coat. He didn't seem to hear me, but when I tugged at his sleeve he stood up and absently shrugged out of it. Dr. Bullard had risen quickly. "That's right. Now why not stay awhile?" He linked arms with Hermann, starting toward the door.

Hermann pulled back. "I don't want to stay here," he told me in a low, strained voice.

Perhaps I could have acted then. "Then you needn't stay," I could have said. But I thought his salvation depended on his staying.

"Don't worry, old chap," Dr. Bullard was booming out. "You'll like us once you get to know us." And Dr. Fromm-Reichmann had moved up close behind them.

Hermann twisted around to give Florence a pleading look. "Remember — I said in the car — I can't be sure what I'll—" His choked breathing muffled his words. Then he gasped out, "Don't let them keep me here!"

"Just a while, to rest," Florence said gently. "A little while."

The magic seemed not to work. Hermann still tried to wrench away. Without relaxing his grip, Dr. Bullard patted his shoulder. "Sure, just a little while."

"How long," Hermann asked Florence, "is a little while?"

"Only as long as you need to rest and get help."

"But *how long?*" His eyes had come to me.

I said what I thought was true. "Maybe a week or so." I looked to Florence; she paused only a moment before she nodded.

"See how you like us," Dr. Bullard said jovially, "before you decide."

Hermann seized on that. "I *can* decide?" he asked Florence. "I can leave if I decide to?"

Meeting his eyes, Florence nodded again. "Trust us, Hermann."

Gradually Hermann was being propelled toward the inner door. He twisted away from Dr. Bullard and reached toward me, his eyes pleading. I caught his hand and he gripped it tight.

"Just give the place the once-over, son." Dr. Bullard was drawing a ring of keys from his pocket. As he unlocked the door we saw a plump young man on the bottom step of a stairway. He was totally bald. In his white T-shirt he looked like an enormous baby. He took Hermann's other arm. "This way, sir." As he spoke he smiled with sudden intense sweetness. Looking over his shoulder Hermann tried to turn. But the young man's arm had gone around his waist, and they had started up the stairs, Dr. Bullard following.

Hermann was climbing steadily now; pride kept him from letting the young man lift him. But he still gazed back at us in an appeal so despairing that I had to respond. "I'll call you," I told him. "Or you can phone me when . . ."

But Dr. Fromm-Reichmann had closed the door and locked it. Florence said sharply that I should not count on telephoning. She then dealt me the first of a different kind of shocks: "Don't forget, the major purpose of hospitalization is to get him away from whatever caused his problem."

Dr. Fromm-Reichmann agreed, saying that for the time being it was better for the patient to escape the untolerated situation.

"The untolerated situation . . ." ". . .whatever caused his problem." They meant me. I tried to take this in.

We were seating ourselves again in the parlor. The dim light, filtered through the trees and the heavy dark draperies, seemed subterranean. I had trouble breathing. The two doctors were leaning toward each other speaking rapidly in terse staccato terms. ". . .paranoid trend, delusional system . . . threat of suicide."

"Suicide!" I stared from one to the other.

"You don't remember?" Florence asked accusingly.

I shook my head. "Did he say it to you?"

"To you. What did you think he meant when he spoke of getting out of your life?"

I reminded her that he had said there were various possibilities. The two doctors gave me the same look — pity for my stupidity.

Dr. Bullard, coming in then, said genially that maybe I should be allowed to think whatever gave me comfort. But Dr. Fromm-Reichmann disagreed, saying that to confront reality was necessary.

"What *is* the reality?" I asked.

"Ah," said Dr. Fromm-Reichmann. "Always they ask the large questions." And Florence warned me not to expect answers at that stage.

When I tried to remind Dr. Fromm-Reichmann of what she said about confronting reality, she answered that the possibility now was only to search. In a kindly voice she made a speech that I would often think over: "Mine is not a science, in which two and two may be brought together to produce finally four. It is rather an art, of gathering the materials and forming a composition approximating a truth which is personal and relative only . . ."

When I looked to Florence she agreed that though some analysts might describe their work rather differently it was essentially creative.

I turned back to Dr. Fromm-Reichmann. Did this search mean finding out everything she could about Hermann's life?

162

Yes, she said. To learn from him about himself was primary. And from others? To an extent, yes. I turned to Florence. "Then shouldn't she talk to Ernst?"

Florence told Dr. Fromm-Reichmann that Ernest and Hermann had a close relationship going back to their youth. Her significant tone made Dr. Fromm-Reichmann lean forward eagerly.

"*Ach,* so . . . And now has come this marriage, which is recent?"

"Very."

"Not really recent." I told them that Hermann and I and my baby had lived as a family for two years.

"But marriage is a different kettle of fish," said Dr. Bullard. "At least to a responsible man." It was true that Hermann had not taken our ritual lightly. Later we had laughed over the ceremony, but it had followed a deeply serious decision. Remembering, I suddenly found tears pouring down my face. The doctors watched me search for a handkerchief. I was ashamed at losing control, especially now, when I must finally tell them. I had postponed the moment by mentioning Ernst, but I couldn't delay any longer. In a gasp I said there was something they had to know.

"Something *I* don't know?" Florence asked.

"I don't think you do. It's very secret."

Dr. Bullard assured me that whatever I told them would be confidential. I said it was a disclosure Hermann would not make, and it could be important. So I had to tell them: Hermann was a Communist.

To my surprise, they hardly reacted. Dr. Bullard made a little speech about this not being a place for inquiring into a patient's politics. And Florence said that of course she had been aware for years of his interest in Marxism.

"But he's not just a theoretical Marxist anymore," I said. And because his membership was secret it might keep him from giving a full picture of his situation.

"My dear young woman," Dr. Fromm-Reichmann said with that pitying look. "I have seen much. Your husband will soon come to understand that I am not one of those who regard to be a Communist as *ipso facto* a symptom of illness."

That was not the point. But Florence was agreeing. "In fact some in our profession might say that for a young man in these days a symptom of illness would be lack of any leftist leanings."

Leftist leanings! Could these doctors have any conception of how little that told of our commitment? But Florence was rising. "We mustn't keep you from your patient." She held out her hand to Dr. Fromm-Reichmann, who took it, then mine, and started toward the door. I couldn't help following. "Can I call you tomorrow?"

"But of course." She gave me a smile then that robbed me once more of self-control. I cried out, "Oh, take good care of him!"

The smile disappeared. "Naturally. He is my patient." She turned abruptly, unlocked the inner door and disappeared. Meanwhile Florence had gone off with Dr. Bullard. I sat on a horsehair chair and waited. It was some minutes before I noticed the carving under my fingers. It showed the head of an animal, a wolf probably, grinning, with teeth of mother of pearl. After some time Florence came back alone. As we put on our coats she whispered, "I got him down to fifty a week, but it took some doing."

I thanked her, trying to remember what was in my savings account, if anything. My salary, which had seemed very good before, came to only seventy-five dollars a week.

The massive door had thudded behind us when I remembered Hermann's suitcase in the car. Florence groaned, tugging the doorbell. The wait was not as long this time. The bald young man came out and took the bag from the car, then stopped still, with that sweet smile I had seen before. "You don't need to worry," he told me. "I saw right away he was a gentleman. They can't fool me, no matter how they . . ."

Florence gripped my arm. "Do come on." But I had to hear everything the young man would say. "Whatever happens tonight," he went on, "he may wake up tomorrow a well man. I've lost several patients that way."

Reluctantly I started the car. As we passed between the stone columns Florence said an orderly had no business talking that way, raising false hopes. My foot slipped off the clutch; the motor stalled on the interurban tracks. "Would they have to be false?" I had the engine going and turned right. "If he's actually seen . . ."

"He may have seen a remission or two," Florence granted. Then added, "I did hope to get over to that drapery place." I must have made some incredulous sound. She gave me a look and decided I was in no shape to shop. She would postpone her slipcovers to her next trip. "That should be when Ernst comes. When he talks to them I want to be there to fill in the background."

"What *is* the background?" I cried out. "How could this happen to Hermann, of all people?"

She warned me sharply against hysteria. And she was right, I thought. I had to hang on to myself or I'd lose control completely. Trying to sound calm I made what I thought was a logical statement that to do my part in this situation I needed to know what we were up against.

"No one really knows," Florence said in a kinder voice. "All we can say for sure about his sort of illness is that it has its roots in the failure of the parents — commonly the mother figure — to provide emotional security in infancy. This causes a weak ego organization, inability to give and receive love on an adult level. . . ."

"But that can't apply to Hermann!"

Again that pitying look. "Even in apparent health there were indications. I myself have seen him show fear of a serious emotional or erotic relationship."

Could she be speaking of her own attempts to attract him? Surely she must have known that Hermann was always involved with someone. His love life had begun, happily and easily, when he was sixteen. As we came into Washington she said she would pick up a taxi to the station. "You're not up to much more driving."

I told her I was stopping off at a friend's house. "Try to get a little rest there," she said gently. I did expect rest at Marion Bachrach's house. But rest was not what I found.

CHAPTER 17

Climbing the long flight of steps from the street I looked forward to Marion's understanding. She could help me fit Florence's statements into some comprehensible picture. As she let me in I saw Vic behind her; I had been naive to expect her to be alone. Charles had stayed seated, but his taut mouth showed suspense. Clearly they didn't trust me. And now I had to confirm their worst fears — confess a sin of the highest magnitude. Yet though the word "sin" had come to me I felt none of the terrible guilt I had felt as a child. Still seeing Hermann on that stairway, looking back, pleading, my emotions had no room for guilt. Even when Marion could no longer hold off the men's questions I answered numbly, giving no excuses for what they found too heinous to believe. "I had to tell," I said. "They had to know."

Charles protested that this wasn't for me to decide. He looked stricken. Vic said in a hollow voice that what I had done might have wrecked our whole organization. And just at the moment when it was beginning to affect key areas of government.

I had no defense. But Marion said medical ethics might keep the doctors silent. She made me recount exactly what I had told them. Though I had been explicit, I said, no one had seemed impressed. At the time I had even worried that they might not have caught the importance of the commitment in Hermann's life.

We could hope so, Charles said, and I remember my sadness at his sigh. Vic told me to avoid Party contacts till further notice. While they went on outlining precautions for the rest of the group

I excused myself to phone. Marion followed me out, concerned. I told her that Carter was waiting for news.

"Be careful what you tell *him,*" she said.

"Well, naturally." Did she have to ask? Then I realized: my status had changed. But this gave me no pang, no remorse, nothing.

At the curb before the Cosmos Club Carter opened my door. "I'll drive." As I moved over I felt slightly comforted, relieved of responsibility.

Asking no questions, he drove to where a gravel path bordered the Tidal Basin. "Let's walk a little."

With his hand solid under my elbow, our footsteps together made a strengthening rhythm. After a time I began to tell him about the trip to Chestnut Lodge. His hand tightened as I described the scene in the Victorian parlor. "The horror — it wasn't anything specific, any threats . . . any predictions . . ."

"That might have been what was frightening."

"Yes!" I told him I had kept expecting something definite I could get hold of. They would seem to hold it out, then when I reached they'd snatch it away. Carter's voice was sympathetic but measured, suggesting that it might be rather soon to expect anything definite. I had to agree to that, but they had seemed to be talking *around* something, I told him. Something they knew, which maybe they assumed I knew too, but I didn't. I lacked some clue.

"Maybe a frame of reference?"

That was it. I couldn't hang what they say *on* anything. Only one person tried to tell me something concrete, and he was talking out of turn. I quoted the orderly. "Florence said to pay no attention."

Carter thought she was probably right. But I cried out that the orderly had known it to happen. "It was only fair to tell me, after I'd seen Hermann dragged up those stairs . . ."

Carter had stopped, his appalled face staring down at me. I realized I hadn't finished my report. But my teeth chattered; he checked me. "Let's find a warm place and a cup of tea."

We walked back to the car under the Japanese cherry trees, bare now, their branches copper colored against the stone-gray sky. It was then that Carter, so judicious all this time, broke out suddenly. "Oh God! If only he weren't so *intelligent!*" The change from his measured manner was upsetting. Yet I felt his words would somehow make sense, if I could figure them out. Did he mean that Hermann caught more significance to things? Probably I should have said "consequences."

Groping in his own way, Carter talked about how Hermann was able to "envision possibilities." He thought this was at the root of his trouble, whatever diagnosis the doctors might give. "He set higher standards for himself than anyone could meet." He was speaking of Hermann's work, in the research project and earlier for the Labor Board. But I thought of Hermann's responsibilities in the Party, with his unit of high-powered neurotics, and the embassy assignment, which had cost him his dream of teaching — a decision Carter had refused to accept as final.

When we reached the car he said he would drive me home. Watching him adjust the side curtains carefully against the wind, I visualized us sitting warm beside the fire. But halfway to Lincoln Memorial he wiped out all comforting thoughts. "Promise me one thing," he said. "When you phone that place tomorrow morning you won't expect to be told he's well."

I imagined making the call. Then I knew I couldn't promise. I shook my head.

"But you must *not* expect that."

"How can I help it?"

"Just don't. Please don't, my dear."

"Now you're the one who's scaring me," I said, and it was true. He was scaring me worse than anyone had.

He understood why. "No, I'm not speaking from any secret source of knowledge. In this area I know no more than you do." He was just applying the reasoning he used for any situation where he lacked facts to base predictions on.

He had stopped the car in the plaza before the memorial, and turned to look me in the face. "Hold steady," he said. "Don't expect, don't hope. Live each day, hour by hour."

The prospect was awful. "Do you really think I can?"

"Well." In his judicious tone he agreed that it would be hard, with my temperament.

"Then I'll have to change my temperament." It was the sort of remark I would have made to Hermann, and he would have laughed. Carter simply said that was easier said than done.

"What must be done *can* be done, as my mother says."

Where Hermann's amused chuckle should have come I heard only silence, like a sort of vacuum, hard to breathe. All this time I had been agonizing over Hermann's plight; now I felt the selfish pain of being without him. I suddenly told Carter I would drive myself home. He could take the taxi that was dropping off some tourists. He studied me a moment, then opened the car door and got out, saying he would call me in the morning.

This showed respect, and respect was fortifying. But after his taxi had driven away I still didn't move. How long I sat there I can only guess, maybe half an hour, just watching the tourists climb the steps, tiny figures silhouetted against the glowing seated giant.

CHAPTER 18

When Ernst came that Friday night it was after ten, but he found me still at the piano. Curious, he came over to look at the music on the rack. "Rockabye Baby?"

I told him this had made bedtime easier for Claudia. She missed Hermann and knew something was terribly wrong. I didn't tell Ernst that I'd used these simple sounds to crowd out the visions haunting me since my interview with Dr. Fromm-Reichmann, which now must be reported to him. I was glad he was delaying this; he stood reading the words of the song aloud:

> When the bough breaks
> The cradle will fall,
> And down will come baby,
> Cradle and all!

When I told him it was Claudia's favorite he said that meant I had given her a strong sense of security. I told him how precarious my own childhood had been, how the song had worried me. This surprised him, for Hermann had spoken of my spirit — as if nothing bad could happen to me.

In my memory of this moment, hearing Ernst's thoughtful voice recalling how Hermann spoke of me, I see the label, "FFV." I am lifting the bottle from the tray, and starting to pour the apple brandy into a glass. The fire is burning well; with sandwiches and drinks on the coffee table the parlor looks festive, falsely festive. When I have poured the two glasses, Ernst raises his, and we speak together: "To his health."

We drank, and Ernst sat down beside me on the sofa. "So . . ." He took another deep swallow. "At least he is in good hands."

I started to answer, agreeing, but suddenly my shoulders began to shake. He put his arms around me, and this made me give way completely. Then I realized that his body was shaking too. We sat locked together, struggling to calm ourselves and each other, until a log fell apart and rolled out blazing on the hearth. He jumped up and put it back.

He had used the same phrases I had used on Saturday to Cora. She had been waiting at the door like a great dark sentinel, her brown eyes full of question. I told her we had taken Hermann to a hospital, where he would be in good hands. She said only, "I feared so."

After all I had been through, the doubt in her voice seemed too much. I asked sharply what she meant, and she said, "Whether they good or bad, they *hands*. Other folks' hands."

I told her this was just a manner of speaking. But as I said it I could see (as I had been seeing ever since I left Chestnut Lodge, and was seeing now) Dr. Bullard's hand gripping Hermann's arm, and then the bald young man's hand coming round to hoist him up the stairs.

Ernst was the first to speak. He asked what I had thought of Dr. Fromm-Reichmann. "In some ways," I said, "she seems like a saint."

Ernst frowned. "A saint?"

"When she talks about her methods."

"But other times? You said 'in some ways.'"

As I told him about the first scene, in the gloomy parlor, it sounded unbelievable. Could my memory be wrong? But I had given a detailed account twice just after it happened. And it must have rung true to Ernst. "No wonder he cracked up afterward."

So he knew. Florence had told him, he said, that Hermann's response to hospitalization was typical. Maybe putting it in these terms made it easier for him. Or she may not have told him everything. Perhaps even she didn't know the worst part.

"Florence said categorically," Ernst went on, "that this reaction was an expression of inner hostility."

"But I never knew anyone less hostile!" I cried.

"That's what I said. But she had an answer, as you might expect." If Hermann had seemed not to be hostile, that was because his hostility was so deeply and dangerously repressed. I couldn't bear to believe this. Mimi's chief, an academic psychologist, once said that the Freudians could fit any fact into their theories, just by turning it upside down. But we had to remember that Hermann himself had gone to Florence for help.

Still we kept on demurring, reminding each other how much pleasure Hermann took in people, even stupid and difficult people. Their humanness amused him, Ernst said. In his life with Hermann they had known people that Ernst found maddening. But Hermann had delighted in their pretensions and hypocrisies. "I think in some way it satisfied his sense of reality."

That was one of Hermann's great assets to the Party. They had assigned men to his unit that no one else could work with. I quoted Hermann's wry remark: "They haven't put all their nuts in one basket; it just seems like it."

Ernst swore then. He hadn't known the Party load had been so heavy. "And then the hullabaloo over his research report."

But until then, I said, Hermann had been able to laugh off his unit's tortuous arguments.

Florence would say that was a mechanism to contain his hostilities, Ernst pointed out. And he had thought of something else: Hermann used to envy him for being able to blow up over small things and then forget them. "He never got angry, you know."

"Not at people." But he had expressed real fury over the graft and profit grabbing that had caused the collapse of the Knickerbocker movie theatre where I had narrowly missed being caught when I was eighteen; and coming back from inspecting the charred hull of the steamship *Morro Castle* he didn't hide his wrath over the lifeboats that had not been kept in condition for use.

Ernst only sighed, and I began to shiver again. How useless this was, trying to defend Hermann from a diagnosis. Ernst refilled my glass. Feeling the warmth spread through me I said I was glad he was here and not at a hotel. At his puzzled look I told him Florence had planned on their coming together and staying at the Hay-Adams House.

"She's crazy!" he broke out, then hastily checked himself. "But very able professionally. You know that, don't you?"

I did; I had seen the way she worked. When I described it as a sort of magic Ernst frowned as he had when I said Dr. Fromm-Reichmann had seemed like a saint. As a scientist he resisted such terms. He was pouring himself more brandy when he said what I could never forget. "So now I have to go out there tomorrow and tell her all about our homosexual relationship."

I jumped. Brandy spilled over my fingers. He refilled my glass. "Ah, Hope. Surely you know how little there is to tell?"

"I'm just jittery," I said, and he reported a moment in the laboratory when he poured fluid into the wrong test tube, nearly causing disaster. That made me wonder if his hands had shaken with knowledge of the details of Hermann's first days in Chestnut Lodge.

I said something about its being better to have to work at a time like this and he agreed; partly, he said, because we would need all the money we could both bring in. This moved me; he was sharing the burden, which had kept me awake. But before I could speak he went on to say that the doctors would be disappointed if they were expecting any interesting revelations from him. "At least as far as overt acts are concerned."

I was still shaken. Only overt? From the way Hermann had talked I thought there weren't even any underfeelings.

I had spoken with care, and he said wryly that "underfeelings" were not so easy to be sure about. "Maybe on his side, but . . ."

"But if you'd had them wouldn't he have known?"

"If I didn't recognize them myself?" Ernst seemed to be thinking back over that time. Whatever the feelings were, he said, they had come closest to the surface during periods between his love affairs. And these vacancies (he would have to tell the doctors) tended to last longer than the affairs.

"But during those times," I asked, "wasn't Hermann always occupied with an affair of his own?"

Ernst nodded. "Hermannn could enjoy a woman for what she was. I asked for the moon." The women that met Ernst's standards, Hermann had told me, were always married, never really free for him. "The doctors will probably think I was not able to fall in love with anyone who would separate me from Hermann."

But they *had* separated, I reminded him. Often, even before Hermann came to Washington. Ernst said it was always Hermann who traveled. "When we were both studying at Columbia I would have wished it to go on indefinitely."

But he had accepted Hermann's coming to Washington, I reminded him, and even seemed pleased about our marriage.

"Any friend would wish it for him. I was his friend."

And yet where did that leave us? There had to be something, some problem. I was facing that now.

"I have no taste," Ernst said, "for discovering dark corners of my psyche. But tomorrow, it seems, I must try."

I had not meant to go with Ernst to Chestnut Lodge, but he wanted my company for the drive. We left Claudia with Mimi, who had invited us to lunch. (From the moment she learned why I had kept apart from her she was all kindness.)

On the way to Rockville I was glad I could be near Hermann, maybe even see him, in spite of what Dr. Fromm-Reichmann had told me. And I couldn't help hoping for that miracle.

Waiting in the doomful parlor, my ears strained to interpret every sound. If footsteps hurried above me, I shrank from the meanings I gave them. When the grandfather clock suddenly chimed the half hour — four harsh clangs breaking off in mid-phrase — I jumped from the horsehair sofa and went to the window. A little snow had fallen in the night, and tracks of some animal led off under the trees. In my mood they seemed larger than a dog's. Trying to calm myself I took up the work I had brought from the office.

175

It was a pamphlet on meat grading. Each chart showed a steer divided into areas labeled according to regional terminology. The fact that no two parts of the country used the same words for the cuts of beef should have given the task enough difficulty to hold my attention. But a line on the first chart suddenly reminded me of one on Dr. Fromm-Reichmann's forehead that looked like a scar. I should have warned Ernst, I thought. On the Wednesday of our consultation my eyes had been fixed on it while she told about the necessity of interpreting, as if it were a language, each phase of an illness. Many psychologists, she said, thought it impossible to penetrate the delusional system. Others doubted the usefulness of attempting to reach patients in this seemingly remote world of their own. She disagreed. To her their very withdrawal, even the hostility, indicated a great need of love.

Her tone became charged, momentous, and ominous as the words she began to use. Panic, she said, could be a form of communication. And then in a quietly reasoning voice, "But cannot we also find methods to communicate, as the patient does, without words?"

I must have nodded blankly, still fighting off her meaning, even though her words registered. "For example, the first evening, when your husband was most agitated, Dr. Bullard entered the ward where the attendant was trying to restrain the patient. He took out his cigarettes and offered one. It was accepted and permitted to be lighted, with a look that spoke much." Communication had been achieved, she said, the symbolic significance of the cigarette fully comprehended. Telling me this Dr. Fromm-Reichmann smiled, as if waiting for me to share her satisfaction.

My face may have been so numbed by shock that she could assume I knew what to expect, perhaps from what she had said the day after he was admitted when I asked to see him. She might have thought I understood the significance of the word she had used then: "disturbed." Now she went on to say that unfortunately in matters so delicate there was the possibility of misunderstanding. Too much had been expected from Dr. Bullard's act of friendship. When Hermann's request to leave had to be denied his panic had become more acute. But she assured me that the friendship — more than friendship, a true form of love — was being transmitted to the patient by the entire staff, not only by herself in the daily hour she spent with Hermann.

As she went on, her way of speaking merged with what she was telling me and became part of the horror. I was almost memorizing her accented words, her foreign inflections. "Can you not see the regression as communicating an appeal? Does not the infant utilize food intake and elimination as major form of expression? Could not then the patient regress to this level due to his need for exerting power over his environment, and to express retaliation?"

She had probably not expected an answer. I could only sit and try to force myself to listen. "So, in response to these infantile signals — there was at that time no intake of food — I offered, when at last came a moment of seeming rapport — the glass of milk. And it was to me significant that my offer was accepted. Of course, the delay to go and get the milk permitted a change of mood. But even when the milk was thrown in my face I was not...."

Here I had cried out in a terrible mix of feelings, incredulous and shamed, apologetic.

She assured me it was nothing in comparison to the reward, his quite lucid, quite humane expressions of remorse. "Can you not perceive this incident, yourself, as very hopeful?" She saw this was beyond me. I had much to learn, she said. They, also, had constantly to remind themselves of the sensitive person living within this outward guise — "this state which your husband himself likened to that of an animal." She raised her hand against what I might say. "I assure you, never do I agree with such statements of these patients. In fact his own statement contradicts itself. The verbalizing, the human speech."

I may have groaned, for she asked quickly, "You dread to know the meaning of the scene?" I tried to say I had to know everything I could. She then pulled herself up, glanced around her and drew herself in, as if impersonating an actor trying to convey squalor. "His meaning was at that moment evident, and to some would be repellent. Though not, you understand, to me. A doctor capable to interpret is not shocked to enter a room where the patient sits naked surrounded by products of his defecations and his. . . ."

Here I surely cried out, for she stopped, asking quite gently, "You wish me not to tell you these things?" And I had to answer once more, when I could speak, that I had to know. At some point I was even able to order my thoughts enough to say that otherwise he would feel burdened with a humiliating secret, later, when he was well. She may have shrugged, dismissing my visions of the future, but said only that it was better to confront the scene in all details. "He sat, as I say, on the floor, and at the moment of my opening the door he was engaged in accomplishing what we must recognize as a release of tension. You understand that his whole organism was in a state of extreme physical tension?"

Unable to meet her eyes, I nodded, then had to hear her explain kindly that masturbation signified only a retreat to "a phase of immaturity which all the world knows is normal." I suppose rational thinking was beyond me by then, for it didn't occur to me to wonder, for instance, why he was naked. In some ritual precaution had they taken away his clothes?

I asked no questions then. Dr. Fromm-Reichmann seemed all-wise and — as I would tell Ernst — saintly. She went on to say that the later willingness to accept milk from her symbolized acceptance of her friendship, which had been proved, she said, by her sitting down with him in his "environment."

"I add also that he warned me in my own interest not to sit down, and when nevertheless I sat beside him he drew a blanket around him, making this statement which I quote: 'Even though I am reduced to the state of animal, I yet know how a lady requires to be treated.' And from that moment, through nearly two hours, he was in rapport with me. Do you recognize how great was this advance?"

I tried, though this was a Hermann I didn't know. Not even when he had been most troubled could I have imagined such a change. I said it was too bad she had had to leave him to get the milk. She explained that letting someone else bring it would not have shown so clearly that she was serving him. And in the end this way might have been better. "The relapse was momentary, providing possibly a necessary shock. He said in a voice of despair, 'I warned you not to become involved with me. Why do you trespass and bring danger upon yourself?'"

These at last were words I could believe Hermann had said. The story became true, even the impossible part.

She was saying in a tone of pride, "You see how articulate he was capable to become?"

"Oh, if you only knew how articulate he *really* is!"

She said rather stiffly that they had recognized his intelligence, even in this state. "He has read, most probably, much psychology?"

When I said he had, she shook her head. It would make the treatment more difficult. "I am feeling in him the watchfulness, the skepticism. . . ."

I couldn't reassure her, and she said she would deal with that in time, when he could discuss this with her rationally. Of course I asked at once when she thought that would be. She shrugged, frowning. "Whether soon or late I cannot say. But eventually. The prognosis is favorable."

I leaned back then, almost faint with relief. But she was getting up, promising to use all the skills of her art. "Compensating in concentrated form for the love and interest of which the patient has suffered deprivation." I was trying once more to take that in when the clock struck the hour and Ernst came back. As he parted the bead portieres he was smiling. I jumped up. "Is he — better?" I didn't dare say "well."

"She says it may not last, but the panic is subsiding." He put his arm around me, told me to stay steady. But when he started to lead me out, I pulled back. "Can't we see him?" Ernst said he had tried. "Thinking it might help if we beckoned, so to say, from the other side. But no."

I knew protesting was useless. But as he started the car I said stubbornly, "I'm sure that seeing you would have helped."

"She said in this delicate stage she could not risk confronting him with someone who might be an object of hostility."

"Did she explain why you would be?"

"Because of having been close to him, apparently." In any relationship, it seemed, each person felt a certain resentment of the other's power. A man's self-respect, especially, required a sense of independence.

I couldn't help protesting that Hermann hadn't been dependent on him. What they did for each other was an even exchange. But Ernst, like Hermann, was more aware of complexities. In talking about this to Dr. Fromm-Reichmann he had thought of his sister and her husband. "He holds the purse strings, is a typical German husband, yet he can't eat or sleep apart from her."

I was glad at that moment that I had to remind him to turn off the highway. He had spoken as if he saw his sister's marriage as equivalent to his relationship with Hermann. He must have felt my shock, for he said we must explore any wild possibilities. Even if Hermann should recover quickly, we should know the cause, in order to avoid a recurrence.

"Recurrence!" I hadn't thought of that.

He assured me that getting to the root of this would keep it from happening again. To this end he had told the doctors all he knew, or even speculated about. Dr. Fromm-Reichmann had finally trapped him into admitting that he and Hermann were close enough for one to sense what the other was feeling. And if Ernst had these feelings and Hermann sensed them. . . .

I broke in, insisting that sensing wasn't the same as knowing. Or accepting.

Ernst agreed emphatically. "That idea — he wouldn't have given it — how do you say? — houseroom."

If he had, I said confidently, it would have meant the end of their "viable working arrangment."

Even as Ernst smiled at Hermann's familiar phrase he said that "viable working arrangment" might seem to the doctors a little too conscious and logical.

Remembering Hermann in our nights together I couldn't believe what Ernst went on to report. Hermann's ego organization was so weak, the doctors said, that he had felt threatened by anyone's coming too close. "They say it's part of the picture in all such breakdowns." Something about this bothered me, but it was Ernst who put his finger on it. "To me this seems like circular reasoning. In science we're taught to start 'without preconceptions,' to observe cases, and proceed from the cases 'toward abstract laws which they all obey.'" Before I could seize on this he said Florence would have an answer to that. She would say she had observed it in Hermann's case before all this started.

She had said it to me too. But now neither of us voiced the reason that had occurred to me. It was too unkind. Florence had put Hermann's need ahead of all her other concerns. She had chosen Dr. Fromm-Reichmann, who had stayed with him through his ordeal and helped him emerge from it.

All the way into Virginia we kept going back to that. The prognosis was good. In fact, when the car turned into the driveway beside Rollo's tennis court I hardly waited for it to stop before I was out and leaping up the stone steps to break the great news.

CHAPTER 19

On Wednesday Dr. Fromm-Reichmann answered my call with the words I had tried not to hope for. "I am coming from your husband," she said, "and I can assure you that his mind is free of delusional content."

Maybe my response ("When can I see him?") was too quick, too urgent. Her tone became more distant. She asked if I didn't agree that there might be danger in confronting him with those to whom he had felt such grave hostility. These questions of hers, which were really statements, always left me without power to speak. I had put my trust in her, truly believed in her superior wisdom, and yet I could not — though I tried, assuming she must *know* — just could not think of Hermann as hostile toward me. In a genuine effort to understand, I asked her how he had expressed this hostility. She answered with another question. Did I think that feelings did not exist if they had not been put into words?

No, I said, but in his disturbed state he could have expressed feelings he had not let come out before. Perhaps my groping for words tried her patience; she repeated the explanation she had given me before, of how the delusional system had been a bulwark against knowledge of his illness. Did I not see, she asked, how difficult the present days would be when he had to accept these painful facts?

Of course I could; his sense of himself would suffer terribly. But part of his worry would be about what others knew and how they felt. "If I could have just a few minutes with him," I pleaded, "I could let him know it's all right."

183

Dr. Fromm-Reichmann asked if I wished to risk impeding his recovery. In the end I had to agree to wait and call her at nine on Saturday.

I phoned Marion the news: his delusions were gone!

She had hoped against hope for this. "Early remissions tend to come — *if* they come — within one to three weeks." She had known that? What else had she kept from me? She admitted that she read a good deal — a course she didn't recommend to me, since it resulted mostly in confusion. "But in studying about neuroses I did pick up a bit about the psychoses."

Psychoses! Ignorant as I was, the word terrified me. No doctor had spoken it. Yet she had known it applied to Hermann's case. I hardly dared frame my questions.

Marion tried to answer reassuringly. Psychoses could be more acute, she admitted, than neuroses such as Artie had, but their advantage was that they could also end, while neuroses, though milder, tended to hang on. "Artie's psychiatrist puts it this way: the psychotic thinks two and two make five; the neurotic knows they make four but he worries about it."

I don't think I even laughed. Marion was making me promise to take her with me on my first visit. Did she think I would need support for a moment of happiness?

On Saturday morning Dr. Fromm-Reichmann said at once, "You shall come at eleven." Then to my surprise she suggested that I bring the child, to show that all was well with her.

Knowing Claudia's sensitivity to atmosphere, I tried to prepare her. But I myself was never quite prepared for Chestnut Lodge. Marion remarked as we drove between the stone pillars, "Cheery layout, I must say."

Dr. Bullard opened the door, with gallant greetings to the "little charmer" they'd heard so much about. He suggested that Marion keep her in the parlor, then led me to a sunny room at the back furnished in flowered chintz with Audubon prints on the walls. A flight of stairs led up from it to dimness and a closed door. Dr.

184

Bullard left me, saying to use my own judgment; his office was just next door.

I stood at the foot of the stairway waiting, my mouth dry. Small noises began to come through the quiet — the faint ringing of a bell, the distant clash of pots and pans, the clang of an oven door. Then there was the soft tread of slippered feet above, along with someone's quick hard heels.

The door at the top of the stairs opened, and I saw Hermann's figure against the light. His hand moved on the railing and he descended a step, testingly, then another. When he was halfway down the door closed above him. He glanced back over his shoulder, then started again, still holding the rail. Only when he was fully in the room did he raise his eyes.

At last he looked at me, intently, with a hesitant, faint smile. It was his own smile, welcoming, but its gladness seemed to struggle with doubt. I went to him slowly. I had made up my mind not to crowd him in any way, and I suppose I moved as I had learned to do with nervous horses. When I raised my hands to his shoulders his arms came around my waist, resting lightly. I pressed my cheek to his.

He was familliar, and at the same time strange, so thin, with this odor of hospital. Trying to catch his own scent under it, I breathed in that mixture of soap and chemicals.

"Angel."

Even spoken so softly as almost to be inaudible, the word filled me with exultation. Yet as I clasped his shoulders more closely I felt the sharpness of the bones. In the full light the bridge of his nose seemed narrower, the indentation at his temples deeper, his eye sockets shadowed. When I murmured "Darling," he pushed me away a little, looking dubioiusly into my face. "You can't mean that. Not now."

I cried out that I did, and he protested. "You don't know," he spoke breathlessly, "— what I've — *become.*"

I gave him the assurance I had planned, that I knew what these illnesses (he grimaced at the word) did to people. I said that part was over, past and gone.

He shook his head, but with something of his old, fond smile, and even the old words: "You make everything so simple."

When I tried to give him the grin that always answered this, I felt tears come to my eyes. *He was so thin.* His collar was too big around his neck, so that the necktie puckered it; his jacket hung loosely from his shoulders. There was a frail look about him that I would never have thought possible. My knees were weakening, and I drew him toward the sofa. "I phoned every day, wanting to talk to you. Did they tell you?"

He shook his head.

"I begged to see you. Wednesday I made a real nuisance of my-self."

"You did?" He was leaning close, intent. "I did too. To the point of humiliation."

I knew how much his dignity meant to him. "Well, we're seeing each other now."

He shook his head again. "It would have been better then." He was speaking more naturally now, but with a puzzled frown. "I can't tell you exactly — there was a different orientation. Possibil-ities." He bit his lips. "I can't bring them back."

"Maybe you will later." I put my hand in his and after a moment his fingers responded. The clock chimed as we sat there, and he said they had given us only half an hour. But there were things he had wanted to ask me.

When he couldn't recall them I gave him the bits of household news I had planned. He listened, intent but frowning slightly, as though distracted. Claudia's name caught his full attention, and when I said she missed him he almost groaned. He missed her too, and wished he could see her. "You can," I told him. "She's here."

He rose quickly, erect and expectant as I had always loved to see him. I went to the parlor where Marion was reading aloud from a child's book she had brought. I had presented the visit to Claudia only as a possibility, but when I came in she jumped to her feet and rushed to me, her eyes lighting with excitement. I nodded, and she put her hand in mine without a word. As we reached the threshold she hesitated just perceptibly, then started toward Hermann with prim, mincing steps, her left hand holding her yellow dress out a little, as if playing some coquettish role.

Hermann sank to his knees and opened his arms. She walked

into them. But after a moment she broke away, as she always did when held close, and pointed down. "Yook. I got new shoes. Padden yeddah, see?"

He nodded, studying them, his eyes bright, too bright. He caught her against him again, buried his face against her shoulder as if to hide his weeping. But his breath rasped and his body was shaking.

For a moment Claudia let herself be held; she even laid a hand gently on his head. But how long could this last? I backed uncertainly toward the hall.

Dr. Bullard's door opened, and he came striding in. "Well, well, this *has* been a red-letter day, hasn't it just!" With the doctor's big hand under an elbow, Hermann stood up, sobbing painfully.

Dr. Bullard was booming out something about its being a pretty emotional moment, "a reunion with two such lovelies." His voice was jovial but behind his back he gave me an urgent brushing signal. I told Claudia to say goodbye, but gave her no time to say it, hurrying her to Marion, then running back.

The room was empty. I looked up the stairs. Dr. Bullard's big body blocked Hermann's at the top. I called out that I would phone tomorrow, and. . . . the door clicked shut.

I stood there trying to take in what had happened, so appallingly different from what I had expected. I hadn't let myself put it into words, but I suppose I had envisioned taking him home, with life ahead as it had been a month ago.

Marion was buttoning Claudia into her coat, telling about the squirrels they had seen out the window. As we emerged into the raw November air, Claudia's hand clung to mine. When I had to detach it to drive she sighed and took her place on Marion's lap, listening politely to the continuing story. But in the middle of the squirrel's liveliest high-wire act she suddenly, contrary to habit, fell sound asleep. If the scene had left her so exhausted, what deeper effect might it have had? She was less than three years old, but her sympathies and perceptions always astonished me. How much of Hermann's suffering had she shared?

After a mile I gave Marion a report coded for Claudia's ears in case she heard it. "His pain came back, apparently, and got worse. He cried a little, and the doctor came."

Marion nodded calmly, saying only that it was a chance I'd had to take. I wanted to ask what effect it might have on Claudia, but she said I must begin thinking of myself. I must get some rest. Because soon I would be starting with my unit. I turned, amazed that she should bring that up now. Anyway, the comrades would surely have dropped any notion of giving me a unit, after what I had told the doctors.

"Whatever they may have thought before," she said, "they agree now with Steve."

"Steve!" I remembered his dark-browed anger that night out at Lee Pressman's. Marion asked if I wanted to know what he had said about me. Anesthetized as I had been to everything unrelated to Hermann, I felt a nudge of curiosity. But it was irrelevant now. I told her I simply was not up to leading a unit.

"Well, my friend," Marion said coolly, "you'll just have to be up to it."

"*Have* to?"

When she nodded I almost stopped the car to fight this out. But Claudia would wake up if we didn't keep moving. I asked what would happen if I just couldn't accept the leadership of a unit.

She said it had been decided that I could.

There was more to our talk, back and forth, but she held firm. As we rounded Chevy Chase Circle I cried out that she didn't seem like the Marion I had known, who had been flippant at meetings when Vic and Charles were so solemn. She had sounded as if at any moment she might kick over the traces.

"Look, my dear comrade," she said. "Let's get this straight. Those traces you speak of — well, I love them." But her feelings, she said, were not the issue, nor mine. "The point is, we're in it. Both of us."

I drove a while, absorbing this. It was like a threat, yet somehow stirring too. "So..." I said. "I can't just... decline?"

She said that if I had been present Steve might have given me a chance to influence the decision. But once the directive was handed down, it stood.

Turning into Nineteenth Street I tried to make all this seem real. She was promising that my unit would not know of my past errors.

I would start with a clean slate. I suppose it may have been helpful to be forced to think about such practicalities just then. Yet Marion herself may have had some doubts. For as she got out of the car she looked into my face, her lips parting as if to speak. But she turned and walked to the foot of the steps, then only called over her shoulder, *"Courage!"*

She pronounced it the French way, and I think that made all the difference.

CHAPTER 20

Dr. Fromm-Reichmann's first words, that next Wednesday, were almost more than I could bear. Hermann's delusions were back in full force. He had become agitated, she said, after my visit.

I realized that even while we were together he had been fighting off that relapse, trying to recapture the "orientation" of the Wednesday before, when he had begged so desperately to call me. "If only they had let him!" I cried out to Marion. But she doubted — or said she doubted — that the regression could have been checked.

Meanwhile Christmas loomed, with aching attempts at cheer for Claudia's sake. I made Hermann a warm bathrobe and was allowed to present it. This was the first of the short, careful visits that became a focus of my week.

He always wanted news. But how different this was from the time when we met after work and he relished every detail of my day. Now I could hardly find a safe topic. With great ingenuity he gave the most trivial incident sinister meanings. I hated hiding my life from him, especially my coming duties in the Party. I not only needed his advice but wanted to share what was happening.

A functionary from New York had given us a sort of pep talk. We comrades in Washington, he said, must never forget that our soft life was temporary, and rare for Communists anywhere, even in this country. Out west Mother Bloor at age seventy-two had just served thirty days in jail for unlawful assembly. The Negro boy Angelo Herndon had been sentenced to eighteen months for his speeches to the unemployed in Atlanta. Ambush was a fact of life in the South, like beatings on the waterfront; employers' goons attacked picket lines everywhere. But the hardships of U.S. Communists were minimal compared to those in the rest of the world, such as the Long March in China.

When the unit leaders came to our house, I had Claudia's blackboard ready. Vic drew a map of China, and with colored chalk we learned to show the rivers, the deserts, and the high Kunlun Mountains stretching along the border of Tibet. We circled the site of the original communes in the south; here Chiang Kai-shek had surrounded them, and we drew the ring showing how his tanks and artillery had kept tightening. The besieged comrades loaded everything they had — even the machinery from their munitions factories — on the backs of hundreds of mules. Fighting desperately, they broke a hole in that fierce military wall, overpowering one of Chiang's crack regiments, letting our thousands of people and animals pour through to start their march. Because Chiang Kai-shek controlled the easiest route northwest, the Communists had to go by a roundabout and mostly trackless path over frozen mountains and across rushing rivers.

Vic and I had done earnest research, using the only reliable sources, Party publications. Dispatches from the capitalist correspondents in Nanking were often based on rumor, reflecting Chiang Kai-shek's hatred of the Communists. They even used his language, calling our leaders "bandits." True, some of the Red Army generals had originally gained their leadership that way. How else could a spirited young man in the chaotic China of that period use his talents? But they had become trusted defenders of the peasants and workers. Some had given their lives against Chiang's cohorts when he set out to "exterminate" all Communists.

Though we tried to take a practical, matter-of-fact attitude to Party objectives, this story inspired us; we felt a need to share, if only in imagination, a more rigorous kind of service. The comrades on the Long March lost much of what they carried from the commune; many of the peasants died of hunger and cold and disease. But thousands of others joined the "poor people's army" and fought to free whole populations from exploitation by ruthless landlords and the tyranny of unenlightened bandit chiefs. The dotted red line on Claudia's blackboard inched its way to the northwest and safety. Out of Chiang's reach they would build schools and hospitals as they had in the south before his army closed in on them. In some of those areas they had made more progress toward literacy for the people in four years than most parts of China had achieved in four hundred. They had abolished prostitution, child slavery, compulsory marriage, and the use of opium. And they were as determined to carry on now as when they started, even though they had arrived famished and ill, their number depleted, after walking eight thousand miles.

As this saga unfolded I felt an exaltation that I longed to share with Hermann. Shut away from the world, literally locked in with his monstrous fears, he desperately needed the support of a belief strong enough to sustain those thousands of marchers along that impossible trail.

Vic read aloud a tribute to Chairman Mao's beneficent wisdom, backed by the indomitable strength and strategic genius of Chu Teh and Chou En-lai. At the end I quoted Chairman Mao's poem that offered to divide China in "three generous pieces":

> One I would send to Europe
> One to America
> And one we would keep in China,
> Thus would a great peace reign in the world.

I wonder now how Hermann would have responded if I had read it to him. Normally he had a realistic sense of the way leaders hold their power. While I, like my mother, wanted to believe in the possibility of a benign governing spirit. But in Hermann's present mood he would have found it easy to weave that poem into his dark imaginings, which were growing more and more grandiose.

I had told him at first, when it was true, that I wasn't seeing comrades, and from then on never mentioned the Party. Yet even though I painted the most innocuous picture of our life he would shake his head over my naive attempt to carry on as if I weren't exposed to deadly danger. Still, his reproaches were loving; there was no sign of the hostility the doctors said he felt. Our moment of parting, when I had to pull away from his arms, was always agonizing.

Drained with disappointment (I must have hoped at each visit to find him well), I often went "home" to Mimi and Rollo, where the boys and guests provided Claudia a lively atmosphere. It was there that I was tracked down one Saturday night by Pat and Dode Jackson, determined to take me to another party of Mary's. I had told her I couldn't face a scene of revelry, but after they had made the long trip out to get me I gave in.

In Mary's living room dazzling highlights were sliding over satin and taffeta the colors of jewels. From a corner I could hear "What Is This Thing Called Love?" played on an accordion by Roosevelt's intimate, Tommy Corcoran. Heywood Broun, monumental and wheezing, sat on a sofa holding court, surrounded by the girls who were always brought to him like offerings. Mary started to lead me over but I remembered her introduction at an earlier party, stressing the Claud connection. I felt a fierce loyalty to Hermann.

At my shoulder someone gave a name I had heard mentioned as having helped to plan the Social Security Act. "What's with Hermann?" he asked worriedly, having learned he was in the hospital. Since Hermannn had spoken warmly of him I decided he deserved honest answers. But even giving him the bare facts I found it hard to shape the words. And on his forehead drops of sweat began to appear as he listened. "God, I can't believe it. Hermann, of all people."

Under his questioning I told about the lucid week when Hermann had seemed himself, then slipped back. "He's fairly calm now, but that only means he's able to use his intelligence to work out his ideas."

"Ideas?"

I described the delusions, which by now I understood were fairly typical. Starting with the people who surrounded him, they had spread until he was convinced that he was the focus of Hitler's plans. "Which puts all his friends in danger, and he blames himself."

"But that's so out of character! I can see why you had to have him committed."

I said I hadn't; he had gone voluntarily.

"And he stays voluntarily?"

"Oh no. Hardly that." My teeth were clicking together.

"I don't get this. What's the legality? Doesn't it have to be one thing or the other?"

I didn't really know. I had gone along with professionals in what they said was an emergency situation. And later I had checked with Dr. William Alanson White at St. Elizabeth's.

"White himself? How did you manage that?"

"I simply called him up; he's very kind." But I couldn't hold back the terrible part. "He said that a mental hospital was the worst possible environment for anybody with these problems, yet in cases like Hermann's there was no safe alternative."

"Do you realize —" (I heard the intake of breath and saw the streaming sweat.) "Do you realize that if this can happen to someone like Hermann it could happen to — *anyone?*"

I knew then why his forehead had been so wet. His worry had been not for Hermann but himself. And I had told him all this because Hermann regarded him as a friend.

To my relief, Jerome Frank had caught my arm. Drawing me to the bar he asked if I was a good repository of secrets. If he didn't tell me he'd be sure to let it out to Mary, who was pumping him. She had already heard that his car had been seen in Henry Wallace's driveway that afternoon. I would have promised anything; Washington gossip was better than my thoughts. He asked if I remembered the day he had waited four hours in the secretary's office.

He was talking about Black Monday, last February, when he and his staff received their letters of dismissal from the AAA administrator. I knew he had gone to Secretary Wallace to protest, insisting at least that they be permitted to resign. Wallace, embarrassed, said he was sure that could be done; he went to speak to the administrator, telling Jerome to wait. But he never came back to his office.

As the tune of "Lazybones" came to us, Jerome pointed to that corner. "There's the source of the stories that got us fired," he said. "Stories about our being flaming reds. Stories spread by a well-placed skunk who wanted to knife me, put an end to any influence I might have with FDR."

I felt a familiar wave of nausea, and suddenly I realized why. His dark tone and glance brought back Hermann's first talk about the office conspiracy against him. Yet what Jerome was saying was undoubtedly true; the results had been real enough.

I picked a sprig of rosemary to cure my queasiness. Did I want to know, Jerome asked, why he had gone out to Wallace's house today? I nodded, sniffing rosemary. He said Henry had phoned him that he had something important to tell him.

I waited.

"He said he had had his secretary find his diary of the 'period of the purge' — you know how he likes alliteration — and realized he'd been deceived by false witnesses. He *would* give a biblical touch to his martyrdom. Doesn't your heart just bleed for the man?"

The false witnesses had told Wallace that Jerome wrote dishonest and subversive opinions. Even worse, that he had brought Communists into the government. I drew back, turning my face from the light. He *had* brought Communists into the government, whether he knew it or not. They were my own comrades.

"I've never had a man on my staff," he went on vehemently, "who didn't know I love this country and loathe any system that denies a man freedom of speech and thought. If my boys ever come out with any nonsense I give them unshirted hell. I tell them to try breathing the air of a dictatorship for a few days if they want to appreciate the USA."

For a minute his ardor seemed attractive. Then I remembered the sharecroppers, and wanted to ask what kind of freedom they had. I held it back, though I knew how he felt about what went on in the South. Even with a real radical I couldn't speak freely. As if his thoughts had followed mine, he sighed. "Well, we lost that round." His lips with their rich curve looked so sorrowful that I had an impulse to put mine against them, to comfort him. But it would have been a sort of Judas kiss. I knew what he did not know about his own protégés. They were not on the level with him, and neither could I be.

Was it then that I thought of the literal meaning of these words? If you were in the underground you could not be on the level with people who were on the up-and-up, open and aboveboard. But these thoughts probably came much later.

"Wallace said he was so ashamed of those days," Jerome finished bitterly, "that he had his secretary burn that part of his diary. As if that put him in the clear."

While I was still taking in this astonishing fact we were interrupted by Rodney announcing a sing-along. I listened until Mary began the song "Co-op-e-rate, co-op-e-rate," which we had composed when we were boosting consumers' cooperatives. She and Rodney had used it for their Christmas card, illustrated by my drawings of suggestive pairs of animals. It had delighted Hermann. The memory sent me fleeing upstairs.

As I stepped into Mary's bedroom I remembered lying there listening to Florence arrange for Hermann to go to Chestnut Lodge. I was trying to wipe my eyes when Lacey Craig came in. (I call her Lacey and her husband Josh because using their real names for what I have to tell would be unfair.)

Josh was the son and namesake of a midwestern politician, a man of many talents with national influence. Josh had worked for him until lured by the New Deal to Washington as a free-lance journalist. Later Josh's dispatches during the war would attract world attention, but now nobody seemed sure just where his work was appearing. Mary said Lacey paid her maid five dollars a week extra for letting herself be called by her last name, as in an English manor house.

On this night Lacey sat down on the bed beside me. "My dear." I could smell the Shalimar she wore, and felt the beads of her dress against my arm. "I know what you are going through. All too well, believe me."

I must have stared. Everything about her from the even blond waves of her upswept hair down to her alligator pumps suggested an assured satisfaction with her status. Yet she had spoken in an intense voice, and now insisted, "I'm in the same boat, you see."

How could she be? There was Josh Craig downstairs, sturdy and solid, with his square jaw that seemed pugnacious until suddenly it gave way to an appreciative grin. Lacey explained that Josh suffered from a psychological problem caused by living under the shadow of a famous father. He might seem confident but this only added to the strain. It was all she could do to keep him functioning at all. And even these efforts were not really enough. He was, for instance, impotent.

I sat listening, bemused. Was I surrounded by normal-seeming people hiding deep secrets? When we heard footsteps on the stairs Lacey spoke hurriedly. "Just remember one thing: you can always use our home as a refuge. Whenever things get too much, just ring our doorbell, day or night."

The offer from this woman, whom I had dismissed as a shallow type, gave me a sense of comfort. Of course I assumed that I would never take advantage of it. In the weeks after our talk I pondered her revelations, even though Josh's problem was obviously far less acute than Hermann's. He was out in the world, presumably going on with his work. The problem of impotence also set his case apart.

Though still under the domination of his delusions, Hermann's feelings for me were as ardent as ever. This was clear from the first of my Saturday visits. When we stood in the little sitting room together his body responded to mine as eagerly as always. And it was our physical separation, I thought, that gave his groans their note of despair.

Wasn't this frustration harmful? I finally dared to put the question to Dr. Fromm-Reichmann. She asked if I was not deceiving myself, since such desires were not to be expected in his case. It was difficult to convince her. I had to speak plainly, and to my surprise — she was a doctor, after all — she blushed. But in the end, after consultation with Dr. Bullard, she agreed to try what they said was a most unusual experiment.

CHAPTER 21

This Saturday Dr. Bullard led me to the stairway, saying that Mrs. Gallup would show me to Hermann's room. We would be undisturbed for an hour. "That is," he added, "unless you ring the bell." I climbed the stairs, trying not to hear his warning. A buzzer sounded somewhere; I wiped my damp hands and loosened my scarf. Beyond the door dishes rattled, then footsteps approached. The key turned in the lock.

A gust of warm air rushed out, heavy with the odor I always forgot to prepare for. A large woman in a tight white uniform greeted me and locked the door again. "I know somebody," she said archly, "that's going to be mighty —"

"Hermann!" I had seen him coming down the hall. But she went on, "We couldn't *pry* him away from that window all —"

"Excuse me." I managed to get past and take his hand. "That's right," Mrs. Gallup said. "You two lovebirds have a nice long hour to bill and coo."

Hermann hesitated, glancing at the people around us in what seemed to be a common room. Probably his natural courtesy made him wonder if it would be impolite not to introduce me. Four people sat at a card table — an elderly man in a bathrobe, two women wearing housedresses, a young boy in dungarees who was studying the dummy hand laid out before him. The others held cards but stared at us. Hermann's eyes went from them to an alcove where a tall man bent over a billiard table. Handsome, with wavy gray hair, he had a curious young look, as if under some sort of spell he had aged without maturing. He smiled now, addressing the three grouped balls in the center of the table. "See, milady, I told you I was too smart for them. They can broadcast but they can't turn the current on me." Then his smile faded. "They can pick up anybody day or night. Turn you right back into a billiard ball."

"Fred, come tell me what to lead," one of the women called, saying that her mind wasn't working today. Thinking about this later, when the picture came back to me sharply — the picture of Hermann's daily surroundings — I thought she had been trying to lure him from his troubled thoughts. Dressed differently, with her hair properly done, she would have been as attractive as any woman walking down Peacock Alley at the Willard Hotel.

Fred made his way to the table. "I was a man who could do anything. In the Olympics I could —"

"There's something *to* that," Mrs. Gallup said quite audibly. "I understand he was some kind of athlete." She gave Hermann's arm a squeeze. "Why don't you just take wifie into your little hideaway."

A clamor of talk followed us down the hall. It seemed Fred wanted me to carry a message to the editor of one of the Washington papers.

"Pay him no mind," Mrs. Gallup said brusquely. "Anyone new gets them all excited." She nudged us into Hermann's room.

It was small and bare, almost filled by the iron bed. But a window looked out into the branches of the beech that overhung the porte cochere. "I love that tree," I said nervously. "It reminds me of the Bois de Boulogne."

"The Bois . . ." Hermann came to stand beside me, murmuring that he would never see the Bois again. I protested, reminding him that last week he had said we should go abroad.

"You and Claudia, yes. To England."

I said I wanted only to be with him, that we would go together. He shook his head. Saddened — even today! — I had to give up. Opening my briefcase I brought out the latest *Consumers' Guide* and some sketches.

He picked up a watercolor. "You did this?" It showed the dead chestnut at the edge of the bluff, the one we had noticed on our first walk. I was suddenly afraid that he would see some dark meaning in the abrupt jagged ending of the branches. But he was saying that the sketch had a freedom and decisiveness that was new in my work. "No fooling around with second thoughts. You splashed the color on." The browns and grays, he said, were subtle, silvery.

He was talking in his familiar thoughtful way, really attending, and — as he always could — telling me something I hadn't recognized. It was true that there was a new quality in my work. And I had felt a new need to paint, and even to play the piano, a need that seemed to draw out ability I hadn't known was there. I showed him a pencil drawing of Claudia. She was asleep, face down, a lock of hair half hiding her forehead. Only the eyelid showed, with its long lashes, and one hand with fingers spread beside the curve of her cheek. He smiled at the drawing as if at Claudia herself. I said I would leave it for him.

He started to speak, then frowned. Envisioning the drawing here on his wall must have made him newly aware of his surroundings. Why couldn't I remember? I sighed, then to cover it I said the room was warm.

"You still have your coat on." Solicitous now, he came and helped me take it off.

"I've been glad of this coat," I told him. It was brown suede, so expensive I wouldn't have bought it except for his urging. He had said it made me look like a young officer in the Red Army. Now I was afraid he would remember that, but he tossed the coat carelessly on a chair and stood looking at me. "Nice."

My dress was muted green-blue — partly rabbit fur, I told him. "Feel."

He ran his hand from my shoulder down and almost as if from habit cupped it around my breast. I stood still, afraid to move. But his arm came around my waist and brought our bodies together. "Angel."

With that word he was himself; I could relax against him. His clasp tightened and held me with a strength I had not felt for months. His mouth moved searchingly against my cheek and I turned mine to meet it. He groped for the fastening of my dress, and

I waited, letting his fingers find the zipper and draw it down. He lifted the dress off and flung it to the chair. His jacket and trousers were laid aside before I was out of my bra and pants. Not for a long time had I seen him move with this easy swiftness.

As naturally as always, we lay down together. In the first moment the bed seemed lumpy and harsh. But almost at once I lost all sense of this, or our bleak surroundings. We could have been anywhere, on the Delaware beach with the salt breeze blowing over us, or safe on our own broad mattress under the down quilt. Hermann's hands and mouth had all their old familiar power. My only discomfort was the starving center of me, pained with longing, then full of luxurious welcome.

But it was over almost at once.

"Angel." His voice was not apologetic; it had all the old after-love resonance. "I wish it had been better for you."

I told him it was wonderful.

"But you didn't come." He knew me too well.

I said that was only a technicality. "The great thing was to be together again. Really together. And we were." I kissed his shoulder, and he smiled. "I'm not in training," he said. "I'll be better next time."

This promise — though he had never had to make it before — was given with his own confidence. But in hearing it he must have remembered how little control he had over his life. He lay back then as if in exhaustion, his arm lax under my neck. It felt like pure bone, and I saw that his ribs thrust up in ridges. His legs had lost their outcurving solid muscle; the shin bones were sharp. And though he had been so quickly aroused, I had felt his frailty there too, a lack of the fullness that had always made me want to cry out, exuberant, "Here comes my intellectual!"

He sat up with a sigh. "There's no use kidding ourselves. This room is meant for a monastic cell."

I made some sort of protest about how opposite from monastic it had seemed a minute ago, but he said the only place for us was home. He had to go home. I told him he would, soon, and he reminded me that I had been saying that for months.

Months! He was right. It was no longer just weeks. I must have sighed again, for I remember his running his finger over the skin below my eyes, saying I had shadows where I'd had none before. I told him quickly that I had been staying late writing last-minute press releases on the Green Belt in Maryland. One of the items I had collected for him was about FDR's tour of the project. He had picked up an old Scottish gardener who recognized the indigenous wild shrubs and begged to keep them in the landscaping. So they had kept them. This, I said, was what I liked about the New Deal.

Hermann shook his head, and I thought he would speak once more about my naiveté, but instead he spoke enviously of the contrast between us — how involved I was, while he was just lying around. His tone was direct and realistic, even though he spoke in shame. I said it wasn't his fault, when he was ill.

My answer made him swing away from me in impatience. "All this talk about my being ill! You've let them take you in with their pseudoscientific jargon."

We were back at the impasse we always reached. There was no way to make him understand my stubbornness. Yet even now, as he dressed, he said he did not blame me. I couldn't help being what I was, youthfully optimistic. It was part of my nature, an asset in domestic life or in any normal situation.

As he spoke he was drawing his trousers on, folding them over in a wide lap and then fastening his belt to hold them up. He did it in an accustomed way. He was *used* to being thin! When he had cinched the buckle the end of the belt looked to be eight inches long; he slipped it under one of the trouser loops, still talking, begging me to see how my credulity had helped to trap him. If I hadn't gone along, he said, they never could have been able to use their processes in reverse against him.

I had heard it all before, but somehow I had not expected it after making love. The "experiment" hadn't worked. I began to put on my clothes while he went on, speaking more and more urgently, as always when he repeated this explanation: "It's been done before with animals — dogs, even pigs can be given neuroses by a carefully planned series of frustrations. Man is presumably a more sensitive animal. Why couldn't he be driven into a pseudomania by a progression of crucial stresses?"

He made it sound almost plausible. I remembered Carter's groan: "If only he weren't so intelligent!"

"Even if they could," I said as always, "Why should they want to? And it would surely be illegal."

He scorned these interruptions, rushing on. "If I were the only victim it wouldn't matter — one man's life. What is horrible is that millions will have to suffer for my mistake — I swear it was a mistake, an innocent acceptance of a well-disguised role — and this, compounded with your refusal to see the consequences —" He had to stop for breath. I seemed actually to be watching the heightened metabolism burn him up, consume his flesh. I pleaded with him not to lose hope. We would somehow work this all out.

Surprisingly he straightened his shoulders and agreed that I might be right, that maybe something could still be done. But almost before I could feel relief he had walked to the window and pointed ominously down at the driveway. "No. It's too late."

A baker's truck was passing toward the back of the mansion. He put his finger against his lips, then turned, picked up my coat and held it out. Mutely I let him help me put it on. Protesting would only upset him more. I kissed him but he was still too distracted to respond.

The common room was empty. Downstairs I found Dr. Bullard waiting. His healthy good looks startled me, contrasting with Hermann's frailty. He asked genially how the experiment had gone. "Hubby fall in with your bright idea?"

I nodded reluctantly. Still, he should know the facts. I said I had thought at first that it had done Hermann good. I suppose the way my voice broke told him the story.

"When you've been around longer you'll learn not to expect miracles." He patted my shoulder. "Look, my girl, have you been following my advice?"

I tried to bring my mind back from the implications of what he had said. He reminded me sternly that I should develop outside interests. "Do things, see people; that's doctor's orders."

As I turned to leave I realized I had left my briefcase. He went to the stairwell with me and as I climbed I heard the buzzer again, and Miss Gallup's voice approaching the door. "Now be a good chap and help me with my trays. Your wife has gone, I tell you. . . ."

The door opened and I pushed past to Hermann. "They wouldn't believe me," he said as I followed him down the hall. For a man like him to have to admit such powerlessness, I thought, must be terribly damaging.

"I love this room," I said as we entered.

He looked around and really smiled. "It's different when you're in it."

I had an inspiration. "Remember, you said it was a monastic cell? And you used to say that to do their best work scholars should be monks? I know how hard it might be under the circumstances, but if you could ignore them and try to —"

He broke in to say these "circumstances" could hardly be ignored. Reminding him that great thinking had been done in prisons, I begged him to make a list of books he wanted. He seemed to consider the idea. But at that moment Miss Gallup arrived with his "nice supper." He glanced down absently at the plate of meat loaf, spaghetti and coleslaw. There were prunes and cake, and a glass of milk. Miss Gallup was chanting about how "we" would sit right down and eat it, wouldn't we? "So kiss wifie goodbye now."

When she had gone I put my hands on his shoulders.

"*Courage!*" I too gave it the French pronunciation, and it seemed to work. His lips trembled into a smile.

CHAPTER 22

All this time we kept coming back to the same question: *Why?* With Ernst, with Carter and some of his staff, with Mary, and with Marion Bachrach, I searched for answers. But even Mimi's psychologist chief was baffled.

Hermann's parents were a kind of exception: they didn't look for explanations to something that could not have happened. Hermann had always been so steady, so successful. How easily he had made friends! And how firmly he had kept them, even schoolmates who might have been jealous of his honors.

And he was so reasonable as a child, his mother said; so "sensible." She told of the summer he was four, when he had cut his knee badly at some distance from their Black Forest cottage. He had managed to make his way home, and while she was treating the knee she said "You must have made a great howl and lament." He had answered calmly, "No, there was no one there to hear."

She told this with a sad little smile as she watched Claudia playing in the snow. Her appreciation was as observant and thoughtful as Hermann's, and I think the presence of a small child was all that made this visit bearable. Hermann's father took a simpler pleasure in Claudia — pure relieving delight in her lusciousness, her bouncing curtseys, her readiness to welcome them as "Oma" and "Opa."

Opa was not tall but stood easily erect, with a fine forehead, clear blue eyes and an appealing smile. His gentle manner had Hermann's friendliness, and with it an air of expectancy that assumed friendliness from the world. During this visit he often seemed bewildered.

Oma's bearing was warier, less trusting, perhaps because she had been betrayed by love, and even by religion. Knowing Oma should have taught me more than it did, and sooner. Only gradually would I let myself wonder if her darker view of the world strengthened her to face catastrophe. She had integrated her experience into her sense of what might lie in wait. Hermann's breakdown was the last thing she expected, but she was not one to underestimate Fate's ingenuity in designing calamities.

I admired her fortitude, but I would have resisted any such reason for it. Underneath, in spite of what was happening, I clung to my optimism. It was much like Opa's, being based on precepts — in my case a variant of the one Mother lived by: "All things work together for good to them that love God." Yet along with her faith Mother had relied on herself to withstand the hardest blows. Maybe now without knowing it I was helped by Mother's courage at the time of my birth.

Hermann's father was most offended at their not being allowed to visit Hermann. When I gave them the doctors' reason he asked, "How could his own parents agitate him?" I couldn't very well say that my own mother could agitate me half an hour after the happiest beginning of a visit. Oma accepted this taboo; she may have remembered clashes with Hermann during his adolescence. But she frowned (and she had a formidable frown) over Dr. Fromm-Reichmann's refusal to see them. Though skeptical about any diagnosis and treatment, she thought that once the responsibility was assumed, the doctor would want all possible information. And who would be a better source than the parents?

I found this hard to answer, since all the doctors said Hermann's problem was rooted in early childhood. I tried to explain the psychoanalyst's theory that to be useful the information had to come from the patient's own memories. Oma was not satisfied. Couldn't they evaluate better what the patient told them if they saw the scene from another point of view? Ernst had said this would have been the scientific method. But I repeated Dr. Fromm-Reichmann's description of her work: it was not a science but an art. And she was sure it would succeed with Hermann.

Opa seized eagerly on this hope, but Oma sat silent in her straight chair, still and upright. Her austerity intimidated me then, before I came to know what strength it stood for, and how much that would mean to me.

All this time Ernst had assumed that his Damon and Pythias arrangement with Hermann still held. His doctorate earned, with a good job at Koppers, he insisted on paying more than half the charges at Chestnut Lodge. He often came for the weekend, saying an hour's play with Claudia was worth the long drive from Pittsburgh. But I knew he came to give moral support — and perhaps to receive it.

Florence Powdermaker did not visit till spring, when I passed on an SOS from Hermann. He thought it essential that she see the history he had written of his case. He had given the notebook to me on a Saturday visit, asking me to make three copies of all but the personal section addressed to me: one copy to go at once to Ernst, another for Florence to see, and the third into safekeeping, for some future unspecified use. It started ominously:

"I do not know what will happen to these notes. They — and I — may be destroyed. Or they may ultimately land in the national archives."

It was the same handwriting as in his first letters to me. From a rigidly level base, the upward strokes rose to abrupt, capricious peaks of varying heights never consistent with each other. A series of words might be strung together as one; a single word might be broken up into separate parts but not by any predictable rule. The effect was of disorder, anarchy, sabotaging his own effort to communicate. Even in those early days, I wondered at the contradiction. How could a man with his forthrightness, his friendly ease as he talked — and talked so clearly and logically — how could he have produced these unhelpful, chaotic symbols?

Now it struck me that I should have read some kind of warning in that contradiction. But wasn't graphology a pseudoscience, like phrenology? And whether or not a graphologist could have predicted his breakdown, it was too late now.

The personal message was brief and loving, forgiving me for taking part, due to my innocent naiveté, in his entrapment. The forgiveness, unrealistic as I thought it then, did comfort me. Also, since its loving tone did not fit into the doctors' assumptions about his illness, it might prove a sort of lifeline.

The rest of the document comprised his delusions, but even his false premise couldn't keep me from marveling at the way he explained how he had been incarcerated. I was eager to see what it would tell Florence.

Almost as soon as she stepped off the train I handed her the folder. Hermann wanted her professional response, I told her, and she nodded. But in the car she took out a memo pad and began scribbling figures on it, using the folder for a desk. When we were on the highway I suggested rather timidly that she might need to know what Hermann had written. At first she did not answer, then said she had been doing a difficult computation. I repeated that Hermann was anxious for her to have his report of what had happened. This time she answered impatiently that she knew everything necessary, having kept in close touch with Ernst. I was worried, but told myself that she must know what was important.

Hermann was waiting for us in the hall with Dr. Bullard. Because of Florence's presence we could take a real walk, out into the town of Rockville. Alert with interest at first, Hermann looked around him at the frame houses with flower beds, clothes on lines, children climbing jungle gyms. His comments were so normal that I was surprised when Florence answered in her special voice of gentle simplicity; it seemed out of place. When after a time Hermann fell into silence, she took his arm. *"Wie geht's, mein Freund?"* And added that it was good that he had started writing.

He asked eagerly for her response to his analysis. She said she hadn't had a chance to read it yet.

He turned to me, troubled, asking if I hadn't given it to her. Before I could answer Florence said she would study it soon and write to him. But he was not satisfied. It would involve too many risks; it was important that they discuss it together. When he glanced at me reproachfully again, I felt that to keep his trust I must tell him I had done exactly as he asked. But Florence was saying in her assuaging tone that in any case she was here and he could tell her whatever was on his mind. He said of course that the first thing was to get him out of the so-called hospital. As if taking this seriously she replied that she would need to know his reasons. He said he could answer in one word: food.

This astonished me, and I started to protest that he had never complained of it before. But Florence was agreeing calmly that institutional diet could be dull. He looked at her as he looked at me when in despair at my innocence. It was not a question of dullness, he told her; on the contrary. Aside from the ever-present danger of poisoning, which he could avoid by abstaining, the people here had worked out an effective form of mental torture, using certain foods to transmit messages; in code, of course.

By now I was sick with dismay. But Florence answered reasonably that in order to understand she would have to know the code. It was partly a matter of scheduling, he said, and partly a matter of shape. On Mondays, for instance, with absolute regularity he was served two muffins for lunch, in certain recognizable shapes. His breathing accelerated as he spoke. When Florence asked what these shapes were, he apologized for what he would have to tell her. One muffin was in the shape of testicles — his father's — and the other in the shape of his mother's vagina.

This was so totally new and alarming that I held my breath for Florence's answer. But she only nodded, without a hint of surprise. He rushed on, asking in an agonized voice how he could be expected to survive under that barrage of messages.

Florence said something about having to think what could be done. When he began again to plead, she told him she would speak to Dr. Bullard and make sure the messages were stopped. He groaned at her obtuseness, pointing out that they would only change the code; then he would have to break the new one. He insisted once more on leaving here. Florence, to my surprise, promised to consult Ernst about making a change. He seemed to believe her, and even I had to ask, as we drove away, if she had meant what she seemed to mean. "Of course not," she said shortly.

It worried me to think he would have false hopes, but before I could speak she broke in to ask if I had forgotten the slipcovers. I had, and I turned the car around.

That drive to Baltimore has a surrealist quality in my memory. While my mind surged — my body, too, with the shock of what I had heard — Florence talked of her plans for repainting her walls off-white, which all the decorators were using. She worried that it might be too cold a background for her. But she could relieve it by color in the drapes and her costumes. Didn't I think that would work?

I wonder now why I didn't protest as she went on; why I didn't ask her frankly how she could think of these things at such a moment? Yet memory shows a young woman staring ahead at the road and listening, making an effort to fit this into some sort of reasonable pattern. Perhaps the answer I found was that doctors had to develop detachment from their patients' miseries.

Crossing Baltimore to a suburb on the other side, I had to ask directions, making Florence restive. But once inside we spent an hour there, as she stood before a mirror holding fabrics up beside her face and asking my opinion, taking it, changing her mind, finally placing a two hundred dollar order.

I was waiting to query her about the change in Hermann's delusions. This sort of sexual element had never come out in his talk before. But it apparently was not new in his thinking about his parents. Could these thoughts have somehow kept him from wanting more hours alone with me in his room? I had told myself that his energy had been burned up by his frantic kind of thinking.

"Don't you need drapes for the winter?" Florence was asking. When she said I could pick up a bargain, I told her nothing would be a bargain right now. As we drove away I explained that I was trying not to let Ernst pay too much. She spoke exasperatedly about his relationship with Hermann. They were like a couple of burrs, she said; if you tried to separate one from the other you were sure to get hurt. Years ago she had given up hope of either of them making a commitment to anyone else.

Unguardedly I asked if she had been surprised when Hermann was able to marry. Only momentarily, she said. After hearing more about it she had realized that with Hermann any relationship would be much more complicated than it first appeared. At my questioning look she said that if he had been simply susceptible to women he had had plenty of opportunity for commitment before. The explanation this time became obvious when Hermann had told her about my child.

I still didn't understand, though I had often thought Claudia had been part of the attraction for him.

Florence pointed out significantly that she was not just *my* child. If Hermann had fallen in love, it was really with Claudia's father. As I tried to take this in she reminded me that Claud was a perfect subject for fantasizing — by either a man or a woman. Already excited by *The Week*, Hermann had seen Claud's child on his first day in Washington, a day when he would be open and vulnerable.

Maybe I gasped out some kind of answer, for she said she hadn't expected me to accept this. "Wives never do."

What made her theory really painful was my fear that there was something to it. Six months before, of course, I would have laughed it off, seeing Hermann's joy in our life together. But the inexplicable had happened; no explanation of his marriage could seem as unlikely as what had happened to him afterward.

Letting Florence off at Union Station I felt that I could not have survived an evening alone with my thoughts. Fortunately Carter was in town for some professional meetings and his staff had invited me to Foxhall Road.

As always with these people I had the comforting sense that I was among friends. But that night it did not last. After we had eaten they decided we should go to a Soviet film everyone was talking about, *The New Gulliver*. Made by photographing three thousand

213

puppets as Lilliputians, its only live actor was Gulliver, the man of the future, who with his strength was able to overthrow the system and drag the whole Lilliputian navy out to sea. I sat between Carter and Wolf Ladejinsky. Halfway through the film I turned to Wolf and protested that his growls made me know how he got his name. But that didn't stop him; as we came out he was fuming. "The nerve of such wish-fulfillment idiocy!" To suggest that one superman, Stalin, could wipe out the whole American navy.

Carter made one of his pacific remarks, about this being only entertainment, but Wolf came back with such revilement that I decided to report it to my unit as the slander we had to fight.

"Nothing is 'only entertainment' over there," Wolf said, accusing the Party of censoring all their best art. Prokofiev's great opera, *War and Peace,* was lost and buried. And the "long arm of the GPU" had finally found Isaac Babel in Odessa. Luckily Trotsky was still outside the country.

Hearing that name I felt only my usual discomfort. Often when I heard criticism of the Soviet Union I knew it must be wrong but was by no means sure what I would have been able to answer if I had been free to try. Tonight this was worse; the others were backing Wolf up, Dan accusing Stalin of selling out the Chinese revolutionaries to Chiang Kai-shek, letting his own faithful comrades be thrown into the fireboxes of locomotives.

Carter might have been watching my face — or perhaps, as I hoped, he was on my side. "In terms of movie criticism," he asked, smiling, "aren't we going rather far afield?"

Dan took the cue and kept the conversation to film technique (which they agreed was superb) till we reached Foxhall Road.

Carter walked with me to my car. Regretting that the evening hadn't given us any chance to talk, he asked me to have dinner with him after his meeting the next day. I decided that with this in prospect I could get through one more night.

CHAPTER 23

When Carter came out of the Shoreham he suggested a restaurant on Chesapeake Bay. Moving to let him drive, I wondered if he could guess the relief I felt at his taking over. (He had his own responsibilities, too, a wife and children.) At the meeting he had given a paper based on the migration study. Hermann's part, he said, had stirred the most interest. He thought this would also happen when the book was published. I said Hermann didn't think it ever would be published.

"It's scheduled for around New Year's, which is lightning speed for a university press." I had coaxed a promise from Hermann to drop his premises if the book actually came out. New Year seemed a long time away.

Carter would not have asked for news, but I had to tell him that Hermann had seemed to get steadily worse after that high point of the first week. Still, recently he had told of a dream he had had. This struck me as important, since he had always said he never dreamed. He was full of the wonder of the dream, which had been just a scene — his being at home, with everything as it had been. He had looked actually happy, remembering.

Carter agreed that it sounded important, though he couldn't believe Hermann had never dreamed before. "Neither did the doctors." I had told them about his interest when I described my dreams of Roosevelt, how intently he had questioned me, trying to learn what the experience was like. "They said he simply forgot his dreams."

"But even granting that," Carter mused, "mightn't it be just as significant? That he had been able to remember this one? And be moved by it?"

I had tried to make this point, but the only response had been a look of forced patience. "Probably doctors have to train themselves not to be distracted by patients' families' ideas." And I must have become more of a bother than most. I remembered a friend describing me as "dynamic," no doubt a euphemism.

Carter was shaking his head ruefully. Many professionals tended not to listen to anyone outside their field. "We can't expect psychiatrists — though maybe we ought to be able to — to let patients shape their treatment programs."

I told him about the elaborate analysis Hermann had written for Florence; it had made me think of what Carter had said that first day about his being too intelligent. "Could it be," I asked, "more the way he *used* his intelligence?"

"Well. . . ." Carter gave this consideration. "Perhaps the intensity. And the wide range. So you see dangers there?"

I thought Hermann had seen them himself. I recalled for Carter as best I could (I had pushed it out of my mind at the time) Hermann's doubts about a bachelor friend's possible marriage. He said a man had to weigh his pros and cons, and there were more cons for a thinking man. He said celibacy was right for a priest, and perhaps for anyone preoccupied with philosophy. "And Hermann *was,* you know. Oh, if only I had listened and tried to *see.* . . ."

Carter laid a hand on mine, which had clenched into a fist. But it didn't stop me. "I should have studied the *words* he used. He spoke of a man preoccupied with philosophy as being 'crazy enough to try to fit everything into a pattern. . . .'"

"But didn't he use 'crazy' sometimes — well, favorably? I seem to remember his using it to describe *you.*"

I felt sharp pain, remembering. "But I think this time he meant 'crazy' the ordinary way, maybe not quite realizing it himself."

Carter was taking this seriously. Nodding, he said philosophy always involved a system. He spoke of how Nietzsche had broken down just after he had written *Beyond Good and Evil* and promised

216

in his next work to tie everything into an all-encompassing system. It seemed to me like male egoism gone berserk. And yet Hermann had never seemed self-important. Did that mean another kind of inner conflict? Everywhere we looked these days I could see dangerous possibilities.

I told Carter about dipping into Hegel when I was putting together some books Hermann had asked for. "Of course by the time I took them he didn't want them. But I wrote some things down to show you." I brought out my notebook and read aloud: "'To conquer cognitively a world experienced as alien and hostile in its objectivity . . .' Doesn't that sound like someone in delirium?"

Carter said it had to be taken in context. I read more: "'The tendency of all man's endeavors is to understand the world, to appropriate it and subdue it to himself, and to this end the positive reality of the world must be as it were *crushed and pounded*.'"

"In other words, idealized," Carter explained. "Taken into the mind and transformed there." But he gave this rather confusing explanation almost absently, as if thinking of something else — maybe Hermann's Marxism, which he had probably guessed. Or could he be thinking of the system Hermann had worked out in his delusions?

But Carter was going on, his voice quickening. "Did it occur to you that a man might try to *save* himself this way?" Not because he was mad already, as I had suggested, but in order not to be driven mad. By the feeling of — and Carter quoted Hegel — "The external world's alienation from oneself." Didn't I see how frightening that might be? And that a man might try to possess it — master it — by knowing?

Yes, even his delusional system — the psychiatrists had said something like this — was a kind of refuge, a protection from knowing a truth impossible to accept. But that system always came too late.

"You can see how frightening such alienation from the world might seem?" Carter was going on. "And that a man might try to possess the world, in a way — master it — by knowing?"

Hermann had been a Hegelian. Should I have seen it as a danger sign? "It still seems crazy," I said. "To imagine you can know *everything!*" I read from my notebook about the "monstrous and insatiable *lust of knowledge.*" And the aim of knowledge being "to divest the objective world that stands opposed to us of its strangeness and trace it back to our innermost self." I asked Carter if that didn't sound sick.

From Hegel, Hermann had gone on to Marx; his need to make life better and more sensible had to be included in his philosophy. Driving slowly along the deep ruts of a sandy Maryland lane, Carter said he had actually tried to hint to Hermann that he should not spread himself too thin. (And he hadn't known about Hermann's Party work.) But "thin" was precisely the wrong word, Carter added. Paradoxically, the very range of Hermann's thinking gave his economics a depth that he himself, he feared, might never achieve. "I had a suspicion that Hermann would become one of our 'movers and shakers.'"

I heard the past tense, and felt it all through my body. "The greater the possibility," Carter was saying sadly, "the greater the risk."

He had parked the car in a meadow and I took deep breaths of the salt air blowing over from the bay. On the verandah of a rambling log cabin where we could look out across the darkening blue water Carter ordered planter's punches and told of Roosevelt's speech at the meeting. "Such ebullience! Such élan!" Yet he had made his way to the podium with enormous difficulty, on crutches and wearing braces, and with the help of two attendants, an ordeal that was never photographed or mentioned in the papers. I knew Carter was trying to divert my thoughts from those last words of his, which left unspoken the fact that not all gambles were won.

"Here was this politician, confronting an assemblage of high-powered economists, most of them critical of his schemes. And his aplomb was perfect. He threw back his head and talked to us as naturally as if we'd been fellow yachtsmen or stamp collectors."

I asked what he had said. Carter laughed and admitted he had realized only later that Roosevelt's points all contradicted each other, leaving nothing substantial at the end. But the audience had given him a standing ovation — hardly the usual behavior of economists.

We talked of the coming election, and Roosevelt's powerful enemies. A Columbia trustee had spoken of him as "a devil incarnate," even though this man was making more money than he had thought he'd ever see again. The Democratic convention would be in Philadelphia, but the next best place to be at that time, Carter said, was Washington. And he would be there, having taken a post with Secretary Ickes for the summer. I was startled by the lift I felt at this news. And then he said, after another sip of punch, that he had worried about me during these months.

His speech was formal to the point of stiffness; curiously this gave it an intensified effect. But when the waiter had brought our crab soufflé, I looked out at the dimly gleaming water and said that there might not be a summer, in the sense that there had been a winter. "Anything can happen."

I didn't like the sound of that. I'd meant only one thing, one good thing. Carter said, "I'll be here, needed or not," and began to plan. A little theatre company would put on plays in Bethesda; should he subscribe for us? And how about the Watergate concerts?

When I imagined us among the clustered boats on the river listening to Debussy I said no to the music, yes to the theatre. His fingers pressed mine again to say he understood. Later in bidding me goodbye he leaned over the car door, his lips grazing my cheek. That was all. So why did I censor this evening out of my Saturday report to Hermann? Was it guilt over my own vague yearning as I had walked with Carter across that starlit meadow? Or my sharp sense of loss as I left him later on Foxhall Road? But I was having so many emotions these days that I'd have found it hard to disentangle loss from yearning.

CHAPTER 24

The number of items I held back from Hermann kept growing. Some I censored without letting myself wonder why. For others, like my evening at the Soviet Embassy, the reasons were clear, but I felt deep regret.

Hermann had always hoped to go there. When editorials had made ironic comments after the opening reception, about the flowing champagne and the fresh caviar in sculptured ice, I had been a bit troubled, thinking of all the hungry people around us. (I gave no credence, of course, to rumors of millions starving in the Soviet Union.) But Hermann reminded me that Marxists judged an action as correct or incorrect depending on its purpose. The Soviet Embassy was making a statement in the only terms understood by the rest of the world: whatever the capitalists could do the Soviet Union could do better.

"So they can enjoy all the *luxe* with a clear conscience!" I said happily. Laughing, Hermann had tried to rid me of this language from my youth. If he had a chance at that caviar, he said, he'd polish it off without reference to conscience. Now I'd have the chance without him.

Jessica Smith's job at the embassy allowed her sometimes quietly to treat a comrade to what was known in Washington as "the hottest invitation in town." So I was both sad and excited as I drove up Sixteenth Street to the mansion that had once been a millionaire's.

If the ambassador wanted to give an impression of respectability, he succeeded that night. An elderly quartet sawed away at the duller music from the time of Handel, while knobs of a gilt chair pressed my spine. When the intermission came I strolled under the crystal chandeliers staring up at the paintings. They would normally not have been my sort of art, much less Hermann's; I wished he could be there to help me appreciate their purpose. This made me miss him so acutely that I decided not to stay for the caviar, if any.

I found it hardest to keep from talking about the labor struggles that became fiercer every month. The New Deal legislation legalizing unions had freed workers to break out against the worst of their old grievances, fighting back when the management's hired thugs beat and shot the organizers. I was bursting with news of the S.S. *California,* whose crew had walked off under the leadership of Joe Curran, to whom Hermann had carried secret documents from the Labor Board. Curran's earlier letter to President Roosevelt, published in all the papers, had actually been written by Hermann. Secretary of Labor Frances Perkins, our first woman cabinet member, from whom we expected so much, had promised to back this strike personally, but in the end she let Curran down. Now the Party had mobilized the indignation of the whole leftist and liberal world; a huge rally was to be held at Madison Square Garden, with Bob Hope as the headline attraction. Imagining the sinister implications Hermann would find in this, I knew clearly why I had to keep it from him. But other censorings were more murky.

During the winter, when the snow was heavier than this countryside had ever seen, I had often had to use my AAA membership to get the car started. It was Larry Oakes who always came, sometimes so soon that I had hardly time to get outdoors again after phoning. Once I asked if mine was the only flivver in Falls Church with a balky engine. Coming around to my window to adjust the spark, he said that everybody had winter complaint that year. He stayed leaning there in the relaxed ease Hermann had admired. Larry was a man of his time, Hermann had said, his mind and body in harmony with the tools and values of his period. Later, remembering, I thought perhaps Hermann's tone had been wistful. In those summer days we had watched the movement of Larry's bare, muscled arms and shoulders, but even in winter, in his hooded parka, his grace showed. A lock of brown hair had escaped and he thrust it back as he instructed me to keep the spark advanced a notch "till she gets in stride." His lips were very red, his teeth as white as the vapor when he spoke. Then one day he asked me to tell my husband that the three of them at the garage were backing him to win.

This left me troubled. Giving such a message — much as Hermann liked Larry — would stir up his anger at being thought a sick person. And if he learned of my difficulty getting off to work he would worry even more about our problems in the cold. Those reasons for silence about Larry were all clear and obvious. But as spring came I had others.

Because of his winter service I always bought gas at Larry's garage. On a day of lashing rain we discovered that we shared a taste for weather, the wilder the better. And one balmy morning in May, with the scent of magnolias in the air, as Larry fitted the nozzle to the tank he remarked that the racing season at Laurel had begun.

Maybe my "Oh?" was not indifferent enough; he asked me if I would like to go on Saturday. Watching the golden balls spinning in the glass globe I told him I was busy, that day and the next. He took this as suggesting the possibility of another time. As he stood there in his confident male posture, like my high school football players, hips thrust forward, a packed look to his low-riding jeans, his broad shoulders seeming to float above his body, I knew I had expected something like this and had let it come. What I said to disourage his plans I don't remember. But he accepted it and gave a little salute, releasing me.

It was not the kind of release I wanted. These months had left me emotionally hungry. Larry was not only sexually compelling; he was kind: a blending with powerful appeal. Any rational modern woman, I thought, would have reached out gladly for an experience that might refresh her, restoring the strength she needed. But I had backed away.

I could have said it was because I believed in fidelity, which was true. But something else was involved — a kind of cowardice. My mother, poor and upright, had armed me with what she would not have admitted was snobbery. Evidently it still held, untouched by Party teachings of respect for the working class.

I imagined raising this as a subject for self-criticism. But the comrades here (unlike New York, I'd heard) were generally puritanical. And any hint of snobbery would add insult to injury. Most of their families had lived in tenements on the lower East Side. One comrade's father was a cutter in a pants factory.

Suppose I consulted Steve. I could see his dark scowl, hear him thunder that this concern with emotions was bourgeois, even counterrevolutionary. He would remind me of the comrades in Spain; in the midst of assassinations and terrorism they were trying to put down strikes from the left while threatened by the army on the right. Was this any time to worry over my mixed feelings about an attractive garage man?

Then without warning I found myself imagining a talk with Hal. I saw his lips soften as I faltered. And suddenly I knew what the outcome of that interview would have been. Shocked, shamed, I told myself that Hal was dead; there would be no problem if he hadn't died. He would have helped Hermann through his crucial time. He meant something to Hermann that no one else ever had, not even Carter.

At the office Mary was talking excitedly about Spain, where she had been a newspaper correspondent. The papers told now of mobs burning churches and dancing over the dead bodies of nuns. I asked if she believed that. She did, because the church had exploited its faithful for centuries, getting rich in the process, and people were desperate. She quoted an old Andalusian saying: "All they have is the night and day, and the cold water in the pitcher." Could you blame them for anything they might do?

"Like the sharecroppers in Arkansas," I said. They had been about to go on what the papers called a "rampage." But they hadn't, Mary said bitterly.

Pat Jackson had brought a delegation to Washington and led them up and down in the rain outside our building for two days.

Black and white together, amazingly, they had chanted "We shall not be moved," and carried signs: AAA Benefits the Rich.

At first Secretary Wallace had been outraged, but when the Cotton Section wanted him to take action against the pickets he refused to call the police. Thinking he could use persuasion, he had sent his faithful Negro messenger to ask Pat to cease and desist, "for old times' sake." ("Jolly old Black Monday times!" Mary had commented when she gave me the inside story.) Pat had agreed, on condition that the delegation be invited in for a cup of tea and a discussion of their grievances. After soul searching, the secretary received Pat, who first had to hear what a noble thing he was doing. But Wallace begged him not to keep it up too long. He was making the folks in the Cotton Section very uncomfortable. Pat had said calmly that this was precisely their purpose. Which had given the secretary his excuse for calling the police.

Hardly an hour after I told Larry I couldn't go to the races because Hermann's friend was coming, Ernst called to say he had to stay at the plant all weekend to monitor an experiment. The picnic the doctors had let us plan must be postponed.

Luckily Hermann had not known about it, and we set off on our usual walk through the woods behind Dr. Fromm-Reichmann's cottage. We had barely started when he said he had something important to tell me. I tried not to show my dread. The new threats he had kept revealing had been hard enough to answer before he told Florence about the coded food. But now his tone was different. He asked quietly if I remembered his last trip for the Labor Board. I did, of course; he had toured the Great Lakes' ports.

"I also went to Chicago." He paused, waiting. It took me a moment to understand. In Chicago he had seen the baby that was possibly his, and the baby's mother. When he had left on that trip I had not even thought of this possibility, hard as that is to believe, even now. Why this confidence in the midst of all my doubts?

He said remorsefully that it had seemed to happen of itself, as if inevitable. I could see how natural that would be. He had once told me that he had tasted mother's milk. When I asked how he liked it, he said, "I was too excited to notice." That should have forewarned me.

I assured him that I understood. Of course, if he had told me at the time I would hardly have taken it so calmly. But today, when I had braced myself for sick fantasies, to hear him speak in his own voice, about something real between us, seemed wonderful. I didn't deserve his gratitude.

With his arms around me he said we must always from now on keep everything straight and clear between us. He was expressing more in words about our relationship than I had ever heard from him before. And it had to do with our future: plans for a marriage meant to go on through the years. His arms around me had their old strength.

But only for a moment. Glancing over my shoulder he stiffened, and his hands dropped. I looked back and caught a glimpse of the orderly disappearing behind a thicket. He was there for a purpose too obscene, Hermann said, to describe.

When I told Carter about Hermann's confession, he was not surprised that I had found the incident easy to forgive. "What else could he do, in the circumstances?" he asked with a smile. "Common courtesy almost required it." But he regarded such real communication between us as a hopeful sign.

I needed his kind of response. I had hoped that hearing of Hermann's tenderly lucid interlude might weaken Dr. Fromm-Reichmann's fateful sureness that he was incapable of love. But she had made no comment on my report, starting at once to set conditions for next week's picnic. It would be at the nearby state park.

All the auguries were good at first. Hermann had chosen the spot beside a stream, saying we could keep our wine cold in a crevice he found between two rocks. Before our first sip he raised his glass with a festive "Prosit!" He exclaimed over Cora's sausage rolls, and appreciated our remembering he liked anchovies on the deviled eggs. It was not till I had opened the basket for dessert that it happened.

I barely noticed the sound of the airplane. But Hermann sat up suddenly, his face white with alarm, listening. Ernst said something about the two-o'clock plane to Pittsburgh. Hermann looked at him, distressed. "But didn't you hear what he said?" When Ernst asked who had spoken, Hermann groaned. This was always the question; they varied the speaker. It was part of their method; but the message was always the same. He would not tell us the words he had heard; they were too terrible, too dangerous to repeat. But in his gasping half sentences the name Hitler kept recurring. Standing up and glancing around fearfully, he would have fled into the woods alone if Ernst had not caught his arm while I packed up hastily and helped persuade him along the path.

Neither Dr. Fromm-Reichmann nor Dr. Bullard was there when we got back to Chestnut Lodge. The young doctor on duty made only a noncommital response to our report. But Ernst, driving home, said heavily, "I suppose you know what that means — his hearing those voices."

Marion Bachrach had once remarked that I could be glad at least that Hermann had had no hallucinations. But now I protested miserably that the doctors themselves admitted they weren't really sure of anything. Ernst sighed. "Hope, let's not pretend that symptom is not an ill omen."

It sounded almost like Hermann's dire predictions. Reaching wildly for a way out of my terror I said I would call Dr. White. Instantly Ernst approved. He must have felt the same desperation.

We stopped at the first phone. Dr. White's secretary answered, though it was hardly office hours. Her voice was friendly, recalling our earlier talk. Dr. White would surely see me, she said, when he came back from Kansas and California. She made an appointment for a lunch hour three weeks hence.

Far ahead as it was, I could look forward to that day. My life now, I thought, was a matter of getting from one stepping-stone to another.

CHAPTER 25

Plunging into work would usually help. I spent hot evenings with Marion on our manual for agitprop writers. Besides livening up the prose, we wanted to correct a fault we thought serious. The Party press seemed always preaching to the converted. Instead of answering specific doubts it simply (and violently) condemned the doubters as tools of capitalist interests. That didn't fit all cases, I said.

Wolf Ladejinsky had now gone so far as to accuse Stalin of pretending to honor Kirov by giving his name to cities and streets, when actually he had murdered him. Yet Wolf himself had been working for years on a practical system for redistributing land and wealth in countries where a few people were rich and most abysmally poor. (Later he would make a successful start at this in Mexico.) He argued for a government takeover of big business, beginning with public utilities. If he was a tool of Wall Street his methods must be more devious than even Hermann's imaginings. But Marion and I both knew it would be hard to get our ideas accepted at headquarters.

Meantime all comrades were worrying about Spain. For a while, when the Madrid telephone lines were cut, we knew little of what was happening, but we learned that Parliament had been disbanded. Antigovernment forces under a general named Franco had taken control of Morocco. Loyalist planes and warships were sent there and to the Canary Islands. A general and a thousand disloyal officers were arrested in Madrid. But it was too late. A full-scale rebellion was under way.

As I walked into the office one morning, Mary asked if I had heard from Claud. When I shook my head, she said that Rodney had picked up a rumor that he was in Spain. The thought of him in the midst of the fighting haunted me as I worked. These last months I had felt a strange resistance to reading *The Week*. Even that night, resolved to catch up, I gave Claudia's bedtime ritual an extra half hour before I settled down and opened the first long, buff-colored envelope. And wished I hadn't, before I finished the first paragraph:

> An ominous piece of information has reached us by a route too circuitous to be believed except by those acquainted with the sinister linkages between the worlds of gangsterdom and high finance. Incredible or not, this rumor has the unmistakable timbre of certain highly placed voices in Berlin. . . .

I had to close my eyes, puzzled at the nausea that had swept over me. After a moment it passed; I started over. But as I read on I felt the same wrenching of stomach muscles, the tightening band around my forehead, and the faintness. Fighting off the malaise, I went on with the story. It blamed the burning of the Reichstag on Hitler's financial agents, who had acted with the aim of causing a break between the Soviet Union and Germany, thus removing from the German market the competition of DEROP, the Russian oil agency.

I knew now: I was hearing the echo of Hermann's delusions. I forced myself to read Claud's explanation of the elaborate book-keeping system by which false figures were provided to the world. The last item described an English flower nursery that grew speci-mens of exotic lilies. The two people who ran it were important Japanese officers in mufti. "The purpose of what can be called quite literally a 'planted' espionage operation is to find out what would happen if the Japanese should take formal steps to constitute them-selves the defenders of Islam. . . ."

Islam! Still queasy, I skimmed through other issues. Though Claud's tone was satiric, with witty descriptions of capitalist blun-ders, he told of malevolent forces, mysterious threats and plottings; he warned of fatal consequences to those who failed to take heed in time. Yet much of what Claud wrote turned out to be true.

Conspiracies did exist. History was full of them. At this moment in Spain a clique of army plotters had schemed to crush the new democracy. The case was as desperate as Hermann could have conceived.

I thought of Germany. Claud had given warning in *The Week* but nobody had acted. Hitler had marched into the Rhineland, his generals pale and trembling as they waited for the French army to strike. But the French army had not struck. Britain had hardly protested. Hitler had resumed his boasting, encouraging Mussolini. Italy's Blackshirts marched into Addis Abbaba, and the Ethiopians helplessly breathed the fascists' mustard gas.

My unit had to learn to distinguish among groups in Spain forming and breaking up and reforming, all fighting for the republic. We learned them by initials, like the New Deal's AAA, NRA, WPA, etc. But these letters stood for the Spanish version of the name, and the CP had to know that POUM, which now stood for the Workers' Party of Marxist Unification — though mainly made up of the old Workers' and Peasants' Revolutionary Alliance — was still as viciously Trotskyite as ever, but not to be confused with the Socialist UGT. If those distinctions — dozens of them — didn't keep my mind occupied, I could turn to the groups involved with religion — the ones on our side mostly anticlerical, of course. The Catholic Action Party tended toward fascism, but not as openly as FUE, which had united with JONS (both monarchist) until they quarreled over leadership. These initials tangled themselves into my nightmares.

Even our American politics had pitfalls. I listened carefully at meetings, read the Communist publications and the *New York Times,* but still could not decide how the Party really wanted us to vote in November. The CP had a candidate for president, but the spirit of the Popular Front seemed to suggest support of Roosevelt.

While Rodney was in Philadelphia covering the convention Mary gave a party where those at home could listen together to the president's acceptance speech. With Lacey Craig, another convention widow, Mary asked me to help balance the sexes by bringing Carter. As we entered we could hear the gleeful voice of Larry Todd, the Soviet *Tass* correspondent, citing statistics to show the superiority of their Five Year Plan to our New Deal.

We caused an interruption in the Todd monologue, and John Finerty took advantage of it. Granting the Soviet Union's material achievements (though he had heard that the material itself tended to crumble), he questioned the ideas it was based on. They were great in opposition, he said, but institutionalizing destroyed them. John usually kept his combative instincts for the courtroom, but now he insisted that power was always maintained by corrupting and abusing ideas.

This was nonsense, said Larry Todd, accusing John of being so used to fighting for the underdog that he couldn't conceive of a country where there was no underdog to fight for. John grinned appreciatively, but refused to believe there was any dearth of underdogs in the Soviet Union.

I hated such arguments; my throat choked with what I mustn't say. Carter may have guessed, for he said it reminded him of academics fearing that modern education would make people too well adjusted. He didn't see that as a problem, he said professorially, in the foreseeable future. Larry Todd said it might well happen in the Soviet Union. According to Dr. Frankwood Williams, they were even getting rid of neuroses over there. I glanced at Lacey Craig, but she was nodding at Mary's offer of another drink as if she hadn't heard what the men were saying. John had laughed derisively. "Don't give me that! In a country where there's a picture of Stalin on every wall?"

I didn't want to dislike John. His lean face, leathery from long days riding in Virginia sunshine, was lively with humor. And as a fighting liberal he had saved many embattled radicals. I had seen him help win John Donovan's case at NRA. Happily Carter broke in, quoting the statement of Lincoln Steffens (only decades later discovered to have been dishonest): "I have seen the future and it works." I watched Carter's mouth shaping those words and noted the sweetness of his full lower lip. Perhaps it was this, combining with months of gratitude, that gave a special charge to the evening from then on.

Mary had turned on the radio, and Roosevelt's voice was instantly recognizable — rather high, with an Eastern twang but a heartiness all his own, and something more, something personal that seemed to carry affection to each hearer. Everyone stopped talking, forks were still, fingers clasping the stems of wine glasses waited as FDR began to forecast "the revolution of 1936."

When he promised to carry on the great fight against the subtle, wily conspiracy of the "economic royalists" I lifted my glass with the others. But as he went on to announce his plans for calling a parley to deal with the drought I remembered the articles I had written about the acres of good topsoil being blown from the plains in great clouds of dust. Nothing effective had been done, and Party criticism was severe.

"Faith, hope, and charity!" the voice answered. "Faith in the soundness of democracy in the midst of dictatorships. Hope renewed because we know so well the progress we have made. Charity in the true sense of the original meaning of that good old word — which literally translated means love. Love that understands, that does not merely share the wealth of the giver but in true sympathy and wisdom helps men to help themselves . . . ."

Only Larry Todd looked unmoved; he wondered cheerfully how anyone could take this guff and like it. John said he could, and Lacey clapped.

"Better the occasional mistakes of a government that lives in a spirit of charity," Roosevelt went on, "than the consistent omissions of a government frozen in the ice of its indifference."

I tried to hear it as demagoguery, but the voice took on a subtly richer timbre. "To some generations much is given. . . . ." We waited in irresistible suspense. "From others much is hoped. Ours has a rendezvous with destiny."

Response blasted the radio: a roar from thousands of throats.

But at the office Mary gave us Rodney's wry reports. In his keynote speech Senator Alben Barkley had spoken of the more abundant life as now being within reach, but when a Negro minister rose to lead an invocation Senator Smith of South Carolina walked out, with the remark that he was "sick of the whole damn business." He came back to vote against the repeal of the two-thirds rule for nomination, its passage being part of the Farley strategy to make sure of Roosevelt's renomination. He threatened to walk out again "if any Negro played any part whatsoever in the proceedings."

Meanwhile Marion Bachrach had secretly gone as a delegate to the Communist convention; her account made me ashamed of my easy response to Roosevelt. Robert Minor had laid out the Party platform, calling for the overthrow of Hitler, the defense of the Spanish Republic, the expulsion of Japan from China, the expulsion of Italy from Ethiopia. Each demand had been answered by a shout from those seven hundred delegates: "RED FRONT! RED FRONT! RED FRONT!"

I wished I could have been there, part of that welded force confronting the great problems of the world. "We will unite the masses of this country for sanctions against the fascist warmakers," Robert Minor had pledged. He urged changes in the army and navy to eliminate fascist elements. He was not afraid to tell the truth behind the Good Neighbor Policy south of the border, Yankee imperialism in a new disguise.

I was in Hermann's study Saturday morning studying this in preparation for the next unit meeting when Cora came to say she was ready to go to town. Behind her Claudia was waiting in the too-large jodhpurs I had bought at a rummage sale. After we had taken Cora to the station I drove to the riding school. There an old stable-man lifted Claudia up and led the fat pony around the paddock while I sailed through the woods and over streams on Blackbird. Driving home, I felt a physical relaxation that I realized afterward, incredulous, had been very close to cheer.

As we stepped into the house the phone was ringing. I recognized the voice of the doctor who had been on duty the week of the picnic. He said not to be alarmed; there was no cause for worry now. But he had been trying to reach me for an hour.

Breaking in with questions, I learned that Hermann had cut himself while shaving. I started to say he often nicked himself — but then I had to let myself begin to understand.

Claudia was standing close, peering up fearfully into my face. I tried to look calm as I listened. He would be remiss in his duties, Dr. Field said, if he did not warn me that this was at least a gesture on Hermann's part "in the direction of taking his own life."

CHAPTER 26

Dr. Field, as I remember him, was a sallow young man in his mid-thirties sitting uneasily at Dr. Fromm-Reichmann's desk. He began at once to speak of the difficulties these emergencies presented. An attendant on duty with a patient who is shaving may receive a crisis call elsewhere, as Terence did today. Terence had not hesitated to respond to it, since up until that moment his patient had never shown any outward sign of his hostility.

Hostility. . . . And this time Dr. Field gave it still more dreadful implications. Such a patient was of course driven by the need to punish those close to him. I may have started to protest, for he went on to say that even positive feelings were always ambivalent. Though the records showed that in some ways Hermann's case seemed "atypical."

As I tried to square these two statements he said Terence had spoken of Hermann's spirit in a tone of devotion "tending toward reverence." I resisted such words, even though they brought tears. Talk so emotional from a doctor seemed wrong; it would have been anathema to Hermann. Maybe a bit embarrassed, Dr. Field turned briskly factual. Although Hermann had had time to do himself more damage, the injuries were slight.

When I asked if perhaps opposing feelings could have held him back, Dr. Field said I must realize that these were complex matters. I suppose I agreed humbly. But even if Hermann had wanted to punish me, and then regretted it, I asked, mightn't he at this very moment be terribly distressed about the pain he had caused me? Wouldn't it help if he could see me, clear things up?

"Quite impossible," Dr. Field said flatly. The procedure in these cases was to return the patient to the "Disturbed" wing under heavy sedation.

There was nothing I could do. How hard this was to accept!

Mary was waiting. Days ago she had planned to drive out with me and visit friends in the neighborhood. Today she had insisted on coming to Chestnut Lodge. Now I was glad of the quick clasp of her hand.

Driving away, I answered the questions she hadn't asked. She listened, but when she spoke it was about the sudden unnatural dusk that had fallen. Strangely, I hadn't noticed. She said I must not try to drive through the storm that was about to break. She had promised to bring me to tea with her friends.

I told her I had to get to town. I had called Carter to say not to count on me for our theatre evening, but his answer was only that he would be waiting in the Willard Coffee Shop till I got there, no matter when that was.

Mary was guiding me into an avenue between tall cedar trees. It led to a long, low-lying house of rose-colored brick with a chimney at either end. As the car stopped, lights went on, giving glimpses of paneled dark wood and bright flowers. Mary urged me go in with her. I was cold, and the glow of the lamps was tempting. At the thought of leaving alone under the threatening sky, I felt imperiled, forlorn. She stood by the car looking into my face, then asked if I was holding something back from her.

It was hard to talk about these things even to someone who deserved my confidence. But I told her what Dr. Field was sure had motivated Hermann. She became as indignant then as I had ever seen her. Doctors, she said, made such pronouncements in the same breath with the statement that nothing in these areas was certain. No one she knew could be as illogical as our friend Florence.

This frightened me; I reminded her that Florence was the one who had decided everything. Mary hurried to reassure me about her professional standing. And in any case I would be seeing Dr. White soon.

Our goodbyes were drowned in thunder. The trees were bending low, and as I drove along the lane they formed an intermittent tunnel of blackness. A branch scraped the roof of the car and my foot slipped. The wind was wild, sprays of leaves flew before it. A limb broke off and crashed to the ground. Luckily it was still possible to steer past. I accelerated riskily to reach the road before another tree could fall apart.

Rain was spattering the windshield when I made the left turn south. Lightning flashed. Visibility was about ten feet, but so few cars used this road that I could keep up speed. Abruptly a trap door seemed to open above; tons of water came crashing down. The noise on the canvas roof almost drowned out the thunder. Rain was like a solid surrounding wall.

I kept the car crawling along the shoulder. When the road widened I followed the curve, then pulled up suddenly, terrified; a figure loomed over me. I gave a cry, my heart pounding, before I made out the shape of a gasoline pump.

Lightning flashes showed a ghostly place, with signs half defaced and rusting fixtures; then the thunder cracked and they were gone. I huddled in the car, the wind tearing at the roof, rain spitting and slashing in from the sides. Now, if ever, I should have felt truly forlorn. But I was strangely caught up in the storm, in tune with its violence.

The torrent lessened; I could drive, though even after I reached the highway the thunder and lightning kept their full force. Straight ahead over Washington, bright crevices in the sky zigzagged down in sharp angles from the zenith. As I watched, one struck straight for the Washington Monument. Then the whole sky went dark.

Again this happened, with a different geometric pattern splitting the sky, but with the same unerring aim. Far away but clearly, I could see that soaring shaft, lighted stark white. I drove slowly, staring forward, absorbing the sight, reveling in each magnificent dazzling flash as if it might be the last. But it went on, gloriously, flash after flash, all the way, even through the city. I drove the length of Sixteenth Street with the monument still a luminous goal.

When I entered the coffee shop at last, Carter rose quickly, his face worried. I told him Hermann was now under sedation, though he had not been really injured.

"Thank God." Carter ordered coffee for me, and after a moment asked about the storm, whether it had been frightening. I tried to tell him that it was like something in the Bible. Like the sign the Israelites were always waiting for God to give, though they never received one like this. He asked if it had seemed to give me any specific message. I thought about this, and tried, but it was too enormous to describe.

"An epiphany," he said. "An affirmation of life." And he felt it had come at the right moment. The great thing was life, that Hermann could still share in it. He said it with a deep sigh that made me guess suddenly that he had feared what I would learn at Chestnut Lodge.

"Doctors have their methods," he said, and I realized how naive I had been. Mary must have had a bad half hour waiting at the Lodge. And Mimi must still be waiting. I excused myself to phone. Carter told me to say that he was taking me to the theatre whether or no.

Claudia, it seemed, had long wanted to spend the night on the "sweeping porch." Mimi could surprise me with her sisterly strength when it was needed.

I don't remember what play we saw, but like the others that summer it gave the audience a two-hour reprieve from thought, especially about the precariousness of life.

Afterward, when Carter seemed unwilling to let me drive out to an empty house I decided to use the key my colleague Anne Carter had urged on me when she set off for Marblehead. The apartment had been closed for several hot days; without waiting to turn on lights we hurried to open the windows. Looking out on Dupont Circle, I could see the violin studio that had once been the regular meeting place of the unit leaders. If anyone in this building had been interested, they might have seen the same people arrive each week. Since Hermann had become a unit leader he had made sure the system changed.

Carter was rummaging in Anne's supplies. "When Polonius said 'Neither a borrower nor a lender be,'" he intoned in his professorial way, "I'm sure Shakespeare didn't have gin in mind." The drink he handed me was strong, and I felt a little light-headed as I looked out into the night, saying something about the romantic way the avenues slanted through the grid of streets to make these circles.

Carter reminded me that Major L'Enfant's design was anything but romantic: these diagonal avenues would make it easier to quell any uprising of the populace. I wished I could ask him if this meant he thought revolutions romantic. But he was saying firmly that rest was what I needed, and drawing me toward the alcove.

The divan was soft under a spread of jade green quilted satin. On the wall above were framed eighteenth-century engravings. The nearest showed a young man wearing a lacy shirt and silk breeches coming on tiptoe into an ornate boudoir where a woman lay in disarranged petticoats, both breasts bursting out of her bodice.

I told him Anne puzzled me. She looked and usually acted like a traditional New England spinster. But she could come out suddenly with an utterly silly "knock-knock" joke. And now these pictures. Carter asked if I expected people to be all of a piece.

I remember this and the rest of the conversation partly because of the importance of the questions it raised — they still seem important, and still unanswered — but also because all conversations with Carter had an undercurrent of expectation, of something impending, a hovering sureness that whatever was said would be momentous.

Perhaps my fatherlessness made me vulnerable to men whose position gave them power. Carter was Hermann's chief, an important figure in the academic world. He was big and solid, but with an air of diffidence, of humor that seemed expressed by the outthrust lower lip like Maurice Chevalier's. I had found him attractive from the start, and then, when I needed it so crucially, he had given me strong immediate support. We had plotted and worked together to bring Hermann back to reality.

All this had given me a sense of closeness to Carter that was like love — *was* love, of course: his sharing of my pain and urgency held us together in a bond so strong that it would last always, through years and miles of separation.

Now when he laughed I heard the affection in his question, and I admitted that I did tend to expect consistency in people, and so had often been disillusioned. But not about Hermann. And it was at this point, when Carter agreed that Hermann had seemed truly integrated, that I began to lose control. In a rush of desperate inspiration I asked if there might be a sort of adhesive that held the parts of people together, a chemical that could be weakened, possibly by another chemical, a disintegrating agent, resulting in illnesses like Hermann's.

I suppose my faltering voice worried Carter, for he tried to say I was in no shape to talk about these things. But I raced on, reminding him of the physical diseases that had mental symptoms — syphillis, for instance. And I had written about pellagra in the South where people with a poor diet even had hallucinations. And fever — in the flu of 1918 my terrifying delirium had been much like Hermann's delusions.

Carter was smoothing the hair back from my temples, begging me not to put myself through this after such a day. But I kept on. Couldn't the doctors be assuming Hermann's problem was due to some childhood trauma, when all the time it might really be physical, and untreated might become worse and worse?

Carter tried to soothe me, saying the doctors must be watching his health. Hadn't they examined him when he was admitted?

If they had, they hadn't mentioned it, or discussed his physical condition. And meanwhile he had been getting thinner and thinner, terribly frail. In such a state, I asked, wouldn't he become more and more vulnerable?

Carter was holding me by then, wiping my face with his handkerchief, begging me not to feel I had to solve these problems all alone. This brought back my doubt of my own thinking, and I probably conceded that if these ideas had any validity the doctors had surely taken them into account.

My thoughts had come out in fragments, painfully, but after a time I was calm enough for Carter to ease me back against the pillow. Still holding me, he began to talk about my epiphany, saying he thought he understood what it had meant. It was not in my character, he said, to live on the bitterness of life. He did not, in fact, think I should. Or even that I could, without damage. I must allow myself a little joy.

The word was startling in the context of my life. Yet as I lay recalling the moment in the abandoned gas station, I remembered how I had given myself to the rush and fury of the storm. Yes, what he said was true. And I wondered now, held so close to his body, if he meant this kind of joy.

But apparently he hadn't. He lifted his mouth from mine, and when I opened my eyes his own were grave as he drew away. He walked to the window and stood there a few minutes silently. Then he came back, saying there were things I should know. Bewildered, I moved over and he settled himself, beside me but apart.

He made a formal speech then — a bit sententious, as he often accused himself of being — about his career (his failed dreams of being a poet) and the responsibilities of family life. Phrases penetrated my blur of exhaustion: "paradoxical loyalty," "weighting of values." When he spoke of the children's "overriding interest" I had a dizzy vision of his daughters on their horses overriding fallen trees in their Adirondack forest.

Addressing me now with gentle directness he said that a casual infidelity would not endanger his marriage. But what this would be — his kiss on my forehead contrasted strangely with the economist's words — could not be so categorized.

When I did not answer — there seemed nothing to say — he murmured "Poor darling" and caught me up close again. In a minute his sympathy had changed, caught fire, demanding as well as giving. But now I pushed with my hands against the solid chest that was so inviting, pushed him firmly away.

He groaned, begging me to count on him in any case, and to promise now that I would go to sleep.

I promised, but lay there for a long time in a state of confusion, not sure what I had really wanted but aching with a feeling of compounded loss.

CHAPTER 27

Old brick buildings lined the road leading through the grounds of St. Elizabeth's. Porches extended from each story, on this July day crowded with patients — all yelling, it seemed. I thought I heard myself called "slut" and "whore." From a men's porch a rough voice told me to get my tin lizzie off the fair grounds or he'd fill it full of lead, backing up his threat with the *bang-bang* a little boy might shout. And he was no little boy.

Women on another porch were shrieking like quarrelsome children, but using words most children would not know. As I glanced up I saw the face of one of the screaming women; she was staring out through the wire netting without expression. On one porch two women standing face to face on the seat of a swing were "working up" higher than I had ever done as a child. At the top of each arc gray hair flew out against the sky. I whispered, "Poor wretches," then remembered: these people were ill, just as Hermann was. But I couldn't bear that thought.

The administration building was much like the others from outside. The interior was bare and institutional, with black-rubber matting protecting the wooden floor of the corridor. A woman was scrubbing it, and I asked directions of her. She gave them, smiling as she spoke the doctor's name.

When Dr. White took my hand I felt steadied at once. He began without preamble, reviewing the facts I had given him in my phone calls. And now he wanted to know what brought me there: a suicide attempt?

243

How had he guessed? "It fits a common pattern," he said, and asked for details. I told him about the shaving scene, and that afterward Hermann had written to assure me that his situation in the sanitarium had driven him to it; only that, whatever the doctors might say.

Dr. White's response took away the comfort the letter had given me. "I wish we could believe," he said sadly, "that they know what they mean." His use of "they" shook me. It put Hermann in the same category with those patients on the porches. He was different! Maybe I didn't actually say that, but I did try to suggest how thoughtful and logical he was, how carefully he had planned and lived his life according to his convictions. Dr. White stopped me there, shaking his head. Those words, he said, could mean danger sometimes.

I wouldn't give up. Even in the hospital, I said, Hermann had not lost the use of his fine intelligence. And to prove it I brought out my copy of his statement. Dr. White leafed through the pages to the end. Turning back to read one paragraph he said he had wondered how Hermann would get over the big hump. He had given an excellent terse summary of the world crisis — excellent if you accepted a leftist point of view — and also made a convincing case for the possibility of psychology being perverted to trap him and destroy his usefulness. But what all patients had trouble explaining, he said, was the grandeur of the delusions, why this particular individual should be the target of these great outer forces. Admitting that Hermann had almost managed it, he read aloud the paragraph:

> We are on the verge of a World War whose outcome is socialism or chaos. Opposing the revolutionary methods and victories — which would bring about the conservation of humanity and its achievements — there are reactionary methods promising opposite results. The latter methods have been improved — beyond the use of outright force and general propaganda — by taking one individual — stable bourgeois background but progressive tendencies — and using modern science and organization to recreate him into a non-individual — preparing by this pilot program for the abysmal self-negation of society.

Dr. White leaned his head on his hand, groaning. "What a waste!" This had struck me with full force as he read; his sharing was a comfort. He would see now why I had to find a way to save Hermann.

Dr. White agreed that it was a "ruinous spot" for a man to be in, but added that he had come to feel even sorrier for the families of the patients. This time I must have cried out against his linking Hermann's case with all the others this way. He just sat shaking his head until I pulled myself together and asked what he had meant at first when he said the suicide attempt fitted into a pattern.

Hermann's age, to begin with: thirty-five when he had the breakdown, and recently married. First marriages at this age seemed to hold some special danger. He spoke of the psychic burden marriage put on a man, the greatest of which was sexual.

I couldn't believe that Hermann had ever felt sex as a burden. Still, to be honest I had to report what he had said to Ernst about not being able to replace Claud. But I quickly added that even after his breakdown his desire was so strong that the hospital had made arrangements for us to be alone together.

Astounded, Dr. White wanted to know how it had gone. And had it continued? I had to admit it hadn't; we were always sent outdoors. This led to the walk with Florence, to which Dr. White listened intently, and then the picnic with Ernst, when Hermann had heard voices. I hardly dared ask him whether that was as bad a sign as we had been told.

Dr. White did not deny it. His voice was almost too gentle, saying I had to face such facts. It was probably then that I asked desperately if these judgments might all be based on wrong assumptions. What if the illness was really physical, one they should be treating?

Dismayingly, he admitted that this might be true. He, as well as others, still worried about it. But psychoanalysis had diverted the mainstream into what might become a dead end. Freud thought physical problems were caused in the psyche, but he had not granted that it could be a two-way street. The real trouble was, Dr. White thought, that no one had ever seemed able to see humans as whole organisms. The very naming of mind *and* body as separate entities had probably held the thinking back a thousand years. He stopped

245

himself, rubbing his forehead wearily with the palm of his hand and saying I hadn't come there for a historical lecture.

In a way I had, I told him, since I knew nothing. I had been advised not to try to read up on it. He said it would take a lot of "reading up," and then I would know as little as the authorities I was reading. He spoke of the frustration of not having any way to help people. One doctor had found it so unbearable that he had taken a hammer to the skulls of demented patients, trying to knock the delusions out of their heads. And it even seemed to work — at least with some, for a while. Probably they were scared into feigning sanity to escape the pain, which of course would be terrible.

I could understand those doctors' impulse. I had felt like shaking Hermann, to shake his ideas back into the right grooves. Dr. White said that dozens of methods had been tried on that principle, most of them forms of torture unacceptable in our society. Which of course left us where we started, with most institutions doing nothing for the patient — or worse than nothing, since it was obviously harmful for anyone, especially someone so vulnerable, to be among deranged people.

This made me even more desperate, and with tears on my face I asked what he would do if this were his own son? Dr. White's answer can never be forgotten: "I'd take him out to the backyard and shoot him."

I sank into my chair, trying to think I had heard him wrong.

He did not apologize. Looking at me levelly he said he had lied, of course, but intentionally, to shock the hope out of me. "That damnable hope" was always a problem, and he saw me as especially prone to it. Didn't I always think things would turn out right in the end? After a moment I realized it was true. Mother may have taught it to me, Mother in her struggling widowhood, counting on God.

Hadn't I, Dr. White demanded to know, ever since last November, wakened each morning expecting to hear news of a miracle? Not exactly expecting, I said, but yes, hoping. He ordered me severely to stop it. If it weren't for that eternal-springing hope, he said, a situation like this would not be so unendurable.

Absurdly, I felt I really ought to promise. I owed it to Dr. White, who in all his eminence had granted me this interview, which I had not made easy for him. He had done his best to give me what he knew from his vast experience. But I couldn't accept it as applying to Hermann, who had been so full of ideas last summer, ready to embark on new projects, even having a baby. Just before his breakdown, I said, he had suddenly come out with a flash of inspiration that Carter Goodrich had thought might change the thinking of economists.

Dr. White only frowned at that, and I remembered how Carter had likened that evening's brilliance to a lightbulb's final dazzling flare. Even so, I couldn't give up. I suppose Dr. White saw this in my face. He let out a tired sigh. I was one of the incorrigibles, he said, and took my hand with that sweet, sad smile.

I don't remember hearing any shouts as I drove out. The patients might have gone in to lunch, or perhaps I was beyond hearing anything. I didn't come to full awareness until I noticed the circling lights of a People's Drug Store and knew I had to use the phone. I couldn't carry on any longer by myself. Marion Bachrach was in Vermont. Carter was with his family in the Adirondacks. My family was sailing on the Chesapeake. Mary had gone with Rodney to the Delaware shore for the weekend. I thought of Pat Jackson and how I would be welcomed in that loving family. He might even have news of Claud, whose danger in Spain made me feel even more alone.

But I was not allowed to associate with Pat. And I knew I should go home and release Cora. But I could not face the hours out there with these thoughts, trying to keep up cheer for Claudia. Then suddenly I remembered the night at Mary's when Lacey Craig had told me she understood my trouble. "Any time things get too awful, remember you can come to us." I turned the car toward Georgetown.

The maid who was so carefully called by her last name, Williams, answered the door with a doubtful stare. When I asked for Mrs. Craig, she said she was out of town. But Josh came up behind her as she spoke, urging me in. I had come just in time to save him from lunching alone.

It was a reprieve, at least. Surprisingly able to eat, I felt a bit better. Josh was a lively talker, and though I'd always been a little intimidated by the bulldog look of his boldly modeled features and the intentness of his eyes, today his voice was softer and his gossip from the Democratic convention seemed chosen to make me laugh. I was impressed with how well informed he was, not at all the uncertain outsider Lacey had pictured, with all those secret problems.

Over dessert we spoke enviously of Mary and Rodney beside the ocean, and Josh suddenly proposed that we drive over and join them. Instantly I knew it was a perfect plan. Part of a foursome with Mary and Rodney, and in any case with Josh's impotence an open secret, we would be above reproach. Yet the idea had a delightful aura of daring and mischief. I went to phone Cora.

I have trouble confessing this part. When I asked Cora to stay on, she protested. And I knew how much her weekends meant to her, after all those long days confined in the country. She was an official church nurse, with a uniform, taking charge of members who were overcome by religious fervor. They needed her, she told me now.

I begged her to understand my need, and when she still demurred, I said I simply had to go. And somehow I used my power to get her grudging assent. This memory has always shamed me. Worse, it started me observing that those who can exploit will exploit, even if they are Marxists. Yet as we set off I was able to put all sense of guilt behind me. I suppose my need seemed to justify anything.

Lacey had taken their car, and Josh was amused to drive my little open roadster. I sat back and tried to let the wind blow Dr. White's grim words from my mind. As we reached the sandy Maryland roads among the Negro cabins, Josh talked about his childhood. His family had been great riders, raising a special kind of crossbreed combining a donkey's surefootedness with beauty and grace from Arabian blood. Dreamily he described the rides with his younger sister in the Colorado foothills. I knew about her death — their father had written a poignant account of it that had become a classic — and now Josh's voice sharing these scenes offered me trust and intimacy.

I wondered if it might also be a plea of some kind from a boy who had not only lived under the shadow of his father but known his sister to be better loved. A child could even feel guilty at having lived on when another child had died. Could that be the source of his problems?

Ocean Beach was strikingly different from Rehoboth, for which I was grateful. Instead of a simple row of bungalows on the water this was a shoddy little imitation of Atlantic City. As we began our search for Mary and Rodney we wondered at the whim that had made them come to such a honky-tonky place.

It turned out, after a while, that they hadn't. We had started with the best hotel and gradually worked our way down until we were inquiring at lowly boarding houses. By that time it was dusk and we were hungry. As we sat over our crab cakes and beer in a small waterside restaurant, we gave up hope of finding them. Curiously enough this seemed no great matter. The happy-go-lucky mood of the place was irresistible.

From the restaurant we wandered along the ocean shore beyond the town until all we could hear was the surge of the waves. I was tired and sank down on the sand, and he joined me, still talking in his dreamy way. Before I was fully aware of what he was doing — so sure had I been of what I had heard — Josh had drawn me down beside him and was holding and kissing me in a way that with any other man I would know must be checked now or never. For a fleeting moment I wondered what to do. Almost by reflex, I started to pull away. But then I thought, if this could be a curative moment for him, wouldn't it do damage to deny him? And in his arms I felt deeply comforted. But it was more than comfort. My own response was overwhelming.

The sand was a gritty bed, and the lovemaking was all rush and urgency, but it was real; leaving me with a sense of promise that was almost a fulfilment in itself. He apologized as we lay under the dim sky, half laughing at ourselves for our haste. He had been deprived for so long, he said.

I asked no questions, though I was as puzzled about this as I had been at first when I realized that he had clearly come prepared. But

249

he went on to tell me that his wife was being psychoanalyzed and the rule was abstinence. Slowly I began to understand that the psychological problems were not his. Evidently one of her symptoms was the compulsion to spread that story about his impotence. And he had borne this patiently. I was already glad about what had happened, but now I knew I had responded to what I sensed in him without being told.

We wandered back to town and took a room in an old-fashioned two-story seaside hotel wrapped in verandahs, its sandy corridors filled with the scent of old wood and salt air. Our mattress seemed to be stuffed with straw not evenly spread, but the bed was wide and we had time to seek, in those long hours, a true escape from both our worlds. I slept at last and in the morning found we had lain in each other's arms all night. The watch on his wrist was pressed against my cheek, and during the next few days my fingers kept searching for the small indentations it had made.

CHAPTER 28

The outside events we discussed at Party meetings couldn't offer any cheer. In Greece a fascist dictatorship had come to power. King George II had collaborated in giving Metaxas total control. The Popular Front government in France, though it had nationalized the munitions industry and expressed eagerness to help the legal government in Spain, had finally decided that "the international situation was too delicate." A rumor was going around that Franco had offered to exchange Ceuta, next to the Rock of Gibraltar, for Mussolini's support of his plans to crush his country's new democracy. According to *The Week* this would turn the Mediterranean into an Italian lake.

Mary wondered how Claud had picked this up. It didn't seem like the kind of news available to a foot soldier.

A foot soldier! Surely he must be a correspondent. No. Rodney had caught a reference to him on the ticker as a member of one of those overnight jumped-up regiments rushed to the front as soon as they could learn to count themselves off, just to fill the breach somehow.

At least Claud had had a little training. In his last year at school, toward the end of the World War, the boys had drilled with wooden imitation guns. I had a vision of his tall figure, an old-fashioned greatcoat flapping about his legs as he makes his way along some ridge among a group of stocky peasants, rifles silhouetted against the sky. This picture stayed with me, mingling with my constant anxiety about Hermann.

The worst world events, if I had let myself recognize their portent, took place in Moscow. Old Bolsheviks, leaders with sacred names, had now been accused of vicious crimes against the Soviet state, even of collaborating in treason with Trotsky. During court sessions that the bourgeois press had started to call "show trials" they were actually confessing to these unspeakable crimes in grotesque detail. A group of comrades held a special meeting to deal with the news.

Henry Collins, our treasurer, lived in what I remember as a converted coach house near Dupont Circle. Approached by a long narrow passageway from one of the numbered streets, it seemed almost too well designed as a secret meeting place. My memory may have added grandeur to his living room, two stories high, three walls lined with books, the top rows reached by a sliding wrought iron stairway. Did this also lead to a gallery with doors leading to other rooms? A mirrored bar held an array of glasses, but Henry never made any motion to serve refreshments until some comrade reminded him that we ought to look like a social gathering.

When I arrived I found all the comrades there but Nat Witt, usually the most punctual of the comrades. The others speculated as to whether domesticity was demoralizing him. Perhaps they were a little jealous (as I knew I was) that his new baby bore the name of Hal. But that could not have accounted for the grimness of their frowns tonight. I'll picture this meeting and those present and the way the talk went as accurately as I can recall.

Without waiting for Nat, Vic announced that Steve had meant to come to Washington but the repercussions from the news were keeping him at headquarters. He had wanted to emphasize that the success of the Popular Front depended on our correcting the widespread misunderstanding of the Moscow trials. Here in Washington we had an important role to play. If we were going to keep the liberals with us in the fight against fascism we must make them see these trials as an absolutely essential part of that struggle.

I had my notebook out by then, and Nat had come in. Our assignment from Steve was a dual one, Vic went on. First, we had to prepare to answer any doubt. Second, we must not expose ourselves as Party members. We groaned, knowing the problems this raised. Even answering at all, John said, marked you as a Communist. Yet he knew he had to take the chance. The trials had all but undone a year's work on his chief, whom he had been allowed to try to recruit.

I remembered the cocktail party Marion had given to help John in this. The comrades had just begun to carry out our directive to become what she disgustedly called social climbers. Arthur, accustomed to having his neurosis the deciding factor in family plans, complained bitterly at being subjected to such an ordeal. But Marion's priorities stayed firm: neither his mental health nor the health of their marriage counted against recruiting a high-ranking New Dealer. And in the end Arthur's habitual manners helped make the party an apparent success. But now John's chief had doubts. A year ago he would not have cared what happened to Zinoviev or Kamenev, John said, but now their fate troubled him deeply.

We had to put up with emotionalism, Charles said, when dealing with confused liberals. And Vic added that Steve had warned that criticizing their position only alienated them. We must first try to understand their point of view and then, as Lenin said, "patiently to explain." This counsel of tolerance came strangely from Steve, by way of Vic. Nat said quietly that people were bound to be misled by the capitalist press, with its legalistic bias. That led Charles to suggest that Nat and John as lawyers might show us how to answer this.

"Most problems caused by legal tradition," I wrote in my notebook as Nat began. The U.S. judicial system was based on the English, which assumed that the accused were innocent until proven guilty. Americans didn't realize that most of Europe — France for instance — assumed the opposite. In Russia the procedure had always been to establish guilt conclusively before bringing the defendant into court.

John broke in with something about this being true in France, but could they really say everywhere, and always? Long enough, Nat said, for our purposes; we must stress those words "established procedure." (I underlined them.) In Russia the trial was really just a formality to give the defendant a chance to make a final public statement before the judge, who had to decide only the *degree* of guilt, and set the punishment.

John stopped Nat again: even Americans who knew this would find it strange that these sixteen traitors were brought into court without any witnesses for the defense. But we could point out that there were none for the state either — except of course the accused themselves. All sixteen had freely admitted being followers of Trotsky. Fourteen of them went further and confessed to participating in a plot to murder a dozen of the most important men in the Soviet government. Not a single defendant asked for clemency, and they all implicated themselves and each other.

That was what bothered his boss, John said, the vehemence of these confessions and accusations. He had called it "obscene."

Rather hesitantly Henry began to point out that the liberal weeklies tried to explain it in terms of Russian history. Before he could finish a sentence he was cried down. "Spare us the Russian soul!" We were through with that Dostoevsky stuff, Charles said, but he thought we should make use of anything we could, even the *New York Times*.

We all knew he meant Walter Duranty, the *Times* correspondent whose dispatches, printed in such a paper, seemed almost single-handedly to demolish the libels of the rest of the press. I think even Party members unconsciously used them to shut out any creeping doubts. True, one of the ways Duranty was able to hold the liberals in line was what Charles called "tripe about traditional Russian theatricalism." But he stood almost alone among newspapermen in defending the legitimacy of the trials. And he never questioned the guilt of the accused. Decades would go by before the world learned that Duranty had been dishonest all along.

Even Duranty, though, did not accept Trotsky's collaboration with the Nazis, which Nat said wryly was the basis of the whole case. Also he saw problems about the hotel where Trotsky was alleged to have met the conspirators. Had it even existed at that time?

I wondered if they could deal with all that as plausibly as Hermann had dealt with the impossibilities of his delusional system.

Charles conceded the holes in Duranty's logic, but his dispatches might help anyway to calm down the irrational resistance of people like John's boss. John demurred at the word "irrational." That resistance had a certain consistency he said. His chief could have accepted the way the prisoners talked — their almost religious rhetoric of having sinned and seen the light — if they had been treated as such, forgiven as repentant sinners. But instead they had been executed.

The statement seemed to resound, filling the room. To me it echoed Hermann's terrible fears, the inexorability of the punishment arranged by malign forces. Everyone was looking at John accusingly. He had uttered words that Party members should leave unsaid. Up to then I had hardly spoken. But now I had to find some escape from those ominous echoes. Timidity had held me silent before. I thought of comrades as so much more advanced politically — a status they all took for granted as males — that I didn't challenge them. If their reasoning about people sometimes ran counter to my experience, I reminded myself that Claud had said bourgeois experience was irrelevant; worse, my ideas were often what Mother would have called commonsensical. But now in this silence I heard myself say that if John's chief was so shocked, a lot of other people must be feeling the same way, the people we wanted to reach. We should be concentrating on ways to reassure them, no matter who they were.

As I spoke I remembered Steve's thundering accusations when Hermann asked an innocent question. From these comrades the best I could expect was the pitying look I met so often at Chestnut Lodge.

The mood did change, but not as I expected. Vic sniffed the air as if taking whiffs of my reasoning, then nodded. And we began formulating effective answers that would sound as if they came from someone who merely wanted to be objective and just, showing the right of any country to save itself from its internal enemies. Even the liberal weeklies assumed that no government would make such extreme accusations in court without incontestable proof of the defendants' guilt. If these traitors abased themselves, it was none of our affair.

255

I accepted all this as means to an end, in the unquestioning way Mother accepted what she took to be divine guidance. Just as her Christian commitment made that her duty, membership in the Party made it my duty not to think for myself. If I had thought for myself I would have seen at once that there was no good answer to the question the papers were asking: Were these men who had been executed actually guilty? If the answer was yes, what would that say about the Old Bolsheviks, about the strength of the ideals and principles by which they had helped build a new society? If the answer was no, what did it say about that society which now executed them?

One possible way of supporting the accusations might have bridged the gap between innocence and guilt. Working it out long afterward, I thought it seemed the sort of answer Hermann might have thought of, if he had been with us that night. He might have said that it was possible for someone to become corrupted gradually, over the years. At first the comrade would try to question or change the Party's policy. But since the Party ruled that out he might try other methods. Then, as those methods involved him with more and more disloyal forces, he'd be trapped with truly traitorous elements.

But of course these comrades would never have let this logical process come to mind. How could they, when it would have meant beginning with the admission that democratic debate on policy was impossible?

I am ashamed now to report my other contribution to the thinking that night. When my turn came I told of having hit upon a quite different answer that seemed effective. I simply asked my doubting friends if they had read the transcript of the trials. They never had, and they always backed down, assuming that my opinion had a firmer base than theirs.

Vic asked worriedly whether I had actually shown the transcript to anyone. Of course I hadn't, because the name of the publisher would have revealed it to be Party literature.

Nat said this wasn't the only reason for not showing it to outsiders. They might expect something like the transcript of an

American trial, with verbatim testimony; this was only a summary, and did not pretend to be impartial. Some of the rhetoric, he said, would make a civil liberty lawyer's hair stand on end. Actually I had not read much of the transcript. It gave me the same feeling of malaise I felt when I read Claud's descriptions of elaborate plots and conspiracies. Breathing became difficult, as if the air had thickened with the evil murk of Hermann's delusions.

Nat was saying that someone must be doing great work in the editorial offices of the liberal weeklies. Dealing with the testimony that the forged passports used by the five assassins sent in from abroad had been prepared by the Gestapo, the *New Republic* reported that this news was received by the German government in "stony silence which is tantamount to the admission of guilt." And one of the writers drew a comparison between our Tories' hatred of Roosevelt and the Old Bolsheviks' hatred of Stalin.

I protested that our Tories would hardly try to sell out their own country. But Charles contradicted me there. The Nye Committee had turned up evidence that when profit was to be made our munition makers did not hesitate to sell bombs and guns to potential enemies.

Leaving, making my way along that dark narrow passage to Seventeenth Street, I felt surrounded by forces as dark as Hermann could imagine. And these were real.

CHAPTER 29

That summer of 1936 the fighting was heavy in the mountains near Barcelona. Rodney heard a rumor that two thousand militiamen had been massacred by Franco's soldiers at Badajoz, first digging their own graves and then falling into them. Peasants nearby had heard the shots.

I'd had no news of Claud. Surely he led a charmed life, Pat Jackson said, cornering me at a party. But could insouciance protect him from bullets?

One night at about this time our fluttery landlady called on me. She had devoted her other visits mostly to delight and awe at having a writer in residence. But that night she said nervously that she had received an offer for the house — one she could not refuse. And since our lease ended soon. . . .

A blow at first, this began to seem what my mother called providential. Marion Bachrach knew of a pleasant apartment in her own neighborhood. Moving left no memory. I must have welcomed the practical ordeal as a distraction from real trauma. The new place, on the second floor of a private house in the Columbia Road area, was sunny and spacious.

Meanwhile Hermann grew more and more troubled over Dr. Fromm-Reichmann's absence on vacation, which he took as desertion. I tried to help him accept it, until one Sunday in August. From then on I waited with even more urgency than his.

Rollo and I were working on the tennis court when Mimi called from the porch that I was wanted on the phone. As I climbed the hill I fought as usual against the hope forbidden by Dr. White. I was still fighting as I began to listen to what Marion Bachrach was trying to say. Before she had finished I gave up the fight for good.

Marion had always been cool and careful in discussing Hermann's case, but this time she spoke in an excited rush. Arthur had just come back from New York, where he had heard amazing news. An Austrian named Sakel had introduced a treatment called insulin shock therapy that was actually curing some cases of schizophrenia. Marion had tracked down Dr. Sakel's report and read it before she called.

He had discovered the method accidentally when a diabetic patient had gone into shock after an overdose of insulin. As Dr. Sakel was bringing him around he found he could actually converse with this patient, who had been out of touch with the world for months. After that they started inducing the shock intentionally, freeing a number of patients from their delusions; some had stayed well for two years. The article gave percentages of apparent cures and improvement. These showed the importance of treatment within the first year. We agreed we had to move fast. Nine months had gone by since Hermann's breakdown.

I phoned Ernst, who was predictably cautious. It sounded dangerous, he said. I agreed that the doctors had to take great care. But Dr. Sakel himself had come here to demonstrate the method in state hospitals. Soon he would start overseeing the treatment at a private sanitarium near New York. Ernst said (quite reasonably, though I gritted my teeth) that we must first consult the doctors at Chestnut Lodge. Meanwhile he would discuss it with with Hermann's parents, and of course with Florence.

Dr. Fromm-Reichmann would not be back for a week. Dr. Bullard immediately advised me to calm down, pointing out the danger of laymen upsetting the applecart by getting in a tizzy about every new fad they heard of, which were, he said, a dime a dozen. But he promised to look up the reference Marion had cited, then talk things over with Dr. Fromm-Reichmann.

The waiting, so hard all along, now seemed just too much. When at last I reached Dr. Fromm-Reichmann she said she had not had a chance to read the article. She would inform me when the staff had

had time to make the necessary study and consultation. But Ernst had good news. Florence had checked with the doctors at the state hospitals where Dr. Sakel had introduced the treatment; all were enthusiastic. She thought we should try to get Hermann into Stony Lodge, in Ossining, where Dr. Sakel was beginning the treatment.

Before I could leap to immediate plans Ernst said Hermann's parents had set two conditions for their agreement. First, we must try bringing Hermann home, at least for a weekend. Second, we must get opinions from the two top authorities in the area. Dr. White would be easy. Mimi immediately named the other, and everyone agreed: Dr. Adolf Meyer at Johns Hopkins, if we could get him.

Dr. Fromm-Reichmann, opposed anyway to the weekend experiment, called it unwise now, when Hermann had complained of feeling ill. Though she had interpreted this as punishing her for her absence, she thought it best to take it seriously. Meanwhile I phoned Dr. White. His secretary said he was out of town. I told her what I meant to ask him; she promised an answer in three days.

When I next phoned Dr. Fromm-Reichman to arrange about bringing Hermann home she said first that she had read the report and that Dr. Sakel's approach was incorrect. A therapy that struck not at the roots of the psychosis but at the surface could not succeed. I brought up the statistics in the article, the percentages of recovery. She said that these must be temporary if they existed. When I tried to say that some had lasted two years she stated flatly that she and Dr. Bullard had discussed the situation and come to a conclusion — Dr. Field concurring — that interrupting Hermann's therapy at the present stage was contraindicated.

Since she had herself interrupted it for several weeks (Hermann still unforgiving) I asked how that reason could apply. I tried to put this with the respect I genuinely felt. But my tact, such as it was, didn't save me from reproof. I had presumed to judge better than those professionally trained. This normally would have shamed me into silence, but I couldn't bear to let her negative statement stand; I reminded her that Dr. Powdermaker was in favor of the change. Unhearing, she said the matter was settled, and hung up before I could protest.

Dr. White, his voice kind as always, said he had made inquiries as soon as he received my message, and had word from several friends in New York. I waited, holding my breath, and then he said, "Girl, I think maybe you've got hold of something." It took me a minute to find words for my relief. The doctors at Chestnut Lodge had turned it down so firmly. Their opposition did not surprise Dr. White. He said Dr. Fromm-Reichmann was trying to prove that these patients could be reached with psychoanalysis. Sakel's approach would threaten all that.

I reminded him that Dr. Sakel tried to reach the patients too, in their lucid periods as they came out of shock. But Dr. White said that Sakel thought something else was involved, something fundamental, which of course would justify tremendous interest. What did I know, he asked, about the history of the human brain?

Then for some minutes I sat in my office learning about the outside layer, the cortex, which had been the last to develop. Only by its use could a man control his savage instincts to the still limited degree now possible. These newer powers of discrimination were not even yet firmly established. They were dangerously vulnerable, and if anything went wrong with them there was nothing to hold back the old savage fears and hostility, which a human being had once needed for survival. They could break out of control and come to dominate the personality completely, according to Sakel, if the problem was not corrected in time. What was new was Sakel's claim that he *could* correct it. And his results apparently backed that up.

I worried about those words "corrected in time." Hermann's breakdown had occurred in November. Dr. White agreed that speed was essential. But he thought Adolf Meyer, given a thorough case history, would do his cogitating in jig time. Those words "jig time" rang through my mind like a happy refrain until events robbed them of their assurance.

The weekend began happily. Hermann liked the apartment and seemed relieved to have us safe from the country winter. He gave no sign of seeing anything sinister about the presence of Mimi, who was there as a precaution stipulated by the sanitarium. She had always taken a teasing, challenging tone with him, but that day she showed just sisterly affection. Censoring her conversation she found topics — science news from a weekly published by her Council — that clearly caught Hermann's interest. He ate hungrily of Cora's chicken fricasee and saluted her apple pie. At Claudia's bedtime, when I got out his flute, he accompanied us as I played "Rockabye Baby."

From the moment he arrived Claudia had not left his side; she insisted on his reading her bedtime stories and tucking her in. Later in our own bed, trying to be quiet, he couldn't stifle his response when at the right moment I murmured "Welcome home." And with a control that amazed us both after his long abstinence he brought me to a sure and lavish climax. But afterward he sighed. "If only . . ." Before he could end the sentence he had fallen asleep, exhausted. And when we woke up Claudia was in bed with us.

His sentence would have ended sadly — I knew this as the morning went on. He was silent, carving the roast, and ate little of it. When Claudia climbed on his lap he smoothed her hair distractedly, biting his lip. She looked puzzled when he failed to answer her questions. Cora, quietly observant, beckoned me to the kitchen and offered to stay on. I shook my head, refusing the implications, but must have heard the warning in her tone, for I persuaded Claudia to come along when I drove Cora to her bus. Hermann hardly noticed when we left.

Returning, I knew something was wrong almost before I entered the house. I told Claudia to play outside and rushed up the stairs. At the door I could hear grunting breaths, sounds of struggle.

In the kitchen Mimi had Hermann locked in a grip from behind, pinning his arms against his body. Hermann's hand gripped the carving knife he had used an hour before. He was jerking and flinging himself from side to side, trying to wrench away from her. I ran and seized Hermann's wrist, but he was stronger than I expected. Slender as his wrist was in my two hands, he was able to twist the knife suddenly, first toward himself and then toward me. I had to step back to escape its thrust. Incredulous, I cried out his name, protesting, but he seemed not to hear. His face was pale and distracted, absent looking, yet with an expression of impersonal resolve. Then for a moment anger contorted it as he summoned the force to break away.

For all Mimi's strength, his body's spasmodic heaves of effort were becoming almost too much for us. As I clung to his wrist I was half lifted off my feet and swung to one side and then the other, the knife jerking in directions I was never prepared for. Hermann really intended, I soon realized, to point the knife toward his own neck. I concentrated on preventing this, forgetting to guard against the rebound, when to loosen my hands he suddenly shifted the position of his. The knife grazed my cheek.

Mimi reproached him. Hermann, his face shocked as he saw the scratch, relaxed his hold. At that moment Mimi let go of one arm and brought her right hand down with a chop that sent the knife clattering to the floor. I caught it up and carried it away. When I had hidden it I came back to hear Mimi trying to argue with him openly against suicide. I begged him to promise not to try it again, but he only looked around desperately as if for another method. Mimi told me to phone Chestnut Lodge. Hermann moaned, entreating me not to phone. His voice had changed from before, had lost all fight and resolve. But I had to make the call, which I had agreed to do if things went wrong.

I hoped later that the next forty minutes did no real damage to Claudia. The atmosphere was tense but quiet when I let her in. Seeing Hermann's desolate face she tried to interest him in *Ferdinand the Bull.* When he hardly glanced at the book she turned to me as if to ask, "What can I do next?" I told her it was time for her nap, and she went quietly, perhaps welcoming rest from what she could sense but not comprehend. Luckily she was asleep when the ambulance came. But others in the house were not.

As Terence and a second young man half-carried him out, Hermann looked back, pleading with us not to do this to him. I could only tell him, after a murmured word with Mimi, that I would follow and meet him at Chestnut Lodge.

But he was nowhere in sight when I arrived. Dr. Bullard was waiting, saying genially that he gathered the experiment had not

gone too swimmingly. My account of the weekend confirmed his
hunch that the timing was no better than when we first came up
with the idea. At least, I said, the delay had given them time to send
the case history to Dr. Meyer.

Dr. Bullard looked blank, and I explained that since Dr. Meyer
had promised to give an opinion on the basis of the case history, Dr.
Fromm-Reichmann had said she would send it as soon as she could.
The time element was important, from what we had learned. Dr.
Bullard asked rather sardonically what we had learned, and from
whom. When I mentioned Florence, he shrugged away the opinion
of a "child psychologist." Not pausing to correct him I said she had
contacts in New York who gave her firsthand information. "And
just what did she pick up in the big city?" Dr. Bullard asked.

I took his question at face value and tried to repeat what Florence
had said, about how they thought the shock gave the patient a sort
of psychic rest. When Dr. Bullard questioned this theory I re-
counted as much as I could of what we all had read and discussed. It
seemed that the patient suffered threats to his ego, panic states and
fears, which kept him constantly mobilized for defense; that part of
his nervous system would be working overtime. When he went into
shock he was spared, for a while, the fruitless spending of energy.

I think it was at about this point that Dr. Fromm-Reichmann
came in, and I faltered. She begged me to continue, saying she found
it very interesting. Her ironic tone struck me as unfair, and maybe a
spurt of anger made me more articulate, comparing the period in
shock to an animal's hibernation, which conserved energy. Dr.
Fromm-Reichmann said she did not concede that this could be an
energy-conserving state, but asked me to proceed. The doctors
listened with the forbearing look they probably gave all patients'
families who tried to interfere. I couldn't really blame them, and I
found it hard to keep on with what we had learned: the vegetative
state that seemed to permit the patient to escape temporarily from
reality — the reality of his own problem — and be able to make
a fresh start after each treatment. Dr. Sakel had called it a protective therapy.

Dr. Fromm-Reichmann was leaning forward, waiting to answer,
and she spoke intensely. If she gave insulin to a patient, which

would excite him at first, then activate his psychotic symptoms and finally send him into the kind of convulsions suffered by epileptics, with the profuse perspiration that surely was associated with massive expenditure of energy, she would hardly call it "protective therapy." An organism under such an assault could not, in her opinion, be said to be enjoying a rest.

She spoke convincingly, as always. But to my own amazement I was able to summon up Florence's answer. She had explained it as a psychic rest, even if physically strenuous. And during the period of coma the patient would be free from those needs to invent systems of delusions to protect his ego, etc. Dr. Fromm-Reichmann asked how anyone could know whether a patient lying in a state of coma was experiencing a psychic rest.

This cowed me; I was suddenly twelve years old, the stepchild in a new school. How could I speak with grown-up dignity? But I clung to Dr. Sakel's results, printed in black and white. I must have sounded like a stubborn child, insisting that the reports told of patients being relieved of their tensions for longer and longer periods; sometimes they didn't recur. There was the usual argument about whether these so-called cures were real, or permanent. Both doctors spoke of the mysterious cases of spontaneous remission, in which the illness simply disappeared, sometimes for good. No one could be sure about what caused them.

The doctors were standing now, meaning to end the interview. But I had been brought up in a debating family, and I couldn't let that opening go by. If Dr. Sakel's cures were spontaneous remissions, he had said, then Fate must have been on the side of his deceiving people, for he had an abnormal number compared to the typical percentage.

I don't remember how they answered that; I was bracing myself to discuss practical plans. Ernst and I had decided we had to, and I did. In the end Dr. Bullard said they would allow — or rather, had no power to prevent — our fooling around with any new therapy, however risky. I turned to Dr. Fromm-Reichmann and asked if she had heard from Dr. Meyer.

She shook her head, her lips tight. Dr. Bullard boomed out that Meyer was a busy man. I couldn't keep them standing; neither could

I leave with this hanging. At the door I turned and dared to ask the explicit question: Had Dr. Fromm-Reichmann sent the history to Dr. Meyer? She hesitated, then said she had been most occupied. Dr. Bullard pointed out that such a history could not be turned out in ten minutes. And that I of all people should think of the demands on her time; she had been seeing my husband an hour every day for a year. That last word scared me. I reminded them that the insulin treatment was most hopeful before the end of the first year.

"The layman always loves statistics," Dr. Bullard said, waiting for me to go. But I couldn't, until I'd asked Dr. Fromm-Reichmann once more how soon she could send the history. She repeated coldly that she had said she would send it as soon as possible. Then there was nothing I could do but leave.

At home, climbing the stairs, I met the owner of the house coming down. She paused, and I expected her usual warm greeting. Her lips parted but she did not speak. Neither did she smile; silently she went on down the stairs. I puzzled over this but not enough, preoccupied as I was, to guess what her look might mean.

CHAPTER 30

Work and Claudia saved me from becoming totally obsessed, those next two weeks. Looking back I see even the election campaign as only a backdrop for the main action — or inaction. Then suddenly I reached my limit. Without calling first I drove out to Chestnut Lodge.

The secretary (I think her name was Bates) said hastily that Dr. Fromm-Reichmann was off duty and Dr. Bullard away for the weekend. She was giving me a wary look, and no wonder. I hadn't even said hello to her, and my hands were shaking. I drew breath and tried to speak calmly. Maybe she herself could help me find out why the case history had not reached Dr. Meyer. I had requested it nearly a month ago, and last week Dr. Fromm-Reichmann had said it had been delayed getting into the mail. What was the situation now?

I would have to ask the doctor, she said. But phoning Dr. Fromm-Reichmann was out of the question on her day off. It took me some minutes of persistence before the plug went into the switchboard. There was no answer. I asked then to see the copy of the history that had been sent. Mrs. Bates jerked up straight and said of course she could not show a case history, even if. . . . Her flush as she broke off, biting her lip, made me almost feel sorry for her as I pushed on, demanding just a glance at the sheets of paper from a distance.

She could only shake her head, hot-faced, and I knew I was wasting my time. Outside, I turned without thinking into the woods where Hermann and I had so often walked. If he had been with me today I would have been trying to stir his senses into the feel of the sun coming through the autumn coolness and the sight of the birch leaves flickering like transparent gold coins between the dark hemlock boughs. He was only a hundred yards from me now, but locked in the disturbed wing, where he had been since the disastrous visit home. But today the pain of that awareness was swallowed up and almost numbed by the drive that had brought me here.

I was walking steadily — marching, really — along the path to Dr. Fromm-Reichmann's cottage. If she had not answered her phone, she obviously was not there. And yet I walked on, my steps speeding up with my heartbeat. Maybe the secretary had given her some sort of signal by the way she rang. But that suspicion was too much like one of the conspiracies that Hermann imagined.

Still, the case history had not arrived. That was a fact, not a delusion. Four weeks had gone by, punctuated by explanations of too many mischances, postponements, forgotten promises. I made myself approach the door and ring the bell. Heard from outside, a silence can have strange echoes. As I waited, this one tugged at some association. Then I remembered: the Sunday Hermann was home I had felt this same suspense before I rushed in.

A lady never rang a doorbell more than once, I had been told severely at age five. Now I pressed my thumb to the button again and held it there. Its steady ringing rasped through my body, yet gave me a sort of satisfaction. The door opened a few inches and I met Fromm-Reichmann's furious eyes. She said sharply that she had not expected to see me there. She had in fact given orders against being interrupted in her studies.

I saw the door begin to close. With sudden strength I thrust my shoulder against it and pushed in, still unable to speak. I was beyond apologies anyway. Remembering the room I entered that day I see it now as light and pleasant. But the chairs and sofa facing the fireplace gave me a feeling of weakness, almost of nausea. The chintz pattern was the same as in the room where I had waited, on that first visit, while Hermann came down the stairs. I found a straight chair and tried to seat myself as if I had a right to.

Dr. Fromm-Reichmann stood by her desk frowning, her pen poised like a rebuke. I saw the lines between her eyebrows as more than ever like scars. Against the light her cinnamon hair seemed to catch fire. As I began to tell her my errand she broke in with a scathing question: Could I be as naive as to expect that the family of a patient could be let to read such documents?

I said once more that I had only needed to assure myself that it had been sent, and the date; the original had not reached Dr. Meyer even as late as yesterday. When she said that most probably it had been received today, I felt a sense of finality, as if something in me had given out. Maybe it was my faith. I had listened to these statements too long. The exchange that followed was quick and urgent, with questions cut off by hasty answers. When exactly had the history been sent? Her answer was evasive, mentioning that she had dictated it. But she must have signed it? Of course. But on what day? She could not tell me; most probably Wednesday, possibly Thursday.

At the time I was not even amazed at her letting this happen, at her defensive tone as she explained her delay after promising last Saturday that it would go out on Monday. She had been busy, but perhaps it had been mailed Tuesday. That would have made it all the stranger that it had not arrived in Baltimore by Friday. She murmured something about routines in large institutions; also the American mail system. I took this up. In case the report had been lost in transit we should send Dr. Meyer the carbon copy.

She welcomed the idea; if only, she said, to relieve my anxieties. I may have tried to protest that my anxieties were not the point, but she was saying kindly that after such a year I could not be expected to see quite normally any situation relating to my husband. That I had become emotional — even possibly hysterical — gave her no surprise. She would in fact be glad to give me professional counsel in her office. But today, even in my anxiety, I must grant her certain rights of privacy at home.

The reproof humbled me. Perhaps I even made a move to go. Whether I heard a breath of too telling relief I don't know, but something brought back the hard resolve that had taken me there. I said I could be calm if she would put that carbon in the mail. Promising to take care of the matter most definitely on Monday, she started to lead the way to the door. My muscles responded, but I found I could check them. I said I must mail it myself, or see it mailed.

Then she whirled on me, angrily asking if I did not trust her.

I could not quite say the word "no," but managed to speak, reminding her that she had said she wanted to help me deal with my anxieties. Now they had reached the point where nothing else would relieve them.

To my surprise she smiled and spoke gently. Of course she wished to relieve my distress. But it was Saturday; the files were in the office, and the office was closed. I pointed out that I had talked to Mrs. Bates on the way here. Surely we could phone her.

Dr. Fromm-Reichmann changed again, and in a frightening way. She drew deep breaths and pulled herself erect until, small as she was, she seemed formidable, standing stiff before me with her breast swelling until it seemed that something fierce would burst forth from her. She turned and walked to the telephone, dialed, then waited silently, expressively, even triumphantly.

Maybe this was one of the times I almost weakened. But I suddenly realized that she might have been dialing any number, one she knew would not answer. I suggested that we simply walk over and get the file. But the office was locked, she said. And inside the office the files were also locked.

With a sort of weary doggedness I questioned her about systems and rules, whether she had a copy of the case history in her own office, whether even if these files were locked she had a key. Her answers became more and more unbelievable. She could not keep her keys here, she said, since the cottage was so vulnerable, as I had proved. I felt curiously unresponsive; by now I knew only that I had to see this through. Vaguely surprised that she kept on answering, I asked where her keys were, and she said they were with Dr. Bullard. Since he was away, then, she had no access at all to her office? This, I said, seemed strange.

Again she became a figure of fury. I had doubted her word. But somehow her anger came too late. Her darkening face failed to affect me. I sat watching in a sort of scientific interest as her nostrils dilated and the cords tautened in her throat. I said I had a feeling that a way could be found to get into her office.

She was suddenly all civility. She suggested that we discuss this like reasonable people. Though I had asked what she could not grant at the moment, I must believe that she was ready to carry out my request, even let me see the copy mailed, if I came on Monday. She would be sorry for the extra trip.

I interrupted to say that the trip did not matter, but the two days' delay did. If the report was sent today it would be there Monday.

She asked why should two days of delay suddenly become so important now? Her inflection told me everything. But I put it into words. Did she mean, I asked flatly, what were two days more, after four weeks' delay?

Her moment of tolerance was over. She began to berate me for breaking into her brief chance to rest. To rest, she went on, from giving care to troubled patients, to suffering with their sufferings, experiencing with them their agonies. I could not imagine, she said, the intensity of their mutual agony. And now she had to bear this from me. That I should accuse her of bad faith when she had given all this devotion to my husband.

I felt humbled once more. True, there was no reason to doubt her devotion to Hermann. I wanted to explain that my coming here today did not mean I was not grateful. But I knew I must not try. I had to hold on to this strange dull control. I remember the feeling of my spine pushed against the wood of that chair as I sat rigid, stolidly silent.

Dr. Fromm-Reichmann began walking up and down the room. The wind was wailing out in the evergreens. Falling leaves and pine needles flashed bright beyond the windows while she spoke. She had gone each day to my husband, she said, listened to the deep troubles he had brought to her. She had devoted all her art to achieve his recovery from these injuries caused by others.

I was moved, even though she meant I was one of the "others." But just as I tried to think what answer I could give without breaking down, she suddenly began to rage again, at my intrusion here, at my doubts of her integrity. And she added an unexpected reproach.

I was trying to destroy her *amour propre,* the strength and sureness that patients needed in their doctor.

I had not intended that. It seemed unfair that I should be blamed for it, under the circumstances. But I told her I was sorry. And felt my control slip. She took advantage of this. Addressing the whipping boughs beyond the window she asked if at this late moment it was enough for one who had done this damage to say that she was sorry. Perhaps it was her histrionic tone that gave me assurance. I answered her rhetorical question, saying that no, it was not enough. I had to ask one more thing. She broke in to say her patience was finished, that I must immediately go.

I sat shaking my head. It may have been a sort of second wind that made me know that I could sit on this chair indefinitely. She cried out that she would send for an attendant, that I would be treated like any person who had become irrational. As she grew more emotional I felt more deeply calm. I sat looking up into her eyes, meeting their irate stare. Then suddenly they closed, and in the moment before her hands came up to cover it her face became distorted, and she was weeping aloud.

The little woman — she was really small now, hunched over, a pitiful figure — was half-falling to the sofa, where she sat huddled, her elbows drawn together as her hands pressed against her face, her hair falling over her fingers. Her shoulders were jerking, and timed with the jerks came sounds that were painful to hear, from this woman I had respected and sometimes almost worshipped. I was all but ready then to take back my demands. But I sat tightly still.

The sounds kept coming, the amazing gulps and groans and snorting gasps, so incongruous from someone who lectured before international meetings. I sat just waiting, until at last on a rush of breath she whispered that I had achieved what I wanted, if that gave me any satisfaction. Even then I had to have this stated openly, as if for some listening witness. I asked if she was admitting that not only had she not sent the case history but had not actually written it. I did not ask why; I think I resisted knowing. It was enough that she nodded her head, wiping her face with the back of her hand as a child would. Did I wish a formal apology? The question came with a sob, and I said no. I knew she would send the history now; that was all I wanted.

Hoping that my knees would hold me I stood up quickly and turned away from her still streaming tears. Only when I was outside did I look down at my own coat and see that running over the brown suede were little trails of pale gray, wetly gleaming like the tracks of a snail.

CHAPTER 31

With all my nerves tuned to hear from Dr. Fromm-Reichmann or Dr. Meyer, I was slow to catch the import of the visit from upstairs. Looking embarrassed and unhappy, my landlady spoke in a tone of careful kindness. She sympathized with my situation, she said, but frankly she didn't feel capable of dealing with the sort of problems that might come up in the future. Though she hated to inconvenience me, she had other plans for the apartment.

At first I was as puzzled as I was shocked; she had seemed my friend, and almost maudlin over Claudia. Why would she do this to us? Then I saw the scene she must have witnessed: Terence and the other young man forcing Hermann into the ambulance. And others had probably seen it too. Perhaps she had heard from a neighbor or two. I was ready to take a stand against the injustice. But even if she relented, could I bear to have Hermann come back here to meet hostility? In any case, the Party would never allow me to make this kind of commotion. A plan began to take form.

With Hermann in Stony Lodge getting treatment, I could find a place near enough for him to come for visits as he got better. I would rent an apartment in New York and earn my living free-lancing. Mary could arrange a leave of absence from my job while I waited to see where Hermann would want to live when he was well.

Mary promised to make sure my leave of absence went through if that was the only way to keep me technically on her staff, though she urged me not to move too fast. I rejected the warning in this advice. But at least I censored my next letter to Hermann's parents, saying only that everything was up in the air while I waited for Dr. Meyer's response.

He was remarkably prompt. A phone call on Thursday asked me to come to Baltimore. I suppose I must have shown my urgency, for I was given an appointment for that very evening.

Memory has perhaps romanticized my first sight of Johns Hopkins because of what took place there. I kept a picture of turrets against the sunset sky, and an inviting glow in the small building to which I was directed. But it fulfilled its promise, from the minute I heard the voice of the tall Scotsman who assured me that I had come to the "rrright" place. This was Dr. Cameron. He said both he and Dr. Meyer had read the case history, and he had been delegated to pass their thinking on. In almost intolerable suspense, of course, I waited for the verdict.

But first Dr. Cameron had questions to ask. He wanted to hear from me, as Dr. White had, about our marriage, my child, our home life. With his encouragement I told him what Hermann had said in the personal note he had given me with his ominous public statement, assuring me of his love in the kind of specifics that made it convincing — about my "dash and vitality," my "daring and confidence," that had been precious until they became a danger. I assumed Dr. Fromm-Reichmann had reported Hermann's close friendship with Ernst, but I felt I had to repeat Florence's assertion that in marrying me Hermann had in effect been marrying Claud.

Dr. Cameron seemed more interested in the disciple relation to Carter Goodrich. The real picture, I thought, should focus on Hal Ware, whose guidance Hermann had lost just when he counted on it for the German Embassy assignment. (Already trusted there, Hermann might next have been ordered to Germany.) But I could not bring myself to speak. With the stern discipline required by the Moscow trials and the war against fascism in Spain, I dared not reveal any Party secrets. In effect, for a moment, I shut out Dr. Cameron's kindly Scottish burr and imagined instead Steve's harsh growl.

Meanwhile Dr. Cameron was saying that Dr. Meyer was concerned about the physical risks of insulin shock. Each day's procedure

— perhaps each hour's — depended on expert judgment of the preceding day's or hour's. But when I said that Dr. Sakel himself would be in charge at Stony Lodge, he spoke the words I was waiting for.

"In that case Dr. Meyer's opinion is favorable."

I don't remember what I said, or even if I managed to form words. Tears were close, and may have come. But after a time I did falter out some sort of thanks for their quick action. Dr. Cameron said he hoped the thanks were not for a prognosis of success, which they definitely could not offer. It was a question of alternatives.

I suppose I didn't let myself consider what this really meant. And he spoke no more until we were walking together down the driveway. As we stood by the car he said in his kind voice that regardless of any therapy we tried, he thought I was on the right path. And I should keep on traveling it, whatever happened. I didn't understand, and his explanation kept me pondering all the way home. He said, as nearly as I can quote him, "It's all you *can* trust to — in one way or another — the giving and receiving of love."

Startling as the words were, they seemed somehow deeply true. It was only when I tried to reproduce the conversation for Ernst that I saw how difficult they might be for a scientific mind to accept.

Ernst was often dissatisfied by the doctors' statements. At his puzzled look I quoted Dr. Cameron's warning about success. "And it's a question of alternatives." At this he nodded with a troubled frown. Maybe at that moment I came near absorbing the full implications. But how could I let such thoughts come to mind then, when he was here to take Hermann from Chestnut Lodge to a possible cure?

Driving out from Washington, Ernst kept reading the road signs aloud — a habit that Hermann had once called maddening. Reverting to it now suggested he was nervous. Certainly I was. Could Dr. Fromm-Reichmann have found some new way to hold on to Hermann?

Ernst began to speak reflectively about history repeating itself. He remembered another time when Hermann had to break the grip of a strong woman, his mother. Never, Ernst said, had he witnessed a scene of such ferocity. Hermann had accepted an invitation from one of his teachers, a young baron. Ernst had come in just as Hermann's mother was angrily accusing him of snobbery, preferring to ski with a *Freiherr* rather than stay home for the rest of his father's leave from the army. Ernst himself, he said, might not have had the courage to stand up to such a tirade. But Hermann had. He wouldn't ever let himself be dominated or manipulated, even by his mother, to whom he was closer intellectually than to his father.

We may have talked then, as we had before, of how frustrating Oma's role of hausfrau must have been. Now I thought that she might have been jealous, too, of this professor, whose life Hermann had once saved on a river trip. But I dared not ask Ernst if he himself had been jealous of that professor. How complicated it all was!

When we entered the gloomy anteroom we found Hermann waiting for us with his suitcase beside him. Dr. Bullard boomed out a jovial greeting, calling this a red-letter day. Helping Hermann on with his coat, he said something about their being sorry to lose him, but on the whole it seemed a smart move. He turned to Dr. Fromm-Reichmann, who had just come in, and asked if she didn't agree. To my amazement she said she did; that now and at all times only the best was wished for him. I believed this. And as I took her hand in leaving I felt sorry for the pain I had caused her.

Once outdoors, as always, Hermann seemed better, glancing to the roadsides with interest. But then his shoulders would tense and he would frown. I don't know what the doctors had told him; with his delusions he must have thought he was being trapped into another tormenting ordeal. Which this time was literally true.

I was no less nervous than before. Ernst was reading aloud a series of Burma Shave signs:

"Keep well to the right"
(then a hundred yards further)
"Of the oncoming car"

(and next)

    "Get your close shave"

(and finally)

    "From the half-pound jar!"

Hermann gave no sign of being either amused or irritated. We arrived early at Union Station, as planned. This was not a day for taking chances. But once installed in the compartment, I wished it could have been later, with the train about to move. As we waited, even now, something might prevent our going. I tried to mock my fears. Did I expect a great clatter of hooves as some sheriff and his posse came riding across the plaza and down the platform?

I was grateful for Ernst's composure. But before I could signal him a warning he stepped off the train to buy newspapers, which I was sure the doctors did not allow. Returning, he tossed a Hershey bar to Hermann, who caught it, pleased: "Ah, almond!" He was unwrapping it as we slid out of the station.

My relief made the compartment seem a festive place. Ernst began to read out the final election results. Roosevelt had won five hundred electoral votes in spite of Father Coughlin's boasts that he would force the decision into the House of Representatives. The president joked about the need of embassies in Maine and Vermont, the only states voting against him; and would the pending appointment of a Maine judge be legal, since the Constitution required that judges be U.S. citizens?

This hardly seemed dangerous for Hermann to hear about, and Ernst made the election last all the way to Philadelphia. With every appearance of enjoying it himself, he laughed (as I couldn't) over the story about Father Divine, whose thriving organization was supported by the wages of his female "angels" as domestics. He had forbidden them to vote, but it looked as if all the other Negroes in the country who had been allowed to vote had gone for Roosevelt. They had ignored the NAACP's warning about the president's bad record on civil rights. For the first time they had deserted the Republican Party. "We paid Lincoln all we owe him. Now we're free."

Hermann seemed less and less interested. Ernst started talking in German, putting the *Times* down. I turned to the inside pages and found what I wanted:

Socialists Lose Ground
Communists Tally Even Less

The Party candidate for governor of New York had not even chalked up 40,000 votes, as compared to 120,000 four years before. Since our membership was far higher now than then, this meant that the great majority had voted Democratic, giving Lehman the edge that elected him. Browder had tacitly expressed satisfaction, which proved that we comrades had rightly discerned what the Party wanted us to do.

It was dusk when we reached New York; Florence had planned for us to arrive after her day at the clinic was over. Hermann seemed relieved to see her; as the hired limousine rolled along the West Side highway he looked out eagerly, identifying the S.S. *Britannia* and the *Ile de France*.

That mood could not last. The autumn evening was melancholy, the suburbs unwelcoming; the warmly lighted houses seemed to shut us out. After a while they became fewer, the roads narrower, deserted, circling around great expanses of black water and then plunging into tunnels of evergreen. At last we came to a filling station where the driver could ask directions. Dimly in the field beyond was a billboard with a tattered poster left over from Hoover days. Ernst read it aloud while we waited: "Nothing can stop US." Hermann must have heard the forced sound of Ernst's chuckle.

Florence angrily criticized the driver. She had given him a map, she said, that plainly showed Stony Lodge. At that, of course, Hermann stirred uneasily beside me. I gripped his hand, murmuring something about people's varying ability to read maps.

The driver came running back, saying we'd be there in two shakes of a lamb's tail. More houses did line the road now, but with fewer and fewer lights as the hour grew late. After the village of Ossining the route was clear, and we followed it up a steeply winding road to arrive in a parking lot walled on one side by woods. On the other was a half circle of modern structures, their cubes and octagons bulking solid against the night sky over the river. On the shore a constellation of lights pricked out the shape of a large institution, which I was later glad that we hadn't recognized as Sing Sing prison.

Here there was only one small naked lamp above the nearest door, and that did not look like an office, as Florence said irritably. I thought I had seen a sign with an arrow as we made the last turn. Ernst borrowed the driver's flashlight, jumped out and ran back. The disk of brilliance stopped on the door of a one-story building. We sat silent while nothing happened. Hermann's breathing was audible in the car.

Then Florence began to talk, to my amazement, about Mrs. Simpson's threatened marriage to Edward VIII. What had *The Week* said? Actually it had told of a secret tip that Claud's office would be visited by one of the king's henchmen in the dead of night. But I answered something noncommittal, appalled that she should remind Hermann of Claud at a time like this. Hermann was drawing his hand from mine and leaning toward the door.

Ernst arrived just then, saying he couldn't raise anyone at the administration building; he would try the lighted door. Florence said that was the best thing; switching to her magically gentle tone she said he would find someone, and everything would be all right. But it seemed to be too late. Hermann sat forward tensely watching the lighted circle on the closed door. Ernst was silhouetted against it, his arm lifting. We heard the dim sound of knocking, then finally his voice, loud, and louder knocking. Suddenly the light disappeared.

The next wait seemed even longer. Florence filled the silence as best she could, her tone soothing at first. But she could not hold back her exasperation, saying she had made arrangements with Dr. Glueck himself. A sudden flurry erupted at the door: voices, female and shrill, figures in confusion against the light. Then the door closed and Ernst came back. There had been a misunderstanding, but it was straightened out; someone would receive us.

Hermann was making small low sounds that were more painful to hear than his most extreme words. A careless ear might have heard them as animal-like, but they were not; this was the only purely human illness, Marion had quoted Sakel as saying. Animals

283

could catch infections and have cancer, but they could not have a psychosis, which was a dysfunction of the human brain. But a reversible dysfunction! I clung to that.

Florence was speaking in her motherly voice about how good the clean sheets would feel to Hermann after the long day. Hermann tried to answer, apparently protesting, but unable to formulate words. To him, I knew, all ahead was frighteningly mysterious and threatening, against which the prospect of clean sheets would hardly give him comfort.

Ernst was coming back with a woman. Lights appeared in the octagonal building on the right. The doctor (I think her name was Metzger) introduced herself nervously, shaking hands with Florence. Her apology was almost incoherent as she turned to Hermann. He shrank back from her, gripping my hand. When I made a move to go with him Dr. Metzger cited a rule that only psychiatrists could visit patients at night. Florence offered her hand in place of mine but he did not let go. In the end I had to detach his fingers. The parting evoked the day we had left him at Chestnut Lodge. But I told myself that this was different. Though Hermann could not believe it now, soon he would be walking out of here once more his real self, confident and sure.

I said something of this to Ernst when we were alone. He looked at me doubtfully; I had to remind him that Dr. Glueck had mentioned a period of weeks. He shrugged, and after a moment of staring into the darkness, began to laugh.

I peered at his face, astounded. All this must have made him hysterical, I thought. But he explained that his absence had been so long because he had been locked in with the women patients — about twenty of them, who had cornered him, some aggressive, each for her own purposes. Either hostile or the opposite, all found him an object of intense curiosity, or of hilarity. The one nurse on duty had a hard time getting them away from him. It was funny, I supposed; but his laughter, I thought, was from nerves.

Florence came back full of enthusiasm. As we drove away she told about the ingenious floor plan of the octagonal building. Each room opened from a central circular hall where someone could keep constant surveillance through one-way windows in the doors. How

Hermann would hate that! But Florence said matter-of-factly that since in any case he always thought people were watching him, he might as well have the benefit of the safety. Hermann's private room was as good as he could have had in a first class hotel. She described the wall-to-wall carpeting, concealed ceiling and baseboard lighting, electrically heated floors, and nonobjective paintings on the wall. "All the furnishings are of the very highest quality." Having seen that luxury, her worry now was how she could hold Dr. Glueck's rates down.

I thought he had assured her about that. He had, she said, in general terms. He had said, after reading the document Hermann had written, that it would be a privilege to treat such a distinguished mind. But that smooth talk had to be translated into dollars and cents. She was planning her tactics now. Here was a man at the peak of his promise, she would tell Dr. Glueck in the morning, who until a year ago...

A year ago. True, it was almost that long. But at least he was here now.

Dr. Glueck was a stout man with rosy, immaculate skin and eyes like black olives. He was dressed as a country gentleman — dark flannel shirt, good tweed suit of grays flecked with orange that matched his wool tie.

When Florence began as planned, saying that Hermann had been finishing a report that was the high point of the Carter Goodrich group's research, and which would be published in January by a university press, Dr. Glueck raised his hand to suggest she needn't go on. Of all the patients they were being asked to help with Dr. Sakel's treatment, he fully believed this might be the mind most worth salvaging. The satisfactions of succeeding would be immense, but he warned that the problems were commensurate. According to Dr. Sakel's theory, to which he subscribed, all the intelligence of that wonderful cortex was now being directed to the destruction of the total organism. Merely to outwit these schemes would be no easy task.

Florence was quicker than I to see where this was leading. She said she assumed the usual precautions would be taken. Not just the usual precautions, he said. These people could be very ingenious.

"These people." I hated the words. But then they began to register. Patients could quiet down, be meek and submissive, bide their time, put on a show of sanity that would fool anyone, "until you'd think nothing was further from their thoughts, then bingo!" They had been all the time on the lookout for a nail file or a piece of wire.

Here Dr. Glueck asked Florence if she had noticed that the pictures were not hung. Instead they were stuck to the wall with suction cups — an idea of his own. But actually these people didn't need anything conventional. They could choke themselves with anything from a butter paddle to a golf ball, or if they couldn't find anything they'd perch up on a dresser and throw themselves off.

Seeing my face he added reassuringly: "But we're always one step ahead." There was not a high surface or a sharp corner in all Stony Lodge. Conceding that she had been impressed by the arrangements, Florence began to talk about costs. Even what he might consider lowered rates could be too much for me. Dr. Glueck reminded her that it wasn't a long-term proposition. In six weeks we might be seeing light at the end of the tunnel, and in eight we might be talking departure dates.

These words may have made me lightheaded; I asked Dr. Glueck if it wouldn't be better for me to have a place in New York for Hermann to come to, rather than Washington with all its associations. He nodded, sliding a paper across the desk and suggesting I sign the waiver so that we might get on with our plans.

I think Florence tried to intervene, telling him I had been under great strain and my plans were a "flight of fancy." One hundred twenty-five dollars a week was more than my whole salary. But in the end that was the rate we agreed on.

As we started down the hill she rebuked me for speaking of the apartment. I tried to explain, as I had not been able to before, that the apartment would not be an extra expense. I knew how to live cheaply in New York, and I had editor friends who would give me work. As we hurried along the path to the station, Florence in her high heels twisted her ankle. Pain may have affected her mood, for she gestured with distaste toward the massive prison buildings, commenting grimly on Dr. Glueck's choice of a view for his patients.

Childishly I resisted criticism of the doctor who had given us such hope. "I like Dr. Glueck," I said, remembering the moment he had spoken the words, "departure dates." "At one point I could have kissed him."

We had reached the platform, and she turned with a short laugh. "You said you felt like kissing him because you felt like killing him."

The train was coming then, and on our silent ride into the city I tried to work out that puzzle.

CHAPTER 32

The next morning I took the subway to Greenwich Village where I signed a lease at $65 a month for the second floor of a brownstone. It had two marble fireplaces, high ceilings with molded cornices, and at the back an accessible rooftop overlooking a pear tree in a garden. I could see the three of us in the spring, sitting out there breathing the fragrance of blossoms. Just sitting, being together — that seemed enough, as it had seemed to Hermann in his dream: "I was just home." Strange how the idea of perfect happiness can distill to its essence.

Since I had promised Mary that I would work as long as possible, I persuaded the New York landlord to start the lease at the time I was sure Hermann could visit. But as soon as I reached home certain realities began to overwhelm me. At the office someone had called me an "iron woman," but the strains were showing. I had been officially promoted to editor, but I still did the same work. Since nobody else on the staff felt capable of radio dialogue, I wanted to leave Mary with a series stockpiled for the future. This meant rushing around for extra interviews, writing them, getting each expert's statements approved, and then persuading the information office to okay the broadcast. My two Party meetings every week involved preparation and then carrying out directives afterward, with the tension of secrecy.

We had been given a month before moving, but I felt uncomfortable in the house, though I tried hard to keep the atmosphere cheery for Claudia. Cora was my strong partner in this, as in all our life — more than I realized at the time. She also relied on me. We had helped her, for instance, to avoid the swindles by which merchants exploited Negroes. Now she had agreed to move with us to New York. I had lured her with a huge Madison Square rally for Angelo Herndon.

One day as I climbed the stairs I met a cold greeting. It probably meant guilt rather than hostility, but I announced impulsively that we would move two weeks early. Without knowing where we would be, Cora and I packed the contents of the apartment for storage. I almost enjoyed the exhaustion; it meant the end of an intolerable period, the beginning of a life of hope.

Those days are so hazy in my memory that I'm not sure now why we didn't take refuge with my family. I know I felt the need of being close to Party comrades. When Mildred and Charles Kramer invited me to stay in their small apartment I fell into their arms. Near them was a nursery school that boarded children in emergencies.

I thought I was acting sensibly — the school was highly recommended, the women were kind, and Cora or I visited Claudia each day — but no end-of-my-tether state can excuse not imagining the pain a four-year-old, even one who has happily attended three schools, would suffer in being separated at night from her mother. She took it bravely, until she caught chicken pox, a real disaster. I was not allowed to come close enough to hug her.

Hermann's parents and I had been communicating regularly, but their letters in careful English were formal. Then suddenly one came from Opa saying he had gone down to Eleventh Street and persuaded the landlord to let him in to measure our apartment. He enclosed a floor plan to help me decide about furniture arrangement. He had even sketched in bookcases, which he offered to build.

Meanwhile the suspense was heightening. Florence had a report of Hermann's physical examination, which revealed nothing striking, she said, except an abnormal lack of adrenalin. Regrettably from a scientific point of view, they could make no comparison with his condition a year ago, since Chestnut Lodge had not given him such a checkup. The doctors had not agreed on a reason for the adrenalin lack. I asked what Dr. Sakel had thought. Florence answered angrily that he had moved on from Stony Lodge. I must have cried out at that. Hadn't Dr. Glueck promised Dr. Sakel's care? Florence, still fuming, said he had implied it, certainly, but perhaps in words that did not commit him. We could only hope Dr. Sakel had trained the other doctors well. Perhaps I pressed her on that, for she ended by reminding me that Dr. Glueck had a high stake in success. I had to pin my hopes on the reputation of Stony Lodge.

It was strange to carry this problem around in a world preoccupied with King Edward and Mrs. Simpson. At every table in the Agriculture cafeteria people were exchanging the latest bulletins on the case. Even *The Week* gave as much space to a scoop about Wally having lunch at the palace with the Queen Mother (later retracted) as to an item about Trotsky being promised asylum in Mexico. In Spain, Franco's forces were pushing into the suburbs of Madrid, and each day the shelling was more intense. Claud was there, in the same hotel with Hemingway and the other correspondents, but I learned that only later.

Franco with Hitler on his side was forging ahead. At Burgos he had declared himself head of the Spanish state; Germany and Italy promptly recognized his government. Since October, when Mussolini sent his son-in-law Ciano to visit Berlin, they had assumed that Madrid was due to fall any day.

Wrong, said *The Week*: now that the Russian airplanes had begun to strafe the Rebel lines, a quick and decisive Republican victory might be regarded as sure, if certain conditions could be met. Then followed four single-spaced pages detailing these conditions. The facts and reasoning were complex, involving dozens of interlocking possibilities, depending on military techniques and strategy.

France was now letting a Yugoslav comrade named Josip Broz (later called Tito) arrange the passage of volunteers over the border. At a unit meeting that would turn out to be almost my last, one comrade asked permission to join this international brigade. After canvassing the unit — they were all in favor — I said I would bring back an answer the next week.

This was the way I treated most questions these days. The unit would soon have a new leader — and a better one, I was sure, one really suited for such a demanding job. Even the routines, such as collecting the literature each week from an ill-lighted basement near the Capitol, were hedged around with conspiratorial techniques that took time. Having learned resourcefulness from Mother I was pretty good at handling practical emergencies. Where I fell short — where I constantly felt the lack of Hermann's guidance — was in theoretical politics. Two years earlier I would never have been considered for a unit. But in this period of the Popular Front my lack of regular Party reflexes had almost become an asset. Experienced comrades tended to be too rigid to fit in with liberals or even fellow travelers. I could guess their likely attitudes and respond according to what Mother would call common sense. Sometimes, against the protests of those who had been brought up in the movement, I would prove to have been "correct" according to reasoning much more complex than mine.

On this question of my member going to Spain, I assumed I would get an okay, since the Party was promoting the Brigade. But the answer was a flat no. The lives of people working in the Washington underground were too valuable to risk. The comrade was disappointed. But he waited till after the meeting to protest privately to me. How much of a man's life, he asked, could be spent sucking up to the boss, cocking an ear for every careless word, even poking into wastebaskets like a scavenger? This was not the right way to describe a Party member's vigilance; it was unheard-of to complain. But I couldn't reprove him. He had made me see suddenly what Hermann must have gone through.

When six weeks had passed since Hermann had entered Stony Lodge, a short note came from Dr. Glueck. Hermann was responding well to treatment. "He relaxes for longer and longer periods, and on emerging from coma reveals a personality so appealing that he has won the affection of all members of the staff who come in contact with him at that time."

292

I read the letter over and over, imagining the sweet curve of Hermann's mouth as he spoke to the nurses. But then I'd read those last three words: "at that time." Did the old delusions come back in full force during other hours? But he had made a start; now my hope felt like a band getting tighter and tighter around my chest.

Two more weeks went by. Carter came from New York for a re-union dinner with the staff at Foxhall Road. There he announced that the publisher had sent proof copies of the book to the usual journals and also to general periodicals. *Harper's* would soon publish an article based on the high points of the study. We could all cele-brate this, but as Carter walked with me to the car he told me what he had tactfully omitted before: the article would feature Her-mann's part of the study. Now I would have this to show him, as well as the book.

Soon *Migration and Economic Opportunity* came in the mail. I could actually hold it in my hands, heavy and impressive. How could Hermann doubt now, with his name plainly identifying his chapters? He would be pleased, too, at Carter's giving me credit in his acknowledgments for the stylistic results of those long hours Hermann and I had spent finding ways to avoid passive verbs.

At the next unit leaders' meeting the comrades talked excitedly about the kidnapping of Generalissimo Chiang Kai-shek. His min-isters described the kidnapper as a young hereditary warlord who had never won a battle. In fact he had lost the Manchurian pro-vinces, they said, after a series of defeats. But Vic said nobody should trust those ministers, a corrupt bunch of liars who sabo-taged the interests of the people. Vic counted on Chiang and the Communists getting together, in spite of the way things looked now. Vic had it wrong, Henry said flatly; others agreed, calling Chiang a bastard bound to betray, sooner or later. (Listening, did I wonder at these comrades using words like "betray" to mark a vil-lain, when they were devoting their days to betrayal of those who trusted them?)

293

A photographer had tried to shoot Chiang from under the black cloth, and one comrade admitted wishing that he hadn't missed. But Nat stopped this talk, saying we must analyze the situation objectively. Whatever we thought of Chiang, he was the only leader who could rally enough support to keep order in China. And the Soviet Union needed order in China. That one fact should clear up any confusion.

I suppose I nodded seriously, maybe even put in a word, but those distant figures were like the ones that moved across the sheet on which Mother used to create a shadow play. My mind focused on Stony Lodge, daydreaming the moment Hermann would come out with me and take the train to New York. I could see him exploring the apartment, looking over his books, putting on a record, then going to the kitchen and finding cold wine. With one hand holding Claudia's and a glass in the other, he would walk back and forth, humming the *Emperor* Concerto, as he had done in Falls Church.

The Sunday when ten weeks had passed, with no more bulletins, I picked Claudia up and drove with her to the Brittens. As soon as she had gone outdoors with the boys, and before I could speak of my worries, Mimi asked me to read proofs with her of an article her anthropologist chief at the Council was publishing.

"Our expedition was not the first," I read aloud, "to undertake the study of the phenomenon of death by the casting of spells..."

As I read on, slowly so that Mimi could check the manuscript, I began to pay attention to the process of laying a curse.

"First, since the community believes in the curse (a necessary prerequisite to its success) the victim becomes an outcast. He is physically separated from his family, avoided by his friends, excluded from the normal routines which up to that time have given him his sense of identity. In effect, he is banished from the world of the living, so that he experiences a kind of foretaste of death. Instead of receiving the support of his own peer group he is cast out of their circle, out of the life of the living community. He cannot preserve himself even physically as a living man against this destruction of his social personality."

Reading aloud the next sentences, about the physical effects of the torpor and anxiety, I couldn't escape their portent.

294

"The body undergoes a particularly intense activity of the sympathetic nervous system, which though ordinarily a useful effort to respond to a new situation, now because of the lack of a known channel for any effective response becomes disorganized and intensified; sometimes even within a few hours there is a decrease in the volume of blood and a corresponding drop in blood pressure, resulting in irreparable damage to the circulatory organs."

I paused, and perhaps Mimi understood why, because she waited patiently till I could go on. The rest of that galley outlined a vicious cycle: anxiety prevented the victim from eating or drinking, this decreased his blood volume further, making him still less able to withstand the psychological pressure. And so on and on, to total destruction.

When we had finally finished, and I sat staring at Mimi speechless, she reminded me that the insulin shock was supposed to have stopped whatever hyperactivity of the nervous system Hermann had suffered. But it was ten weeks now. Did Dr. Glueck's silence mean the treatment had failed? And I had heard nothing from Florence, who had promised to keep me in touch.

Mimi simply pointed to the phone on the kitchen wall. Florence answered as if she had expected my call. She had not had any news, but she said she would phone Dr. Glueck.

The next morning I found a night letter from him on my office desk: VISIT PERMISSIBLE STOP PHONE SECRETARY FOR APPOINTMENT.

I took the noon train.

CHAPTER 33

At seven that night I was in Dr. Glueck's office. He came around from behind his desk, stocky and neat in his pepper-and-salt tweed. Seeing how breathless I was, he said I should get more exercise. As he went on about the benefits of a regular regime I was reminded of Dr. Bullard's advice to take up a hobby. When I tried to get in a question about Hermann, Dr. Glueck shook his head warningly. I was in a state of tension, he said, and pointed to my hands. The fingers of my left hand were clasping the back of the right, the fingers of the right gripping the left thumb. Dr. Glueck asked significantly if I knew what that thumb represented.

Was he hinting that my grip meant I wanted to emasculate Hermann? But he said only that relaxing would make me fitter for what was ahead. When I asked quickly what *was* ahead, he begged me not to expect miracles. Still, his eyes held a jovial twinkle suggesting he might have a surprise in store for me.

Perhaps he had pushed a button earlier, for a woman in a white jacket appeared then. In the nervous voice I recognized from that first night, Dr. Metzger said she would take me to Hermann, and I followed her out through the icy dark.

She talked all the way to the octagonal building, but in unfinished sentences that I could not concentrate on enough to interpret. A nurse let us in and I crossed the soft beige carpet in Dr. Metzger's wake. She tapped on a small square pane of glass, the door opened, and Hermann was there.

His eyes lighted up as he saw me, and he caught my arm. Drawing me in, he studied my face eagerly, as he always had after even a short separation. He was still thin, but not frail as he had been before. His cheeks had color, his hand felt strong holding mine. He was better! There was no doubt of it; much, much better.

Dr. Metzger stood beside us as with a smile that seemed wistful, even envious. She was younger than I had thought, with light-lashed, gray-blue eyes and a gentle mouth. In such a moment, of course, I felt a rush of good feeling, and said something vacuous about its being a nice room, which was true. Dr. Metger gestured toward the broad studio couch in the corner, and this time there was no doubt about what she said. I could stay the night here if I wished. With Hermann's arm around me now, his lips quivering in the effort to hide his emotion, I told her that of course I would. She said goodnight and left.

Hermann kept on examining me, hungrily, commenting on my hair — it was longer — and disentangling a strand of it from an epaulette. He carried the coat to his closet with a step that seemed almost as buoyant as a year ago. I had seen him lose that buoyancy. Now it was coming back!

When we sat down together on the couch he asked about Claudia, and I told him how Roy had taken her to the Smithsonian, where she had tried earnestly to understand how the *Tyrannosaurus rex* had become extinct. As I finished I went tense, from habit, worrying that he would see something darkly significant in that extinction. But he was smiling, amused, relishing the picture. And his arm around me tightened, holding me closer.

I remembered that I had planned to show him, first of all, the book and the reviews. Now it seemed he hardly needed this reassurance. I didn't want to move. But I had promised, and it was unfair to hold back something so important. Reluctantly I left him long enough to get the book from my briefcase, opening it first to show the table of contents, and then the parts signed with his name. His smile came slowly, half incredulous. But no more than anyone would have felt: "Can it be true? After all that struggle it's actually in print?" He turned the pages in the savoring way he always had with books, tipping his head, commenting on the chapter titles, approving the binding, and finally turning to the acknowledgments. Seeing my name, he said I deserved it, and gave me the grin I loved, sharing, comradely, bringing back all those hot nights we had toiled over his manuscript.

I showed him then the article in *Harper's* that focused on his chapters. He shook his head as he scanned it, but his lips were twisting, restraining a pleased smile. He was responding, I thought, just as I had dreamed he would. Better still, in a few minutes he put down the book and the magazine and took me in his arms.

It was like the afternoon on the train when I had come back from England. With Claudia sleeping nearby we had sat together like this, his fingers playing with my hair while we made our plans to be married. Then as now his hand had dropped after a while to cup my breast; I had laid my head in the curve of his neck and rested there, knowing we had the night ahead, and the rest of our lives. Now as his lips pressed my temple, my cheekbone, moving to my mouth, softening luxuriously, I felt a sense of time expanding: we could take each moment as it came, build slowly to a joy so imperative it must be approached with caution, gradually.

It took a moment to come back, to hear the sound. The tapping was light, timid but persistent, then Dr. Metzger's voice, excusing herself for interrupting. When she came in she apologized again, but said she must take me to my room. Hermann, still breathing fast, was frowning, as puzzled as I was. I tried to say I had expected to stay here, but Dr. Metzger shook her head, picked up my suitcase and led the way to the door.

Why didn't I refuse to follow her? I have wondered often since. But that would have meant making a scene, which from habit I avoided as dangerous for Hermann. Yet wasn't it worse for him to be roused this way, then left suddenly frustrated, deprived of physical release and what he might need even more — the intimacy he had called "our fortifying flame?" With my old respect for experts I told myself there must be a reason; probably Dr. Metzger's first offer had been a serious error. Arguing would only make her unhappy and spoil the atmosphere completely.

299

I tried to tell Hermann how disappointed I was. But with Dr. Metzger standing there I couldn't make him know how much I wanted him, how I had longed for that night together. What I did say was so inadequate as to sound false. When I added that I'd see him in the morning Dr. Metzger murmured something about arranging breakfast. But that would be a mockery, I thought dismally as I left, compared to a breakfast after a night of love.

I followed Dr. Metzger into another building, down an uncarpeted corridor to an iron door, which she unlocked. The room was a sort of cubicle, with only a narrow passage between a built-in bunk and shelves recessed in the wall. The emptiness here was not merely lack of comfort; it was aggressively and cruelly barren. The atmosphere had its effect. In bed I had to fight off the kind of loneliness that is also fear. I told myself that Hermann was better, was himself; my loneliness didn't matter.

But what about his? Surely the sudden separation had been a shock — shock with an element of betrayal. It fitted his description of how a sane person can be broken down. It was even like what I'd read in the anthropology journal, the outcast under a curse. As I was thinking this I heard a scream. It was from somewhere near, a high shriek, female, wild, prolonged, rising in desperation until suddenly it was cut off, unfinished, as if a hand had closed over a mouth.

Two hours passed, maybe three, before I slept. When I woke up my watch said nine. No sunshine had come in the small window; the sky was pewter gray. I dressed hurriedly, afraid I had missed breakfast with Hermann. But when I tried the door it would not open. No one who hasn't been locked into a cell can know what it is like. Fighting panic, I searched and found a button by the light switch. When I pushed it nothing happened. I pressed it again, then sat down. I would wait five minutes. They went by, too slowly. I picked up the *New Republic* I had absently carried away, and started reading a review of *Green Hills of Africa*. "Something frightful happens," Edmund Wilson had written, "when Hemingway casts a sentence in the first person singular."

Too nervous to read on, I glanced down to the poem at the bottom of the page. Malcolm Cowley seemed to be saying it was less terrifying to hunt hippopotami on the banks of a jungle river than to stalk the enemies within the mind. Hermann must not see this, I thought. At least my maddening wait was serving some purpose. I turned to the review of *Migration and Economic Opportunity,* tore it out and dropped the rest of the magazine in the wastebasket. Then I began to beat on the door.

After a few minutes I heard a key in the lock. A nurse appeared, looking surprised. When I told her who I was, she said she thought I was staying with my husband. I was more and more confused. What had happened, who had made the change? Dr. Metzger, on her own? She had seemed so kind.

Hermann was waiting, his head tilted in question. I apologized for oversleeping. He said I must have been tired, and asked if I had had breakfast. With my hands on his shoulders, my cheek against his, I said of course I wouldn't have eaten without him. But his lips did not search for mine. And at that moment a nurse knocked and brought in a tray with coffee and rolls.

I had hardly taken a sip when Dr. Glueck came in, exclaiming with all Dr. Bullard's heartiness about how Stony Lodge was proud to provide coffee for lovebirds at any hour. Slapping Hermann on the back, he asked me if I didn't think he was doing fine. I started to answer, but he had turned to Hermann, speaking louder, as if to someone hard of hearing, asking him if he was going to show his lady wife around the place. With a laugh he said he could skip the gym, then turned to tell me (speaking in a normal tone again) that some people didn't take to jumping leather horses. And they might even balk at occupational therapy.

I hesitated, troubled by his using that word "they," and addressing me as if Hermann weren't present. But he had swung around, his hand still on Hermann's shoulder, proposing a trip to the Lodge's farm. He would be going out there in half an hour.

To my surprise — at first, before I realized that his old courtesy had come back — Hermann agreed, after making sure that both of us were invited. Of course, Dr. Glueck said, and again used the phrase "lovebirds." That and his suggestive laugh made me wonder if he knew what had happened last night. He left, reminding us once more to meet him on the driveway at ten minutes to ten precisely. His booming voice echoed in the silence when he left.

I began to give Hermann a censored report on Christmas. It had been a painful day for me, but Claudia was happy with the old-fashioned red sled Mary had given her, the kind pictured under the tree in nineteenth-century children's books. He smiled, asking about the boys. I described the festoons of paper-clip chains Roy had hung in the basement, through which he sent an electric charge that made sparks for Claudia's excitement.

I was sitting on the divan where we had sat together last night, but instead of joining me he walked restlessly around the room. While I was talking he listened, but when I paused he became preoccupied. Yet not — though I couldn't put my finger on the difference — in the way of this past year, as if beyond some invisible wall. It was more like the times when he took walks to think out a problem in his work. He kept glancing at his watch, and at twenty minutes to ten said we should go out to the driveway. He got my coat from the closet, helped me on with it, and put on his own. I wondered why he was so eager to go to the farm. Had he established such a rapport with Dr. Glueck?

The day was cold and raw. As we walked up and down the driveway I tried for a light note, imitating Cora: "Shua gonna snow befo' nightfall." Hermann's smile was his own. He said the difference was that when she had said it would snow it always had. I hated that past tense and hurried to tell him that Claudia had learned from Cora how to smell a change in the weather hours ahead, and announced it the same way.

"People probably possess this kind of sensitivity in inverse ratio to their literacy." Hermann's reflective tone, which was so much part of what I loved in him, made my throat tighten with joy. And he went on to say that Claudia would probably lose that ability when she learned to read.

Then Cora might too, I told him. She was doing more reading these days. At this Hermann's interest sharpened, bringing back my caution. For he asked quickly what she was reading. I dared not tell him she read the *Daily Worker,* a habit that had started when Claudia, having found our secret cache, had tried to flush a copy down the toilet. Dutifully drying it on the radiator, Cora had noticed a story about the Scottsboro boys. Next day she calmly asked for the following issue. I gave it to her, poker-faced in my guilt. My carelessness in hiding the papers was unforgivable.

Still, the Party made a point of recruiting Negroes. We had a plank in our platform calling for them to have a state of their own in the South. The big obstacle to recruiting was their devotion to religion. But Cora's seemed not to check her; she was learning fast. I wanted to tell Hermann, ask him how much to encourage her. But all I said was that she always read the *Consumers' Guide* from cover to cover. I hated going on with the deception; perhaps before the visit was over I could drop it for good.

He was speaking of how vulnerable intellectuals were, unaware not only of physical currents in the air but of others less tangible. He wasn't speaking in the ominous tone I dreaded. He sounded intent, simply concentrating, as he might have done at any time, on the idea of intellectuals being cocooned in their own theories. Still, "currents in the air" came a little too close to his delusions about mysterious large forces. I reminded him that it was already ten o'clock. Why hadn't Dr. Glueck come? Were we waiting in the wrong place?

No, Hermann said. The arrangement had been that we should wait in the driveway just outside. But he worried about my standing around in the cold. He took my arm and started down toward the administration building. By then it was nearly half an hour after the time we had been told to meet Dr. Glueck. The secretary had gone to the commissary for coffee. We sat waiting by the window, but no car passed. Hermann seemed troubled, but his lips did not move in the nervous way they had when he was struggling with his delusions.

At 10:30 the secretary came back. Asking if we had come to see the doctor, she said he had gone to the farm for a wood-chopping session, but should be back soon. I asked if she was sure. Of course she was, she said. He had taken the beach wagon, as usual, and had to be back here for an eleven o'clock appointment.

When she asked if we wanted to see Dr. Metzger, we said no. Neither of us felt like telling her what had happened. I think now I should have, and asked about the reasons for last night. But at the time I thought of the damage it might do to Hermann's relationship with Dr. Glueck. Besides, I was none too sure of myself in these encounters with authority.

Outdoors as we walked aimlessly up and down the drive I said the sort of thing I had learned to say during this past year — that doctors had a lot on their minds. In my heart I couldn't excuse Dr. Glueck, and Hermann nodded without much conviction. After a time the door to Hermann's building opened and a group of people came out. An elderly woman ran across to Hermann and tugged at his arm, urging him to come to lunch. "Saturday baked beans, kiddo."

Hermann said we'd better eat, that the baked beans were actually quite good. My spirits rose at this. His old appetite must have come back.

The dining room was large and light, with two window walls. Almost filling the third was a huge stone fireplace in which great logs burned. Dr. Glueck had probably cut those logs, I said, feeling better about him. We sat at a table for two; none seated more than six, and there were flowers on each one. Nearby were four women, three silent and one steadily talking. But at a quick glance the room held no more signs of eccentricity than I had seen in a New York automat.

The beans were good, and served with baked ham as juicy as Cora's. I asked if they raised pigs on the farm. Hermann said he thought so. He had been meaning to join the volunteers who went over there to work. Then he added that the trip had seemed just right for us today. His face was troubled, and I couldn't blame him. After all, if Dr. Glueck had succeeded in getting close to him, the relationship would be important. And if deep meaning could be read into the smallest action, as I understood their theories insisted, what must Hermann be reading into what happened last night and today?

At the end of the meal everybody rose at once and quietly started to leave, apparently at some signal so discreet that the departure might have happened of itself. I was impressed by the dignity of the occasion. Could these humane arrangements make up for Dr.

Glueck's lapse this morning and the broken promise that we could stay together? I was afraid not, for Hermann was silent and subdued as we walked back to his room.

To revive last night's jubilant mood, I found the review from the *New Republic* and read aloud the beginning:

> Professor Carter Goodrich and his associates have produced a comprehensive report which for richness of material, ingenuity in handling data, and general all-around fruitfulness in usable results, is among the most valuable produced in our century.

Leaving him to read on and enjoy the praise for his own part, I went over and sat down at his desk. On it, to my surprise, was the *New York Times*. If he was now allowed to read the papers, they must think he was practically well. I tried to feel elation, but couldn't quite lose my fearfulness. Did Dr. Glueck keep aware precisely of what was in the news these days? And he could hardly guess what significance some of it had for Hermann.

The front page told of Britain's banning of volunteers going to fight in Spain. But Franco's drive on Madrid had been halted. The Flint sit-down strikers and General Motors had declared a truce; Walter Reuther claimed victory for a sympathetic action in Dearborn. A dispatch from Hong Kong bore the headline: New Plot Shows Inner Anti-Chiang Cabal.

According to the dispatch, the kidnapping of Chiang had been carried out as a desperate last resort by a patriotic idealist who saw Chiang caught in a conspiracy among his own ministers. They had prevented him from carrying out either the domestic reforms he had promised or a real defense of his country against the Japanese invaders. The kidnapper was not the failed soldier that these henchmen's statements pictured, but a hero who had acted courageously out of regard for China's future. He had captured Chiang only to get him to a safe place away from his ministers, where he could listen to reason. The young man had stood respectfully before him half a day at a time, patiently pleading the cause of his country, while at home Chiang's ministers had plotted against him, organizing a "punitive expedition" ostensibly for his rescue but actually with the hope that in the fighting Chiang would be killed and they could seize power.

If the doctors knowingly let Hermann read stories like this, they must feel sure his recovery was firm. But even as I thought this I felt something wrong about Hermann's silence. I glanced over at him. His head was bowed over the page and I couldn't see his face. If the review had gladdened him, it didn't show in his posture.

"Isn't that a marvelous send-off?" I asked, going over to him. But he shook his head, holding out the page and pointing to one paragraph. Frowning, he asked what I thought of it. I knew what it said, but I read it under his eyes:

> . . . While fertile in suggested expedients for short-term solutions to unemployment, the study plainly points out that the problem cannot be solved in the long term by existing rules of production and value. The key to a solution lies in modern technology, as Mr. Brunck shows more convincingly than anyone before him. The trend toward automation makes feasible — if accompanied by democratic action now beginning — a new pattern that will permit the work of man's hands to be measured and paid for on the basis of *goods* produced: goods not only in a material sense but goods of a higher order — benefits to the society in which the worker lives.

I asked if he didn't think this was great.

"It would be," he said in a low voice, "in other circumstances."

I don't know whether it was the words themselves — they echoed so much of what he had said in this past year — or the tone, almost of despair. I think now I should have brought it all out into the open, asked what had troubled him, tried to answer his fears. But it had never done any good to argue against his delusions. Besides, this room was probably wired so that nurses and doctors could hear. I'm not sure what I did say. It must have been something meant to be reassuring, something naive like "How can anyone see anything wrong about presenting the truth?"

He shook his head (as he had so often this past year) at my obtuseness. Then suddenly, apparently giving up hope of convincing me, he said we must talk of other things. He led me over to the divan and sat with his arm around me, asking me to tell him more about Claudia. If his delusions had been threatening him a moment before, they had relaxed their hold. He spoke dreamily, recalling scenes in Virginia — Claudia on the fat white pony and me on Blackbird, our attempts to play his Bach duets for piano and flute, our boat trip to Virginia Beach. My hair hadn't been so long then, he said, and lifted a strand from my shoulder.

But his hand dropped away, and he reached for a copy of *Consumers' Guide* with Claudia on the cover digging potatoes. Her mouth was pressed tight with effort, the sweat had dampened her hair around her forehead, and the sun highlighted her round bare shoulders. He smiled at it, then looked up at me and said I had done well with my project — as well as he had let me. I told him that the best she had was what he had given her, and it would be all the more important as she grew up. He didn't deny it — not in words, anyway; but when I remembered afterward how he had smiled, it seemed to distance him from what I had said. Just as in our first days he had smiled in a sort of unaccepting tolerance of my extravagance.

I turned my face to his, and our lips touched briefly. All yesterday's ardor was gone, leaving only affection. I thought it was our forced separation that had numbed him. If we had stayed together, made love — not just once, I knew from the slow deep ease of the beginning — we would have wakened to the lovely languor that turns the sensations of the body — the bruised burning and fatigue — into a changed feeling about the world. The stirred center seems to send waves spreading out and up to the brain so that we see things differently, with tranquillity and sureness. No news from anywhere could have touched that serenity.

I turned in one more effort to rouse him, but at that moment there came another timid tapping on the door. When Hermann opened it Dr. Metzger came in with one last halting apology. The visit had already lasted longer, she hinted, than had been intended.

Hermann told her we'd be out in a few minutes. His voice was so firm that she left us at once. But when we were alone he only picked up my bag and stood holding it, preoccupied. I said I would be coming back soon, and his head moved slightly; I thought he nodded. I had wanted to tell him about the apartment in New York, but at this moment I found myself holding back. The idea of change might be too much, and he seemed to enjoy picturing Claudia in a familiar background.

Without a word he led the way into the hall where Dr. Metzger was waiting. As we followed her his steps slowed. He took my arm and held me close as we walked. A girl was coming toward us, dark-haired with high cheekbones, rather like the daughter of Hal Ware who had gone with us on that picnic when Hermann had been assigned to the German Embassy. It gave me a bad feeling.

This girl's beautiful oval face was devoid of expression. Her eyes met mine in a cool stare that was startling in its lack of contact. She had her arms bent at the elbow and folded across her chest; something about this made me turn and glance after her when she had passed. The sleeves of the clean, white jacket ended with canvas straps securely buckled together at the back.

Hermann had paid her no attention; he might not even have seen her. We were almost at the door, and Dr. Metzger opened it. As I stepped out on the gravel I looked over her shoulder and met Hermann's eyes. Their look of appeal was different from that first day when he was led up the stairway at Chestnut Lodge, but just as intense. I turned quickly, pushed the door open and went back in. With my arms around him I said the words I had kept saying, about his coming home soon, for good. And now he held me with his own strength, his lips were alive on mine at last. If only this could go on, if only we need not separate, I thought, but Dr. Metzger was waiting, murmuring about my train, and finally our bodies parted and the door closed.

CHAPTER 34

On the train from New York I resolved to do my Party duty by reading the *Times* from front to back. But I couldn't concentrate. I kept going over the visit, trying to believe Hermann was as well as he had seemed at first. True, he had later become subdued and silent. Still, he had had reason; the doctors had let him down, not once but twice. Yet it was while we were waiting for Dr. Glueck, knowing he had forgotten us, that Hermann had talked so animatedly about Cora and Claudia predicting weather. Even when he spoke of intellectuals not being sensitive to atmosphere his voice hadn't given the words sinister meaning.

How soon had I begun to worry? It was much later, at the way he shook his head over my naiveté, just as he had so often in the past year. And some of the words he spoke echoed the dread and foreboding of his delusions. Maybe fatigue affected me, but I sank back against the train seat, discouraged. Dr. White had been right: my hope was incorrigible, and unrealistic.

In the office next day Mary's look was a question she didn't try to conceal. I told her how well Hermann had seemed on first meeting, how delightfully himself. She just waited, studying my face as she inserted her cigarette into the long holder.

I suppose I started with all the good signs I had listed on the train. He was physically more robust, eating well, being allowed to read the paper, and responding happily to the publication of the book. But under her gaze I found myself telling about the times he had seemed to slip back. I added quickly that I thought those lapses were temporary and part of the recovery progress.

She wanted to know if I had that from Dr. Glueck. I had to tell her that he hadn't been available when I left. Had I talked to Florence? No, I had hurried through New York to get home. (But I had really had time. Why hadn't I called?)

Mary was bringing the Washington paper forward on her desk, pointing to the headlines about Spain, saying something about the news these days being not exactly curative. I hardly gave the paper a glance. It was bound to have the latest on the new trials of traitors in the Soviet Union, which I avoided discussing with Mary. But I remembered what I had read on the train. The seventeen now being tried had been Old Bolsheviks whose names I had heard from Hermann's talk of his reading: Sokolnikov, Piatakov, Karl Radek. In fact, during the summer of 1932, when Hermann was in the USSR, Julian Huxley had had an interview with Radek that had made him a strong supporter of the Soviet Union. But now mobs in the Moscow street were yelling "Kill the mad dogs!" And they were only repeating the words the prosecutor Vishinsky was saying inside at the start of every session.

All this must have been going through my mind as I tried to answer Mary. I suppose I said what I had been telling myself, that if the doctors let Hermann read the paper it must mean he was well enough to take it. (But had they checked on what he'd be reading? Did they know what it might mean to him?) If Mary was convinced she didn't show it. I remember her shrug and change of subject as she picked up the paper again. She said Rodney thought Claud was still in Spain.

The phone rang then; it was Dan Creamer. Knowing how eager the staff was to hear how Hermann had reacted to the book, I invited him to lunch. In the Agriculture cafeteria his homely face across the table created an oasis of quiet affection amid the clatter. I told him that seeing the book had given Hermann reassurance, though at that moment I hadn't thought that was needed.

Dan did a double take, his eyes brightening at the first words, then the brows meeting over the beaky nose in a worried frown. What did I mean, "at the moment"? I didn't know how to say what

I wasn't myself sure about. I may have stalled a little, telling how arrangements had gone wrong in the visit, shadowing the mood. Those incidents struck Dan as unforgivable at a mental hospital. Did the shift of mood send Hermann back into his old haunted world, out of touch?

I realized I was shaking my head, saying no before I thought. And this confused me. I had been so sure that Hermann had slipped back, at least briefly, into his delusions. But concentrating once more, trying to study Hermann's face in my memory, I couldn't help feeling that his grim look then was different from the times when he was seeing sinister visions; he seemed really *present*.

I told Dan that this time when we talked Hermann answered on the same level, even though he was excited, which could be explained, I saw now, by what we had been talking about. When I broke off Dan waited, naturally wanting to hear what that subject had been. And again before I thought — Dan had this effect on me, I couldn't help trusting him — I said it was when he was reading the *New Republic* review. That astonished Dan. He'd have thought it was exactly what would gratify Hermann.

How could I answer? I dared not talk politics with Dan. I could hardly say it might have been the part that seemed to require a New Deal kind of reformism, which was anathema to Marxists. Seeing my troubled face Dan kindly tried to help. Hermann was probably very vulnerable, he said, at this stage of recovery. The sight of his name in print might have made him feel the way some primitives did — exposed, unprotected.

That was truer than Dan knew. But fear of exposure to the Party — the Party of those trials in Russia — was not a primitive superstition. I felt more and more confused; steam seemed to be rising in my brain, blurring everything. And Dan was going on, saying what was again too true — that Hermann could have been disturbed by seeing his position summarized, simplified, whereas in the actual study he had arrived at it gradually, supported by his figures.

We were on dangerous ground, and I could only nod. Luckily Mary came over to the table then, bringing her coffee, and I invited her to sit down with us. She began talking about Spain, and I was relieved, though the news from there was desperate.

CHAPTER 35

Strangely enough, I didn't try to get any answers from Marion Bachrach, my most knowledgeable friend, my closest comrade. On the phone I reported only that Hermann seemed much better. She was about to leave for Vermont to see a builder about an addition to their summer place, and I didn't want to delay her.

Actually I resisted talking to Marion without really knowing why. If I had looked ahead to explaining my puzzle to her I would have seen that it would lead to possibilities I couldn't bring up with Marion, though she was much less rigid than the other comrades. Even in my own mind I didn't dare confront those possibilities. If I couldn't decide whether Hermann's dark sense of threat was a sick imagining or a rational fear of the Party's response to his writing, what should that have told me?

Talking to Mimi made me feel much clearer. When she had finished counting seven peppercorns into a kettle of vegetable soup she turned and called me a worrywart. Hermann had gained weight and was enjoying his food. Wasn't that enough at this stage? Was I doing him any good by imagining signs of trouble? Just assume he was getting well and go ahead.

Her tone was bracing. That night I wrote to Hermann about the New York apartment. Describing its large rooms with marble fireplaces and molded ceilings, I told how his father had visited it to draw the floor plan. I could see the tender way Hermann's lips would curve as he pictured his father measuring for bookcases. And so I am sure they would have, if he had read the letter.

Two days later Mary arrived at the office waving the newspaper. "Hey nonny nonny!" She laid it on my desk, open to the column, "My Day."

Mrs. Roosevelt began by recommending the current *Harper's*. In it she had read an article about a study that might turn out to be the most important piece of research to be published in this decade. I scanned the column in excitement mixed with apprehension. Hermann's name was mentioned twice, and three paragraphs were devoted to his part of the study. Lighting her cigarette, Mary was watching me read. She told me not to be put off by Mrs. R.'s tendency to oversimplify. She said I should think only that millions of people would read a strong argument for social change, and all due to my man.

My man. . . . So Mary was willing at last to call him that, now that he might become as well known as Claud. But this wry thought was only in the back of my mind as I read on: ". . . After all, the most vital question to many people in this country today is how to keep people at work and put our young people as they come to working age into jobs which will provide them a living wage . . . We as a people must solve it by deciding on the type of social and economic philosophy which we wish to see established in this country. When we know the changes we want, we can then set government machinery to work to accomplish them . . ."

Mary was urging me to shoot it off to Hermann PDQ. Then she saw my face and stopped. Before she could ask any questions her phone rang and I slipped out, relieved. Again I was seeing Hermann's frown as he read the *New Republic* review, and hearing his ominous voice as he said it would have been good "under other circumstances."

In the stenographic pool Emma had finished copying nearly all the radio programs I had stockpiled. As I picked them up I answered the question in her dark eyes. Yes, he was better. It wasn't the time or place to go into detail, for which I was grateful. I must have felt the same resistance I had felt to discussing the visit with Marion Bachrach. For Emma was now a Party member. In the way all comrades recognize each other I had guessed from her tone and look in the months since I had assured Charlie that she was ready to be recruited.

Carrying the finished scripts I walked slowly back to the office. As I neared the door Anne Carter came out. Seeing me, her eyes widened and her fingers flew over her mouth. I asked what was the matter and she hesitated, then gasped that Mary was looking for me. And instead of going on where she had started, she took my arm and turned back, leading me in. I felt her hand shaking. But even before I felt it, before I saw Mary's face, my last moment of not knowing was over. Yet I didn't believe it, even with Florence's voice at my ear, stating it precisely, and angrily. The most elementary routine precautions had been neglected, and Hermann had used a belt to hang himself.

CHAPTER 36

On the way to New York Claudia fell asleep, exhausted perhaps by the emotion around her. Or maybe she was just relieved to be home again, even though home was a train compartment with telephone poles flashing past the window.

Mimi had made the atmosphere almost cozy. She was able to talk, as I couldn't, and she talked reassuringly, normally. But after Claudia was asleep she went on. Trying, no doubt, to help me understand and thus accept what had happened, she spoke of men's need to extend their knowledge beyond their own capacities. For of course (she assumed then, as I did) Hermann had slipped back into his illness. Her last statement (I couldn't take any more) was something like this: "Men go on thinking and thinking, we try to laugh them out of it, but they keep beating their brains until they die, and we survive." At that point I was pressing my fists against the sides of my forehead. Mimi drew my hands gently away and let me sit quiet, concentrating on not being sick.

We met Ernst in New York, and the hours moved on as if prearranged, as if this was what people did, meeting each other at hotels, calling doctor cousins for prescriptions, taking pills and sitting at restaurant tables and getting to another train on schedule, arriving and being met and finding that a place never seen before could seem the right and only place to be.

Somewhere in all this the cue for Mimi's exit must have come, for she had disappeared when I woke the second day with my mind clear, too clear. Outside my door Claudia was telling somebody about a puppy. Whoever answered, inaudibly, apparently encouraged her for she went on, kind and informative, moving away.

The sedatives had not quite worn off, but it was possible to bathe and dress. Oma was waiting with coffee. Beside the window Claudia sat with Opa in the sunshine. She announced that he was brushing her hair, and I saw the flash of it in the sunshine as his hands moved. From the brush clung an electric web of light.

I also saw, though Claudia had spoken proudly, that her eyes were watchful. Yes, and hopeful, I thought as I sipped coffee and spoke to Oma about the picture they made in the sun. Claudia was hoping for a normal mother. And this she must have.

I couldn't any longer ask of fate, as I had the first day — demanded, obsessively — to give up everything, everyone, in exchange for the fact not being true. This futile cry was not permitted; it was as taboo as yesterday's temptation to follow Hermann.

Oma was apologizing for her appearance. She regretted that this should have been the week of her extractions. She quoted someone who had observed (was it Leonardo?) that the fewer teeth one had, the fiercer one appeared. Claudia had found that amusing, she said, and asked her to impersonate a lion, which she had done, and not just once. I marveled at her composure. She had even smiled. I said I too had had a dentist appointment, which I had felt an urgent need to keep. I had *wanted* the drilling. Oma did not seem to find that strange. And when I asked her if she was still in pain from the extractions she said, "Not much. Not, so to say, enough."

Claudia was complimenting Opa for being a good brusher, and I murmured about her contentment here. Children knew, Oma said, where they were needed. I looked at her as she sat so erect in her chair, her dark eyes deep above the thrust of her cheekbones and the shrunken mouth; I saw her as an ancient wisewoman, like some lost Mayan priestess.

But now she was talking about practical arrangements. Ernst had gone this morning to the funeral home where they had taken Hermann's body. Stony Lodge had made sure, she said bitterly, that it was in another county. The doctors wanted no tales told. Her bitterness was implacable but without surprise or indignation. It seemed to be part of some knowledge already within her, as if like Mithridates in the poem, she had tasted poison drop by drop all her life. Nothing could happen to her that she had not in a sense anticipated.

This was not true of Opa. Each minute brought him new agony, newly unendurable, for which he was never prepared. It seemed always to be touch and go, with Claudia's presence narrowly saving him. When he took her out into the garden Oma and I stood watching the two figures move among the bare hummocks where Opa was apparently telling her that flowers would be coming up. He had always believed, Oma said, truly believed in spite of all the blows that had fallen on him, that everything would sooner or later work out well. He had lost his position in America when they went on vacation to Germany just before the war, had gone through that war, and afterward the inflation, in which he lost another business. Each time he had been puzzled, reviewing his actions. He could not understand; he had followed all the rules. Yet he had kept his faith in the rules, starting over in America at the age of sixty. "And now comes this."

Ernst rescued us by arriving then, and we had to think about lunch. After it was cleared away I lay down with Claudia. Through the bedroom door I heard Ernst talking, and some names came through: Elsa and Clive Wing, Florence, Goodrich, Bach. Trying not to understand, I fell asleep.

In the morning, when Opa and Claudia had left to get the paper, Ernst came again. Drinking coffee while he waited for Oma to dress, he asked if I would like to join them. Just for the ride, which was short, only to the next suburb; I needn't go in.

Westchester was at its bleakest; the snow had melted away and there was no sun. Only the delicate bare branches held any beauty. After a few miles Ernst turned off the highway into a street marked Dead End. At the foot was a white mansion with tall columns at its entrance. Ernst parked, took Oma up to the door, then came back and got in beside me, his arm along the back of the seat, his hand clasping my shoulder, not talking at all.

After what seemed a long time Oma came out between the pillars. Ernst ran up and helped her down the steps. She was a little less steady than when she had climbed them. But a few minutes later as we were moving away she said quietly that Hermann had looked really like himself. "He seemed to smile, as if he would speak."

I went with them the next morning, resolved to go in with her. But at the last moment I sat still. When Ernst came back I spoke of my shame, being younger but not so brave as Oma. To my surprise he said that Oma's kind of bravery was good for certain occasions, but other qualities might have been needed more from day to day. He spoke as if he had been giving it thought.

It was too late to try to figure out what had gone wrong in Hermann's life. Too late even to tell Ernst my puzzles over that last visit. Instead I said that Mimi had quoted someone who called man a thinking reed. Ernst said Pascal's statement did apply to Hermann, whose thinking was ambitious. He himself had lived more on the surface of things. Then he drew my head down to his shoulder and we fell into silence.

When Oma appeared between the columns I jumped out of the car and ran up to her, in a panic that I might lose this last chance to see Hermann. But she shook her head and said not to go in. He was no longer like himself. "He resembles one of his uncles."

On the third morning Mimi appeared, and again it seemed all according to some plan in which I moved through my part as the unknown script unfolded. In a limousine we rode once more to the columned mansion. Instead of three, this time, we were four. Opa sat in the back between Oma and me. His hand was gripping Oma's the way Hermann's had gripped mine that night we left him at Stony Lodge.

Then we were in what was meant to be a chapel, which without my being able really to think about it shocked me with a sense of sacrilege. Light came through raw colored glass and fell in blood-like splashes on the blond folding chairs. An organ began to play as we went in — Bach; I thought, "St. Anne's Fugue" — and I couldn't help crying. Maybe the tears were partly in anger. I could only be glad Hermann was not hearing his treasured music translated into these whines above him.

It had taken me minutes, resisting, to see the closed mahogany box, though it stood on an open partitioned square directly before the row of seats where I sat with Oma and Opa. Hermann's mother was gazing at the coffin. Her eyes seemed not focused on the wood itself but seeing through it to the face that on the day before yesterday had seemed to smile but yesterday had resembled an uncle. My tears kept pouring but failed to blind my imagining.

The service was beginning. The German language hurt my ears. It was a little relieving to recognize the voice of Dr. Corell, who had introduced me to Hermann. But he had also introduced Hermann into the Nazi embassy. He was reading the poem of Rilke's that Hermann had once quoted to me in English:

> We shall all of us fall. This hand of mine must fall.
> See for yourself the others; it will be the fate of all.

But now Dr. Corell was reading the last lines, which Hermann had not been able to accept:

> *Und doch ist Einer, welcher dieses Fallen*
> *unendlich Sanft in Seines Handen halt.*

Hermann could not believe in that One who would hold these fallen ones forever gently in his hands. I wanted to be comforted, as I think everyone did who listened, for their sighs seemed a palpable wish to believe, a longing I shared just then, while at the same time weeping in the unbelief I shared with Hermann, whom in a way it had doomed to this maghogany box.

Clothes rustled, footsteps came near, instruments were tuned, and after a moment a woman's voice rose above a cello. I heard a whispered question behind me, then Ernst answering: "Elsa."

I felt sudden deep pain, angry pain. I was hearing her voice for the first time, a high voice, and (I told myself) rather thin, forced beyond its range. It was presumptuous, I thought, for her to sing in

German with such pretentious perfection. She had taken over the occasion — with the complicity of Ernst, of course. They had conspired in a plan that assumed her right to express Hermann's taste, the right of prior relationship and her subtle appreciation of him, a recognition of her ability to do justice to his memory.

These reactions were as brief as the flash of a knife through sore flesh, but followed by a thought as searing. Perhaps she did have this right, as the woman who most truly would have met Hermann's needs. Perhaps he had never really recovered from the loss of her. And our marriage had not helped. Perhaps done harm.

"Hier schlummert seine stillen Frieden," Elsa sang, her voice softer and fuller now. I remembered Hermann's record, with the chamber orchestra, and a chorus that thundered, *"Ist Todt. Todt. Todt!"* The massed choir in huge repetition gradually lowering to a whisper had pronounced the finality of death. Just when I felt I couldn't bear more, Opa moved beside me, and I knew he was hearing the same dire words. He was leaning forward, leaning too far. I laid a hand on his arm.

"Here sleeps in his sweet peace the great sufferer." Elsa sang in German, and I knew the meaning was all too clear to Opa. "The sufferer who on this earth could not without wounding himself break off one rose."

Opa gave a groan and lurched forward. I caught him with two hands, and as he half-fell I saw what he had seen. The floor was giving way beneath the coffin. It was slowly sinking.

I tried to hold him, but Opa wrenched away. With unexpected strength he plunged forward from my hands, flinging himself upon the mahogany, and lay there with his cheek against the wood, his right arm reaching to embrace it, the fingers scrabbling to seize and hold his son from disappearing.

The cello soared up and joined the voice blindly singing above and behind us, unaware. Two men had come and were lifting Opa up from the coffin, which went on sinking slowly. Elsa sang on. The coffin was almost out of sight. Opa's face was buried in his handkerchief, stifling his sobs. Oma had her arm around his shaking shoulders.

The coffin disappeared under closing doors, and cello tones overpowered all small sounds of anguish as Elsa's high voice sang on: "... the great sufferer who carried under his full heart the well-being of mankind ... carried it in pain until the end of his life ..."

Lebensende.... Elsa made the word beautiful.

Opa had become quiet, as somewhere down below a furnace door had opened and Hermann's body was being given to the flames.

EPILOGUE

I wonder if I can make the next two years believable to anyone who has never been part of a close, secret group like the Washington underground. The strength of the commitment held me to life; I shut out any thought that might lead to losing that bond.

The days after the funeral, the move to New York, are lost to me. When the stopped clock of memory starts again we are already in the Eleventh Street apartment. Cora is living with us; Claudia goes each day to a nursery school at the settlement house around the corner.

I find myself wishing the old rules for widows still held. I remember 1917 in Washington: the heavy, all-encompassing black cloth that sheltered so many women in church. Now I wish I could hide my grief behind those mourning veils. I wear my only black dress, made over from one worn to a party given by Alec Waugh at the Rainbow Room. But it fails to protect me from lighthearted talk.

Irrational sometimes, through most of the hours my mood is simple endurance, of effort to be a mother to Claudia. Yet she begins to come home from school too weary, too apathetic. When Opa goes on a business trip she worries, keeps asking about him. She has a dream of being run over in the subway — a frightening dream, though she doesn't remember hurting. "I just didn't want to be not anybody." I take her temperature. A low-grade fever, only a degree or two, it is regular, every afternoon, without any reason the doctor can find.

We keep her home from nursery school, I spend more time with her, her spirits rise and and her temperature goes down. She is happiest on the weekends we spend in a near subarb with Oma and Opa. Is it because Opa is like Hermann, does she feel sheltered by family?

Jessica Smith, now editing *Soviet Russia Today,* asks me to help her create a new magazine for women. It will never appear; our ideas for women's future may not accord with Moscow's. But such a task connects me to the Party like a diver to an oxygen tank.

Meanwhile Jessica becomes a personal friend; she invites me to a family dinner for Mother Bloor. I know she is grateful for the help she can count on from me, such as a page of humor, new and unlikely in a Communist publication, and not easy for me just now. I have an appointment to interview Sergei Prokofiev, but just before our date I receive a letter from him regretting that he has been called back to Moscow.

On another assignment I edit interviews with the Soviet aviators who have made history by flying nonstop over the North Pole to the United States. My editing consists largely of pruning sentences like "Comrade Stalin himself spoke to me, took my hand. Comrade Stalin embraced me. Comrade Stalin kissed me on both cheeks." I write to a comrade, "I am becoming the nation's expert on de-Stalinization."

I write this without losing any faith in the Soviet Union. But such irreverence is possible only among the kind of comrades I am meeting now in New York — writers and artists whose technical connection to the Party I never try to figure out. None of them seems to belong to a unit or branch, doing open work such as picketing, handing out leaflets, or selling the *Daily Worker* on the street. I'm not surprised, having experienced in Washington (without really thinking about it) the sense of being part of an informal elite with privileges.

It occurs to me that if the Party is to reach the "masses" we must publish in the magazines they read. I begin to write "confessions," told in the first person, purporting to be real-life histories. Actually they do show the dreams of a working-class girl and her meager choices for fulfilment, with an honesty ruled out by the taboos of proper women's magazines.

At first I have to follow the "sin and pay" formula. But after a time I manage to slip in a message, and soon will be able to use the real drama of the class struggle. I'll sell the poignant story of a Flint, Michigan, autoworker who, trapped into becoming a stool pigeon, betrays his fellow union members. In one scene, after realizing what he has done, he passes a fruit stand, sees the words "Northern Spy," and has to vomit. I have based the story on testimony about labor spying by witnesses before the Lafollette Committee, for which Charles Kramer now works.

I will travel to Harlan County where thugs hired by the mine owners ambush union organizers and shoot into the homes of sympathizers, even a minister of the gospel, crippling him and killing his son. I will go south to the highway encampment of striking sharecroppers and talk with the real people I had tried to defend in Washington. I'll write about the children ill with pneumonia in the cold tents, their parents threatened by lynch mobs as they try to break away from their legal slavery. Four-part serials based on these true melodramas will appear in *True Story,* with its millions of readers.

This writing is done on my own, without directive or indeed attention from the Party. I haven't been approached officially by any functionary. Party members are supposed to be "under discipline," but I assumed they thought me unfit, knowing through Jessica the stresses of these past months. They are waiting — it will later be clear — measuring my stabilty, judging whether I have the absolute reliability needed for the kind of assignment that is in fact ahead.

On days we can afford it we buy flowers from the cart on Bleecker Street. Josh and Lacey Craig bring a large spray of white stock, pure and fragrant. They also bring their Scotty, who "sings" for Claudia. The visit is perfect for her, and for me. Josh's eyes meeting mine express only concern. But months later a blurred voice against a noisy background refuses to give a name but insists that a July night is not forgotten.

Howard Selsam, Hermann's philosopher friend who visited us in Virginia, has joined with Communist colleagues to found a Marxist intellectual journal, *Science & Society.* I give them Hermann's collection of books (some rare ones Howard had coveted) as a nucleus for the magazine's library. Whether this library ever materializes I can't bring myself to check.

Colleagues from Washington keep turning up. The latest consumers counsel, Donald Montgomery, a restless, eager man in his early forties, drawn to New York, he says, by Beethoven's late quartets at the YMHA, takes me to dinner at a gypsy restaurant. He drinks and talks of his discontent; another poet manqué, he feels trapped in marriage and fatherhood. I can summon up little sympathy for someone ready to throw away what Hermann and I treasured and lost. Later I hear that he and Mary are in love. They marry, and are happy. The happiness lasts until suddenly Mary develops a tumor on the brain. Don helps her learn once more to walk and dress herself; she brings back speech by trying to recite the "Hey Nonny Nonny" verses she loved. But the tumor grows again, and she dies. Don asks me to come to her memorial service, but I fail to find a way to make it possible. When I write to him again, what I receive in response is a sheaf of clippings from his lawyer. They report that after the service Don went back to their house on Capitol Hill, telephoned the police to make sure his children were not the ones to find him, and shot himself in the head. The note he left said simply "I cannot live without her."

But this is far in the future; Mary has yet to lose her Rodney (dead at his Scripps-Howard desk), and to build in his memory the Dutcher pier at Menemsha for the fishermen of Martha's Vineyard. In 1937 I still have only my own sorrow to bear.

Marion Bachrach comes often, and in June we go to the congress of the League of American Writers. Walter Duranty, seeming furious at the criticism of the trials in the Soviet Union, shouts out "Give them a chance to cultivate their garden!" In the burst of applause we beam at each other, exultant with an enormous relief that we would not put into words. We hear the desperate news of Spain from Ernest Hemingway and the Dutchman Joris Ivens, who show their film, *The Spanish Earth*. We listen earnestly to Earl Browder, chairman of the CPUSA. Wistfully I imagine Hermann asking, "Isn't the Party expecting too much, to take him as a literary figure?" But neither Marion nor I wonder how he comes to be speaking at a congress of writers. The husband of one of my best new friends in New York is the executive secretary of the League.

Marion hurries home to Artie, and at the last session I sit with a new friend from Detroit. Harriet is an unusual comrade — blonde, sophisticated, wearing a subtly cut blue linen suit that may have cost more than *Modern Romances* pays for a fifteen-thousand-word "book-length."

In the lobby afterward she hails a slender red-haired young man who invites us to the Brevoort for a drink. As we sit at an outdoor table watching the Fifth Avenue strollers I listen to his accounts of tactics in the teachers' union at Harvard, where he is an English instructor. He talks seriously, but with irony untypical of Communists. His Boston accent and aquiline features make me see him as a blue-blooded New Englander, a true Harvard man. Then casually he mentions taking his aunt to the dog races. I laugh — and the sound is strange to my ears.

His glance is alert and speculative: when it comes my way I turn the talk to Harriet, who is about to be published in a Detroit magazine. Sipping my julep, I feel swathed in widowhood. I find myself declining another drink. I am a third party; I say I must go home to Claudia. And I do leave, somewhat to my own surprise. I walk home slowly.

My circle of acquaintance widens. I meet Joe Freeman, the literary editor of *New Masses,* which has published my account of being shown through a Harlan County mine as the guest of the owners' public relations officers. Joe invites me to have a drink with him at the old Martha Washington, in these days the dowager of lower Fifth Avenue hostelries. I am impressed to be with someone of Freeman's importance in the Party. Beside me on the divan in the dimness he lets a curved forefinger run lightly down my cheek. I quickly speak of politics. And in my confusion I let him draw me out on Washington, and reveal too much.

Almost at once I realize that I have broken the inviolable rule. In Washington it was burned into us: nobody, not even a husband or wife, or the most trusted outside comrade, could be allowed to suspect the existence of the Washington underground. My guilt weighs heavy, becomes unbearable. Though this thought is never allowed to enter my mind, I feel the same distress I felt as a child when a review of my day showed an undeniable sin.

Each sin, no matter how tiny, had to be confessed to my mother before I slept. In the winter I would force myself out of the slowly warming bed and creep downstairs through the cold. The only way to relief was confession. And now, again, it is the only way.

When I tell Jessica that I must meet Steve she directs me to the Communist headquarters on Fourteenth Street. I'll find J. Peters on the ninth floor. *The ninth floor.* Those words send shudders through me. For three years in Washington I heard them with awe: "This is a directive straight from the ninth floor." Or, terrifyingly, "He's been called to the ninth floor to explain."

As the freight elevator slowly climbs, groaning with portent, I remember that night at Lee Pressman's. I can see Steve's dark-browed fury at Hermann's question. How will he look now, when he learns of my loose talk? Hermann's error had been well-intentioned. Mine, though a slip, is inexcusable. ("I didn't mean to" was never permitted by Mother. "You must mean *not* to," she would answer, with a sharp cut of the switch on my bare leg.)

Entering that dread ninth-floor office I wonder what fearful consequences I have brought on myself. My voice falters as I begin.

Steve listens but the frown does not appear. I speak more calmly, leaving nothing out. It does not occur to me to remind him of Hermann's breakdown and the long ordeal that followed. As a Communist I'm above that. (Mother never permitted excuses.)

Suddenly, to my amazement, Steve leans forward with a gentle smile and lets his hand rest softly on my hair.

I can't believe it. Am I being relieved of this aching weight? Yes. That much is clear. Steve's reasons, of course, are not. The Washington secret, however secret it may be, is safe with Joe Freeman, whose brother, I later learn, is a seasoned Soviet agent.

Steve's actual words of release, and my answers, are lost to me. But not my gratitude. At that moment his authority, accepted technically before, becomes emotionally real.

He takes no advantage of this at once. Nor would I have expected him to trust me with a task after my gross error. I don't realize that to a shrewd organizer like J. Peters my confession chiefly proves my reliability. Experience must have taught him that the conscientious type of comrade, brought up to "do right," could best be depended on, even to lie, steal, and deceive successfully, persistently, and with less danger of detection. It is as if one's conscience, already functioning, need only be given a quarter-turn so that the needle points east instead of north, and then the world can be faced with a look of clear-eyed rectitude.

Trying to economize, I have moved to a cheaper apartment on Bank Street. It lacks the openness of Eleventh Street, with only a fire escape at the back where I can sit and watch Claudia playing with the three little Montague boys. On the autumn day Jessica first visits the apartment, Claudia is adjudicating a quarrel, reasoning with the older boys while she stands with outthrust hands protecting the youngest.

As we stand talking of the mysterious effect one child can have on others, Jessica suddenly frowns and asks how old Claudia is, exactly. Nearly five, I tell her. What happens, Jessica asks, when Claudia is sick and can't go to school? If I can't be here, Cora comes. "Cora," Jessica nods, relieved.

Later I will understand. Now a member of a Harlem unit, Cora is known to be dependable. But at that moment I wonder at Jessica's questions and the interest she takes in the layout of the apartment. She stands for some time staring into the small inner windowless room. This all comes clear when a few days later she asks if I can let that space be used by the Party. They need a place not likely to be raided, where someone can store and use certain important documents. Of course I agree. It means I am really trusted by the Party.

In the darkness a few nights later a new file case is installed next to mine, this one impressively locked. And the following morning a stranger arrives. He is a dark-haired, solid-looking man in his forties, his mouth set in seriousness that can suddenly change to sweetness when he smiles. I find him somehow touching, and after a time learn why. His wife and little boy are far away in Moscow. A naturalized American, once an immigrant hatmaker from Latvia, he is now in this country without any human contact except me and (separately) Earl Browder. He takes a tender interest in Claudia from the first day she spends at home. When he holds my hand wistfully, saying goodnight, I suspect that the Party hoped to give him more than a safe place to work. Meeting his smile I wish I could offer what he needs. But he sees it is not to be, and I learn to ignore his presence in the next room as I sit at the dining table writing.

Dutifully incurious, I never let myself wonder what an important secret emissary from the Soviet apparatus can be doing, day after day, leafing silently through documents in my inner room. Only a few lapses give me a clue. Once he can't repress an angry exclamation, and I hear the name of Trotsky. Another day he mutters that Trotskyites are "sick. Just sick." That doesn't surprise me; this name can rouse the Party to fury far fiercer than could be stirred by the most villainous capitalist. I myself have caught this spirit; a Trotskyist I meet at the home of one of Claud's early friends is described in one of my letters as "a jack-in-the box, with abnormally short legs."

Around this time Frankwood Williams, the Party's favored psychiatrist, makes a trip to see for himself the triumphs of the Soviet Union in eliminating mental illness. What he learns there nobody ever discovers. On the way back, traveling on a Polish steamer, he dies of a sudden undiagnosed gastrointestinal problem, and is buried at sea.

In the fall of 1938, Claudia sits in her bath listening to huge branches crack and crash in the hurricane. While the world waits for Hitler to take the Sudetenland, she listens to the radio and cries, "Poor Czechoslovakia!" Hearing so much talk of war, she wants to know what this means. Late at night she comes weeping out of sleep asking why there should be war. "Why can't people just be nice and good to each other?" Neither I nor my comrades who are present — Richard Wright among them — can find a consoling answer.

The work in the inner room ends after several months with no dramatic revelation. (That will come later.) On his side the parting is undoubtedly painful. But I am preoccupied.

Everyone is giving parties for Spain. Listening to their music as we walk through the Village, we look in at the posters showing a female figure with clenched fist held high. "La Pasionara!" Claudia

332

cries. I wish Hermann could hear her correct pronunciation. At one fund-raiser on a penthouse roof I meet Sid Perelman again. He is bemused, trying with difficulty to switch from surrealist to socially conscious, in tune with the times.

After a kindly conference with William Maxwell I publish an account in the *New Yorker* of hiring, through New York's Out of Wedlock bureau, a charming "O.W." who cleans and babysits and gradually reveals the complex twists and turns of her all-too-true confession.

By the time of the 1939 congress of the League of American Writers my class struggle serials have appeared in *True Story*. I am asked to give a talk showing writers how they can use their talents to encourage and educate the people really on the front line. It is my first experience of winning laughter and applause, being greeted afterward by such idols as Sylvia Townsend Warner (whom I will visit later in England). Many well-known American authors belong to the League, and in my daze it seems all of them are excited by my proposals. Happily I am unaware that none of them will ever follow my tips on reaching the masses.

I sit at the last session with the chairman of the League, Donald Ogden Stewart, and his wife, Ella Winter, widow of Lincoln Steffens. With us is the red-haired young man from two years ago. This time I am no third party, if I ever was. We four go to dinner; we dance and drink champagne. Later, after writing about this evening to a comrade in the south, I will receive an answer seething with bitterness, contrasting this New York gaiety with his life among the sharecroppers, every moment in fear of ambush, eating meals of corn bread, drinking nothing more festive than buttermilk. And reading that letter I will recall remorsefully that on this night no such thoughts had come to my mind. The mood was all celebratory. I suppose I feel I have a right to celebrate; those serials are hard work.

And perhaps I am celebrating something more: the slight lifting of a cloud darkening these years — my sense that life is over. Sitting beside the young man who was called "Red" as a boy, I hear about his teaching at a Workers' School in Boston. In my answer to his first letter I write that this "is the kind of thankless task that tells much about people in our gang." Our gang, of course, is the Party.

Claudia and I go for the weekend to a comrade's cottage in Katonah, and he is invited. Claudia, now age six, studies him from below the rim of a white sailor's cap set at a rakish angle on her shining hair. Approving, after an hour, she suggests that he stroke her arm. It is round, apricot colored, blondly glinting in the sun; he strokes it, marveling. Driving back to New York I point out to Claudia a Massachusetts license plate; wanting to go on, speak his name, I hold back. But she says it, adding, "I feel so sorry for him, all alone in Massachusetts."

Actually he does feel alone now, though teaching in Harvard Summer School. Deadlines and editorial conferences keep me in New York, as well as Claudia's goodbye visit to Oma and Opa before she goes to camp. Far off in Germany are their own grandchildren, whose father, a composer and conductor, has been losing one post after another under Hitler. But with Claudia, Opa can show the sunniness that gives her such contentment and gives me such pain. Watching the handsome old man helping her water flowers I see so much of Hermann that I cherished.

In French the word *dénouement* means the untying of a knot. Such dénouements are never simple and easy. But the mood of many weekends is idyllic, finding cabins on the Cape or down some New Hampshire lakeside road lined with signs saying Night Crawlers For Sale. Idyllic, that is, until the last one, in New York. It is late August, and this time we meet in shock, incredulity, then slow, unwilling belief, followed by angry hopelessness. Von Ribbentrop has traveled to Moscow to meet Molotov and sign a non-aggression pact between Hitler and Stalin.

Riding on the open top of a Fifth Avenue bus we see Richard Rovere across the aisle. His face is the color of concrete. He can hardly speak. We seek out other comrades, who find as little to say. Even the *Daily Worker* is caught unprepared, and at first expresses dismay. Then it seems to gulp as it comes out with the official line of acceptance, even enthusiasm. But fellow travelers are falling away, scorned by the Party, described as being "thrown off the train of history."

At the end of the month we drive to Buffalo, where the teachers union is holding its national convention. Long under the influence of the Party, its sessions now go through turmoil. Faithful comrades, fewer by the hour, wrestle to hold their power over the many waverers. Liberals who during the Popular Front have respected the Communists' lead now sternly call this a betrayal of everything antifascists have worked for.

The comrades are hard put to answer. Inwardly shaken, they insist that the step was necessary for self-defense. The Soviet Union has been refused a nonaggression pact with the Western powers, who sold out at Munich, did not support the Loyalists in Spain, and obviously hoped for a war between Russia and Germany.

The sophisticated comrades know that the directives followed by the American Party could all along be summed up in the slogan that ended most speeches at Party meetings and *Daily Worker* editorials: "Defend the Soviet Union!" Those still loyal to the Party accept this. The Russian comrades have achieved Communism "on one sixth of the earth's surface," and it has represented the hope of the world. They are more experienced, have more at stake, understand the only options open to them. But not all these arguments can be used with liberals, who keep on shaking their heads.

Meantime my friend Crystal Bing, Claud's office mainstay, has come to America as an emissary from *The Week*. On September 3, 1939, the day Britain declared war, Crystal attends our wedding in an upstate village. The minister is a socialist, though our host, Granville Hicks, until three weeks before, had been a magisterial Communist. Crystal weeps all through the ceremony, sure that her husband will be called up. (After heavy combat he will go through years of surgery to rebuild some semblance of a face.)

For members of secret Party units, breaking away is more than difficult. My case is eased by moving to Massachusetts. Though the rules say members can leave the Party only by being expelled, I am not followed by questions or reproaches. Johnnie B., Marion's son and John Abt's nephew, will come to call when his Merchant Marine ship puts in at Boston during the war.

Are the comrades still friendly because they don't guess my changed views? How can they guess what I myself don't surely know? Time and events will have to show me. The Soviet Union in effect has taken over Estonia, Latvia, and Lithuania. Finland resists, and is invaded. I have nightmares, seeing the Soviet troops in their ghostly white, skiing over the snow-covered mountains. We feel sick when we hear our friend Donald Ogden Stewart, whose Broadway comedies have been both lighthearted and right-thinking, jeer callously "Poor little Finland!"— a frightening echo of "Poor little Belgium," the lament for the atrocities of 1914.

Naturally I want to face facts honestly. Of course. But it has taken me years, out of range of pressures, to free my conscience from its blind loyalties. Even when much later I was given reason to believe that Trotsky's assassination had been planned in my inner room on Bank Street, I could only hope I would not have agreed to its use if I had known.

When blind people suddenly are given sight they often find it painful at first — the harshness, the garish light; it hurts to look at what they have to see.

We who were self-blinded suffer the further pain of shame. Not shame that we joined in the fight, which indeed must be renewed and renewed, as long as people are still ill-fed, ill-clothed, ill-housed, and brutally tortured. My shame is in the terms of my joining: I forfeited my most essential freedom, to think for myself. Instead of keeping my wits about me, I gave them over to others, believing big lies and rejecting truths as big as millions starving. No excuse can lighten the knowledge that I used my brain and talents in defense of Stalin.

Had Hermann seen this, that autumn of 1935, when he found truths that conflicted with his commitment to the Party? In confronting that choice he retreated into madness. When I look back at my last visit at Stony Lodge, his frown of fear and foreboding seems all too sane; his ominous words express dread of a terrible reality. I even wonder if he saw this risk from the beginning, when I was so fervent, so eager to take the step from which his nature held him back. I laughed at his caution, at his need to consider consequences. Might not his foresight have added unbearably to the conflict between his Party duties and his loyalty to those who trusted him?

336

We can never be sure of a final answer. But in writing this history I have learned enough to ask the question. And the question is important, not just in its implications for one man's life. Hermann's history becomes a major tragedy when we see him as an early sacrifice of a whole generation of young believers whose lives were damaged by disillusionment in the Soviet Union's false promise. Their loss went far beyond the loss of their years of effort to help keep this promise. It was an irreparable loss, a loss of faith in their own integrity.

A NOTE ON THE AUTHOR

Born in Iowa in 1903, HOPE HALE DAVIS has studied art,
painted scenery for the theater, edited magazines, and written
criticism, memoirs, poetry, and fiction. Her work has appeared widely and ranges from a 1938 interview with Lou
Gehrig to stories in *The New Yorker.* A collection of her short
stories, *The Dark Way to the Plaza,* was published in 1968.
Mother of three, grandmother of four, she lives in Cambridge,
Massachusetts with her husband, Robert Gorham Davis,
where she teaches writing at the Radcliffe Seminars.

A NOTE ON THE BOOK

The text for this book was composed by Steerforth Press using
a digital version of Granjon, a typeface designed by George
W. Jones and first issued by Linotype in 1928. The book was
printed on acid free papers and bound by Quebecor Printing~
Book Press Inc. of North Brattleboro, Vermont.